Agrarian Structure
and Political Power
in Mexico

Roger Bartra

Agrarian Structure and Political Power in Mexico

Translated by Stephen K. Ault

The Johns Hopkins University Press

Baltimore and London

This book has been brought to publication with
the generous assistance of the Pribram Fund.

The Johns Hopkins University Press
701 West 40th Street
Baltimore, Maryland 21211-2190
The Johns Hopkins Press Ltd., London

Library of Congress Cataloging-in-Publication Data
Bartra, Roger.
Agrarian structure and political power in Mexico / Roger Bartra ;
translated by Stephen K. Ault.
p. cm.
Material originally published in Spanish between 1974 and 1987,
substantially reworked by the author.
Includes bibliographical references and index.
ISBN 0-8018-4398-7
1. Agriculture—Economic aspects—Mexico. 2. Peasantry—Mexico.
3. Land reform—Mexico. I. Title.
HD1792.B387   1992
338.1'0962—dc20   92-11605

A catalog record for this book is available
from the British Library

Contents

Illustrations

Tables

Tables

Preface

Over the last twenty years a lively debate over agrarian problems has taken place in Mexico and Latin America. It is no coincidence that researchers and politicians have been embroiled in serious arguments since the beginning of the 1970s: at that time it was already apparent that agriculture had entered a new and critical period of development and that the official theories regarding the peasantry then in vogue provided no understanding of the new direction in the countryside. The reformist aura had given way to the stark facts: the dynamism of the capitalist system was threatening to lead the Mexican government's economic policy down a dead-end street.

Controversies and new research helped destroy the myth that the agrarian question turned on the problems of land tenure and called into doubt the central, heroic, and efficient role of the *campesino* (peasant). Capital was revealed as the axis of the agrarian process, and it was shown that the real peasant had little to do with that unique mythological figure programmed by official bureaucratic discourse to be the permanent, static demiurge of the Mexican countryside. It was obvious that capital was quickly overwhelming his roots in the land and that the peasantry was proving to be a living, heterogeneous movement, enormously differentiated and disparate.

This book brings together my research and polemic writings on the links between agrarian structure and political power in Mexico. In compiling this volume for publication in English in the United States, I have updated, corrected, expanded, reworked, and reorganized a series of texts published between 1974 and 1987, almost all in Spanish.[1] Since the publication of these writings, a great deal of ink has flowed, many discussions have taken place, and a variety of experiences has accumulated.

One of the central concepts of my studies on the Mexican countryside is the existence of an original historical articulation between a dynamic process of accumulation of capital and the syncopated refunctionalization of the small peasant economy, that is, the existence of an integration between the process of proletarianization and the system of reproduction of the peasantry. Those studies proved that the dominant tendency resulting from this "permanent primitive accumulation" causes, over the long term, the extinction of the traditional peasantry and the forms of political power linked to it. Our studies revealed that the old commonplace according to which Mexico is still a peasant nation was a falsehood and that it was necessary to introduce rigor and imagination into the study of the agrarian question.

Naturally, these efforts had to confront populist interpretations, in their official, statist version as well as in their leftist version, which had transformed the peasant into a vulgar metaphor that would suit any "revolutionary" slogan. The controversy spread and became polarized into two major strains of interpreters: the *campesinistas* and the *descampesinistas* (or *proletaristas*), according to the definition of the controversy given by Ernest Feder.[2] Suddenly, in opposition to the interpretations that rejected such traditional dogmatic orthodoxy (and that were tagged as descampesinista and proletarista), there arose what the alarmed Feder labeled a "strange alliance" among the World Bank, various government agencies concerned with "rescuing" the peasant, and several strains of populism. The reaction against my interpretations maintains that there is a distinct, central place for the peasantry within the capitalist economy and that, far from becoming extinct, the peasantry shows a tendency toward becoming the principal alternative to the agrarian crisis. This notion has been based upon an unreal definition of the peasant (a hoax exposed and criticized by Manuel Coello) and upon closing one's eyes to the complex, random process of proletarianization (quite nicely analyzed by Luisa Paré).[3]

The leftist, orthodox version of *campesinismo* clung to the view, much in fashion in Latin America during the seventies, according to which we in Mexico find ourselves with a "dependent capitalism" that, unlike other capitalisms, is structurally incapable of developing on its own and of resolving some of its internal conflicts. Thus, this bastard capitalism would, by definition, find itself limited in absorbing agrarian contradictions and diluting them in the logic of the accumulation of capital. This view assumes, then, an incompatibility between this supposed variety of capitalism and modern agricultural development, which would involve a stimulus to well-to-do peasants of the new type (*"farmers"*), entrepreneurial accumulation of capital, and proletarianization of the rural masses. In accordance with this logic, given that "dependent capitalism" can neither enable the peasantry to become bourgeois nor proletarianize it, the inevitable result is that the rural mass, as a whole, appears to be structurally revolutionary and radically antagonistic to the system.

But good intentions can neither halt the avalanche of conclusive facts nor change the course of history. This interpretation has foundered largely for two reasons: (1) dependency theory has not managed to explain how, despite the famous "structural limits," capitalism has developed in Mexico; and (2) its economism, which derives political theses from economic facts, has exploded in the face of the enormous complexity of political life. The inescapable fact is that in spite of the specific and singular traits of Mexican capitalism (and, I believe, to a large extent because of them), the process of capital accumulation reaches unanticipated heights, and the system of exploitation is being modernized, branching out, and becoming more complex. What is more important, the Gordian knot of the traditional agrarian struggle is being swallowed whole and digested by capitalism, which apparently has not resulted in fatal congestion. Contrary to what was foreseen by populist orthodoxy, during the recent years of intense economic crisis, the peasant movement properly speaking—with an agrarian orientation—has not become a global alternative to the system, has not had the initiative, and has not become widespread on a national scale. Nor has the struggle for land become a spontaneous unifying force. On the contrary, rather than concentrating on the "peasant question," the rural movements have branched out, invaded new areas, and presented a rich, heterogeneous spectrum of fronts articulated, instead, around the struggle for political democracy. The course of the struggles and conflicts in the countryside has shown that we are witnessing a bankruptcy of agrarianism, in both its populist expressions and its technocratic strain. The agrarian theses of the campesinista stripe that have taken on an orthodox Marxist formulation have only managed to introduce enormous confusion. All their efforts have gone toward proving that the peasant's existence is logically possible within capitalism for the simple reason that he struggles for his existence. This tautology is usually surrounded with such a jumble of dogmatic double-talk that it is almost impossible to take away from it anything clear-cut—except, as a Leibniz of the poor would say, that the peasant lives logically subsumed in the worst of all possible worlds.[4]

How did the crisis of agrarianism come about? The hegemony of technocratic currents in the government that was consolidated in the late seventies gave way to a policy that could be labeled a true attempt to "disamortize" (or expropriate) peasant assets. As in the case of the Indian communal lands affected by the Lerdo Law of 1856, the López Portillo government initiated an aggressive economic policy against the peasants, whose lands were viewed (from the capitalist perspective) as being in the possession of "dead hands." This is the significance of the Agriculture Development Act, which began a process that culminated in 1991 with the modification of Article 27 of the Mexican Constitution.

When I began pointing out in 1972 that the rental of ejido land was a necessity of the voracious processes of the expansion of capitalism in Mexican agriculture, to many it seemed an abstract, theoretical polemic remote from reality. Today, those processes that we were observing have been embodied in an alternative whose power and reality no one can doubt, one that is usually referred to as "modern policy" in the terminology of the technocrats. This policy began with the Agriculture Development Act, which openly authorizes the renting of ejido parcels, as well as the use of wage labor on lands that were distributed "to those who worked them." The new legislation allows the land to belong, not to the one who works it, but to the one who makes it produce, a slight nuance that hides the abyss that separates the battered peasant economy from the capitalist economy.

Even though, for bureaucratic reasons, this law has not proved to be very functional, it had great importance in legitimizing the rental of land and the expansion of entrepreneurial forms of production in the ejido zones. It is worth the effort to describe briefly the way it was formulated, for it is revealing of the contradictory terms in which the Mexican state argues with itself. In the introduction to the legislation, "rentism" was demagogically rejected, although it is obvious that by "attacking it through its causes," what the bill did was simply to establish in a sham fashion regulations for what was already occurring on a massive scale. Under this law, the ejidos and communities can make agreements with "small property owners" in order to create units of production with legal capacity to "hire laborers" *(wages)* and to distribute the "earnings" *(profits)* among those who contributed the land *(ground rent)* and the material resources *(capital)*, which "will be valued in accordance with their importance in production."[5] There we have, then, all the classic ingredients of agrarian capitalism, which was invited by law to take into its own "living hands" the production that the "dead hands" of the peasants participating in ejidos and working communal lands are not capable of developing. The economic policy related to these ideas displaced and marginalized the Ministry of Agrarian Reform from these matters. The modernization of agriculture is watched over by the grand bastion of the agrarian technocracy, the powerful Ministry of Agriculture and Water Resources.

These technocratic tendencies finally succeeded in 1991 in introducing into the constitution the legal changes necessary to permit the sale and rental of ejido lands as well as the investment of domestic and foreign private capital in the ejidos. Furthermore, the process of land distribution was declared at an end.

Nevertheless, the Mexican government did not totally abandon traditional agrarian rhetoric. With the aim of "revitalizing the alliance between the state and the peasants" and of solving the problem of the nutritional deficits of the population and the country, the López Portillo administration implemented the so-called Mexican Food System (Sistema Alimentario Mexicano, or SAM). On the eve of the agricultural crisis, the rural population went to sleep with the comforting populist dream of the SAM, but it awoke to a cold technocratic morning with an agro-capitalist development law. The administration of Carlos Salinas de Gortari repeated the operation with even more daring: it put in place a populist National Solidarity Program to mitigate the discontent of the marginalized masses but immediately thereafter opened the way for the disamortization of ejido lands. Perhaps the SAM and the solidarity program, with their streams of promises, were nothing more than a soporific to mitigate the pain of a brutal entrepreneurial surgical operation on Mexican agriculture? Or was it a question of a bitter internal struggle between sectors of the technocracy that assigned to themselves, in some cases, the representation of peasant interests and, in others, the interests of efficient agriculture and modern livestock-raising? Surely both interpretations are valid: they complement one another.

The advent, and subsequent calamity, of the SAM is a process that enables one to confirm that the theses developed in this book strike sensitive nerves and allow one to understand some of the basic aspects of the agrarian structure and the political system in Mexico. What has the SAM been in reality? In spite of its guise as a happy peasant food utopia, the SAM never got beyond being a price and distribution policy aimed at increasing production of basic grains and at strengthening the situation of the strata of well-off peasants. (Of course, large agricultural producers also benefited from this policy.) In a veiled and grudging manner, the authors of the SAM themselves recognized that "a portion" of the agricultural producers could not be made the subject of plans for development: "a segment of the producers at infra-subsistence level, because of their extremely diminished resources (from one-half hectare to two hectares of poor dry-farming land) *will not be able to subsist as farmers.*" The SAM's authors do not clarify the point, but it so happens that in 1970 the so-called infra-subsistence-level peasants with fewer than two hectares totaled almost one million producers (without counting their families), that is, 65 percent of all infra-subsistence-level producers and more than one-third of the total number of producers. What did the SAM propose for them? "Here it would be appropriate," they said, "to *consolidate areas* in order that a portion of them might attain viability as producers, and other segments of them would have to be made *subjects of employment and food subsidy policies in other spheres.*"[6] What this means, in other words, is *concentration of property and proletarianization-pauperization of the peasantry.*

An excellent study done for the Economic Commission for Latin America (CEPAL) reveals a considerably more somber situation: 72 percent of the agricultural production units in 1970 are "units in the actual or potential process of disintegration," and it concludes by agreeing that "this important sector corresponds to what some authors characterize as 'the peasant sector in disintegration,' as does the agricultural semi-proletariat or the poor peasant sector."[7] This sector, which "requires extrapraedial income in order to be able to take care of its own consumption as well as the reproduction of the peasant unit," cannot be considered to be composed of "entrepreneurs with meager resources" in whom a traditional agricultural policy might discover some hidden efficiency: 83 percent of those whom the CEPAL study cited above classifies, in spite of everything, as "peasants" are to be found in this terrible situation.

Thus, even being quite optimistic, one can apply the technocratic policies for agricultural development to more than a quarter of the agricultural production units in the country only with great difficulty. Yet, even within this sector, strong polarizing tendencies are at work to restrict the operative spectrum of the dominant technocratic policy: in fact, the majority of these plans contribute gradually to the polarization of the units of production, to the increase of inequities, and to the ruin of many peasants.[8]

As can be seen, Mexican political reality and agrarian structure are extraordinarily complex. This book offers an interpretation that arose out of a renewal of Marxist analyses. But I want to point out some flaws and some risks that have slowed down research and discussion along the path that I propose, which ought to be a road open to multiple possibilities. Many of the arguments over the agrarian question have set out along a rugged path that in my judgment leads nowhere but into the swamp of dogmatism. This path has been the somewhat frenetic search for a "revolutionary subject" endowed with such virtues and located in such structures that it ought to lead us inevitably to the Promised Land. When it became evident that the multifaceted peasantry contained complex, heterogeneous contradictions, the specter of the rural proletariat appeared; it seemed like a changing of the guard, in which the exhausted peasant was relieved. This is a half-truth, and like all half-truths, if not explored in all its aspects, it can lead to great distortions.

The Marxist studies have run a grave risk here: they have come close to the danger of replacing campesinista populism with laborist messianism, which is, in the end, nothing more than the urban, modern slant on the old scheme: populism and laborism are two faces of the same coin. The difficulty resides in the fact that Marxism evolves in a doctrinaire environment that imprisons even those of us who struggle to liberate ourselves from dogmatic restraints, for the dogma flows everywhere, into our surroundings, and it influences the meaning of concepts and the course of research. For example, the use of the concept *mode of production* led to enormous misunderstandings because it represented a set of magic words that, once pronounced, unleashed a ceremonial fetishism among the zealous guardians of the structural key to society. But, correspondingly, it prompted the holy furor of those who believed that by casting a spell with the notion of *class struggle*, they were obtaining the sure password to revolutionary struggle. The same thing has occurred with the concept of the *proletariat:* as a result of being used to invoke revolutionary movements, it has ended up obscuring from us the real, living forms that make up the modern working class and hiding the always unpublicized processes by which revolutionary events are generated.

What I am labeling *proletarianization of the peasantry* is something rather more complex than the mere replacement of one revolutionary subject by another, new one. It is the opening of a new area for struggles, correlations, and contradictions, the opening of a space that contemplates what has been called an expansion of the revolutionary subject. I would say that this expansion is also a formidable explosion that annihilates the very notion of *subject*. That substantially *proletarian* character that the rural mass acquires is not a unifying stamp that indicates a homogeneous subject but the heterogeneous result of the explosion that occurs in agriculture when modern capitalism expands. One should not be deceived: the unifying fact of the expansion of wage relations generates a sociopolitical and cultural space that, precisely because of its relatively homogeneous support, opens an unsuspected multiplicity of new situations and alternatives. In contrast, the great dispersion and disunity of the classic peasantry—described by Marx as a sack of potatoes—has historically generated political spaces much more homogeneous than those created by the omnipresent modern capitalist market.

Translator's note. English translations of key Spanish words in the text appear in parentheses following the Spanish. Some of these have been supplied by the translator.

Chapter 1

Agriculture and Capitalism

He suffers from four or five illnesses, but the most serious of them is his robust health.

—Mario Benedetti,
El cumpleaños de Juan Angel

AGRARIAN structures and the political situations that find their origins in them have been and continue to be a challenge for Marxist analysis.[1] Not a few have lost themselves in the labyrinth of rural life without obtaining anything but simplistic outlines or interminable descriptions of more or less incomprehensible phenomena. In the case of Latin America, this statement is particularly true; but it is also noteworthy that Marxist researchers have almost completely ignored the tools that Marx developed for the purpose of understanding the evolution of agriculture. In fact, in many cases the analyses of Latin American agrarian situations have been limited to studies with a populist slant. Today, the situation is changing, even though the vices of the past persist. In this study I attempt to show how the classic Marxist interpretations of agrarian problems represent an indispensable point of departure for understanding Mexican and Latin American rural reality. Nevertheless, as can be surmised, the theoretical problems that they have bequeathed us have been numerous.

Although this study is fundamentally theoretical, it represents a compact synthesis of concrete research experiences. I am convinced that only through the stimulus of these empirical studies could I have reached the point of setting up the analytical models proposed here.[2] These models are offered as valid for Mexican agrarian reality, but I believe that to a certain point they can be generally applied to Latin America and to some countries of the so-called Third World.

Paths of the Development
of Capitalism in Agriculture

A reading of the last chapter of *Capital* will not have ceased to hamper those who try to understand the agrarian structure of a capitalist country like Mexico: "The owners of mere labour power, the owners of capital, and the landowners, whose respective sources of income are wages, profit, and ground-rent—in other words wage-labourers, capitalists and landowners—form the three great classes of modern society based on the capitalist mode of production."[3]

And where should one of the most numerous classes of our rural areas, the *campesinos,* be located? In addressing this question, two simplistic escapes have been used: (1) in the countryside, precapitalist forms of production survive, and thus it is necessary to use the model of the feudal mode of production to explain the situation; (2) the capitalist mode of production predominates; ergo, the peasants are in fact proletarians. From either of these perspectives, the application of the fundamental concepts utilized by Marx in the analysis of class structure—wages, profit, and ground rent—has been abandoned. We will attempt to demonstrate that given that Mexico is a capitalist country, it is not possible to understand its agrarian structure except by starting with these concepts. That fact notwithstanding, the second alternative mentioned (i.e., that peasants equal proletarians) is fundamentally false.

The three concepts that I consider indispensable for the interpretation of Mexican agriculture (wages, profit, and ground rent) will oblige me to restate the basic premises of the development of capitalism: (1) the separation of wage labor power and the means of production (which generates, on one hand, wage labor and, on the other, the concentration of the means of production such as capital); (2) the process of the commercial accumulation of capital, prior to the development of the capitalist mode of production; and (3) the evolution of systems of ground rent.

Nevertheless, if anything is clear in the Marxist interpretation of agrarian evolution, it is that this evolution cannot be understood in strictly economic terms: the role of the political dimension is so important that without examining it one cannot manage to understand the background of the problem. This is especially true in Mexico, where the modalities that agriculture assumes cannot be understood without a prior study of the roots of the agrarian reform that originated in the heat of the Revolution of 1910. A good example of the decisive importance of the political dimension of agrarian processes can be found in Lenin's analyses.

Lenin stated that capitalist development in agriculture takes two paths: (1) the old landholding economy, tied to serfdom, is slowly transformed into an entrepreneurial capitalist economy (of the Junker type) thanks to the internal evolution of the latifundio; and (2) a revolutionary process destroys the old landholding economy, the forms of large property, and the systems of servitude, giving way to the development of the small peasant farm, which, in turn, will begin to break down before the assault of capitalism.[4]

Either path leads to the capitalist agricultural enterprise, in a process of de-peasantization and of replacement of the system of payment in labor (or other precapitalist forms) by the wage system. De-peasantization is in reality the birth of an agricultural proletariat torn from the land with greater or lesser violence; this can only occur parallel to an accumulation of capital and a concentration of the production that has wage labor as its basis. This process follows the outlines of what Marx labeled the primitive accumulation of capital.

But absent from the panorama painted by Lenin and from his brilliant analysis of the evolution of Russian agriculture is the concept of ground rent, which for Marx represented the key to capitalist development of agriculture and to what we might call "the English path." It is apparent that Lenin was familiar with this concept, as several of his texts demonstrate.[5] However, the references to the concept are theoretical in nature; it is rare to find ground rent applied to the Russian agrarian problem.

Furthermore, Marx dedicates many pages of the third volume of *Capital* to explaining, on the basis of the English example, the birth, development, and features of capitalist agriculture. The key concept is that of ground rent, which offers an explanation of the existence of a landholding class that receives such a rent without affecting the realization of a normal (average) profit on the part of another social class: the agrarian bourgeoisie. On the basis of the English example, it can be said that three classes are found in agriculture: the landholder, the capitalist, and the agricultural worker. Only the existence of a superprofit in agricultural production can explain the fact that the capitalist can earn the *average rate* of profit and pay rent to the landowner as well.

To put matters simply, the origin of this superprofit in agriculture is explained by two factors: (1) production on certain lands offers special advantages (fertile soil, proximity to markets, possibilities for more accelerated turnover of capital, etc.), which generates the various forms of so-called differential rent. But it is also true that even the worst lands produce rent: (2) the low organic composition of the capital in agriculture (technological backwardness, greater investment in labor power) produces a surplus value greater than the average profit in a country. This absolute rent has its origins, ultimately, in private ownership of land. The absolute rent only disappears upon the disappearance of private property, but it *tends toward zero*, given that the long-term tendency, imposed by technological development, is one of a constant increase in the organic composition of agricultural capital. Further on I shall provide a more detailed explanation of this process, in conjunction with its application to Mexican reality.

In the three paths of development of capitalism in agriculture—Junker, revolutionary, and English—we find situations that imply a complex, clashing articulation of social classes, forms, and modes of production. Only from a methodological perspective that accepts as a point of departure the existence of a *heterogeneity* of social classes, modes, and forms of production will it be possible to comprehend the phenomenon of capitalist development in those countries in which agriculture is still one of the principal underpinnings of the economy. This variety of situations and contexts arises from the overlapping of relations of production with phenomena that we may label extraeconomic and that are expressed in correlations among political forces and the forms of land ownership. Thus, it will be necessary to examine, although perhaps only briefly, the theoretical implications of transitional processes that enclose an articulation of different modes of production. In this fashion we will be able to understand the way the peasants are inserted into a process—the development of capitalism—that seems completely alien to them or in any case alienates them.

The Articulation of Modes of Production

It is a commonplace to state that Marx never developed a theory of social classes, but it is a falsehood. The Marxist theory of the modes of production is in fact a theory of social classes. The concept of mode of production is the theoretical matrix that makes possible an understanding of the class struggle. In a famous letter to Joseph Weydemeyer dated March 5, 1852, Marx made clear that he was not the one who had discovered either the class struggle or the anatomy of such struggles. Marx recognizes the originality of his own contribution to the theory of social classes in three points: (1) that the existence of the classes is linked only with predetermined historical phases of the development of production; (2) that class struggle necessarily leads to the dictatorship of the proletariat; and (3) that this dictatorship itself is only a transitional phase in the process leading to the abolition of all classes and to a classless society.

Lenin, however, in his famous definition of social classes, characterizes them primarily in terms of their relationship with a historically determined social system of production. I would not want to begin a Talmudic debate over terminology here, but I have no doubt that Marx's concept of the "determined historic phase of the development of production" and Lenin's concept of "historically determined social system of production" have been crystallized in the term *mode of production*. Let us consider, as an example, Marx's definition of the term:

> Scientific analysis of the capitalist mode of production proves . . . that this is a mode of production of a particular kind and a specific historical determinacy; that like any other particular mode of production it assumes a given level of social productive forces and their forms of development as its historical precondition, a condition that is itself the historical result and product of a previous process and from which the new mode of production proceeds as its given foundation; that the relations of production corresponding to this specific and historically determined mode of production—relations into which men enter in their social life-process, in the production of their social life—have a specific, historical and transitory character; and that finally the relations of distribution are essentially identical with these relations of production, the reverse side of the same coin, so that the two things share the same historically transitory character.[6]

However, certain of Marx's texts refer to the concept of mode of production as an abstraction that expresses a "model" that has no "pure," real existence in any society. In this sense, the mode of production would be, in Marx's own words, an "ideal average."[7] Is there a contradiction between that ideal abstract character and its specific, historically determined character? Is one actually dealing with two different concepts under a single name? On the basis of this apparent contradiction, there have been attempts to detach these two concepts from one another: on the one hand, mode of production, which refers to a formal, abstract object, and on the other, the economic formation of society, which refers to a concrete, real object.[8] This means that the dividing line between what Marx called the simple abstract determination and the concrete as synthesis of multiple determinations,[9] as two levels of the process of knowledge, would enable one to distinguish between the abstract concept of mode of production and the concrete concept of economic social formation. In accordance with this position, what Marx achieved in discovering the laws of the capitalist mode of production would be barely an intermediate step in the process of knowledge that sets out from the *concrete represented* and arrives at the *concrete-real*.

The difficulty with such interpretations is that in accordance with Marx's method, the economic formation contains within itself the specific, historically determined articulation (mode of production) that enables one to understand the complex of social relations in a given society. How, then, is it to be supposed that the abstract element represents the specific embodiment of the concrete? There seems to be an inversion here. Marx wrote:

5

In all forms of society it is one specific [form of] production which itself and so likewise in its relations determines the position and influence of all the rest. It is a *general* illumination which bathes all other colors and modifies their particularity. It is a special ether which determines the specific gravity of all existence which is conspicuous in it.[10]

In the famous 1859 Preface to *A Contribution to the Critique of Political Economy*, Marx assigns to the modes of production (Asiatic, ancient, feudal, and capitalist) the historicity (periodicity) and specificity of the development of the economic formation of the society. Thus, the mode of production is the concrete synthesis of multiple determinations that enable one to explain the particularities as well as the generalities of an economic formation. The concept of economic formation, if understood as a combination of various modes and forms of production, is not a concept that indicates greater concreteness, since such concreteness is expressed in the dominant mode of production. The concept of economic formation of society expresses a global reality by means of a greater dissociation from the terms of the particular-general synthesis; therefore, the concept enables one to recognize the historical and logical links of the parts of one whole and permits one to locate the specific features determined by the whole and the conditions of the generalization of the specific features of the different social forms. The concept of economic formation represents a "combinator" of different elements, in which the traces of a still-abstract level of the process of knowledge are recognized. The true synthesis, which is expressed by the concept of mode of production, erases the impressions of a classificatory combination in order to make way for the conceptual representation of the historically multidetermined concrete totality.

From the foregoing observations, it can be discerned that the category of mode of production refers fundamentally to the economic bases of the society. This means that the outline of the levels mentioned (economic, political, and ideological) is not used here as a direct function of the mode of production (i.e., each mode of production with its respective three internal levels). In my judgment, the complexity and relative independence of the superstructure prevent one from going forward to analyze and classify it in exactly the same way that study of the economic formation makes possible. The principal reason is that the superstructure is firmly dominated, united, and welded together by that which represents the synthesis of modern society: the state. The "combinator" of political and ideological categories responds to conditions that do not automatically arise out of the "combinator" of modes and forms of production.

That is, the concrete character of a mode of production—which is conferred upon it by its historical articulation with other determined modes of production as well as by its own specificity—does not in itself assist the formal reduction of the political superstructure to the economic base. Much less is it possible to situate the functions of the political apparatus as a mediation between two or more articulated modes of production. The idea may seem attractive: the state would be the mediator between the world of the specific precapitalist modes of production and capitalism as the only truly universal mode of production, between feudal peasant barbarity and modern civilization. Actually, this is how bourgeois ideology presents the problem to us. In reality, the mediation (therefore, the unity and the contradiction) between two modes of production is not represented by third elements (politics, circulation, etc.), much as the state in its contradiction with civil society does not require true mediations (social classes, etc.). The "articulation" between civil society and state, just like that established between different modes and forms of production, itself generates—within the spheres that are being articulated—the necessary conditions for their contradictory union. This does not mean that, in fact, the conditions of a historically determined articulation of modes of production are not going to influence significantly the configuration of the political superstructure. It is especially interesting to emphasize here the importance of the process through which the articulation between the peasant economy (with or without feudal remnants) and the capitalist economy contributes to shaping specific forms of political power and ideological expression that appear in a mediating guise. These forms produce perfectly real—that is, historical—illusions, as real and necessary for bourgeois society as, for example, the economic category of exchange value. The commodity, in effect, behaves in the same mysterious way in which political mediations appear to us: like something "physically metaphysical," as Marx said, which, notwithstanding the fact that they exist through the independence of different spheres of production and of the superstructure, appear in one deceptive form and express the social character—the unity—of the process. The articulation of different modes of production does not in itself imply anything mysterious. The mysteries and the illusions arise historically as the fetishized expression of the coherence of the transition process, which, although it articulates different productive spheres, takes place in the same society and upon the basis of the essential unity of the social and economic relations that create the passage from one epoch to another.

These reflections seek, more than anything else, to clarify the terms of the argument developed in this essay, with the aim of avoiding confusion and advancing the understanding of the clashing situations that involve articulation of different modes and forms of production.

An articulation of two or more modes of production implies

a. that the subordinate modes and forms of production take on a double character (their own and the one their subordination confers upon them); and

b. that the dominant mode of production, through its historical determination, contains within its internal structure mechanisms specific to its own form of exploitation as well as mechanisms that simultaneously link it to and separate it from other modes of production.

This is the way in which the specificity of a mode of production (its concrete, real character) expresses the structural contradictions of the entirety of the economic formation. Thus, the problem resides not in the fact that the modes of production never appear in a "pure" form (a problem that is, basically, nonexistent) but in the way in which such "impurities" are converted into the historically determined specificity of a mode of production.

The best example I can offer is that of capitalism, focusing the discussion on the process of transition from precapitalist society to bourgeois society. Marx explained this process by means of two complementary conceptual tools: his theory of the primitive accumulation of capital and his theory of the transformation of absolute into relative surplus value (of the transformation of formal subordination into real subordination of labor by capital).[11]

The theory of the primitive accumulation of capital explains the transition process in its entirety, in its general characteristics; in turn, the theory of formal and real subordination of labor by capital explains the process concretely, as it manifests itself within the capitalist mode of production. For this reason, I will discuss briefly the special features of this latter aspect. Marx defined it this way: "It is in contradistinction to this last that we come to designate as the *formal subsumption of labour under capital* what we have discussed earlier, viz. the takeover by capital of a mode of labour developed before the emergence of capitalist relations."[12]

Marx suggests that the various precapitalist modes of production are transformed into processes of production of capital by means of a purely monetary relation that, nevertheless, situates the direct producer (peasant, craftsman, slave) as the personification of labor subordinate to capital. This occurs without modification of the noncapitalist conditions of production:

> However, the specifically capitalist mode of production has yet other methods of exacting the surplus value at its disposal. But given a preexisting mode of labour, i.e., an *established* development of the productive power of labour and a mode of labour corresponding to this productive power, surplus value can be created only by lengthening the working day, i.e., by increasing *absolute surplus value*.[13]

Of Marx's theory of the formal subordination of labor to capital, we can conclude as follows:

1. That the capitalist mode of production expresses in its very specificity the articulation with other modes of production, under the form of absolute surplus value. This demonstrates the *concrete* character of the concept of mode of production, which is capable of expressing its articulation with a prior, different mode of production, without altering its specificity because of that fact, by means of a category that only makes complete sense for capitalism: absolute surplus value.

2. That this type of subordination indicates a transition structure in which, despite the fact that the capitalist mode of production is already dominant, the old mode of production as such remains. "There is no change as yet in the mode of production itself. . . . The *labour process* goes on as before, with the proviso that it is now subordinated to capital."[14]

3. That the innovation in the relations of subordination of labor, with respect to the previous conditions, consists in the fact that such relations are reduced to a pure monetary character, eliminating all vestiges of a patriarchal, political, and religious nature. This difference between the new subordination to capital and prior relations represents the embryo and the bases for the typical forms of exploitation of developed capitalism: real subordination or relative surplus value.

At first glance, Marx's analysis might seem to identify—in the case of formal subordination—the monetary relation as essential and as mediating. But what does this monetary relation express? It expresses the substitution of extraeconomic coercion of the direct producer by a new form of purely economic domination, in which the capitalist consumes, watches over, and directs labor power. However, the monetary relation reveals, simultaneously, that the relation of domination has changed only *formally*, purifying it of extraeconomic political and social elements; but it forms the necessary base for the reduction of the necessary labor time (relative surplus value). In sum, the monetary relation between modes of production is, in reality, a form of (absolute) surplus value, in effect a form of exploitation that is explained, not at the level of circulation, but by the conditions of production. These conditions indicate that the dominance of capital still does not change the forms of production typical of other, previous modes of production. Purely monetary circulation does nothing more than express this particular articulation of production, which is still in the process of transition.

The Simple Commodity Mode of Production

It is important to take up again the problem of exchange value. I will attempt to link the examination of the concept to the definition of the simple commodity mode of production. I use the example of this mode of production because I believe that of all the noncapitalist systems of production, this is the one that takes on the greatest significance in the contemporary history of the so-called underdeveloped countries. At the outset, I believe it necessary to note that this mode of production is considered to have a secondary, subordinate character. Even in eras in which capital did not yet dominate the whole of the society, this mode of production did not achieve dominance, for one of its specific characteristics is precisely its secondary nature. In this system, typical of the smallholding peasant and the craftsman, the producer possesses the means of production (tools, land, etc.), works directly in the productive process, and sells in the market a more or less significant portion of his production. This mode of production is secondary by nature for a simple reason: it is not a class-based system; that is, no dominant class that can subjugate the entire society arises out of it. It could be argued that in preclass societies this mode of production could be dominant; it certainly could in a case where, in similar societies, there was a mercantile system, itself a fruit of class-based society.

But what is interesting here is its articulation with the capitalist system. From this perspective, its connection appears at the level of commercial relations and is characterized fundamentally by a relation of exchange of nonequivalents that transfers to the capitalist sector the surplus labor generated by the work of the peasant and the craftsman. The law of value typical of the capitalist economy cannot be applied to noncapitalist forms of production unless powerful reasons exist for doing so. When we find articulation of the capitalist and peasant economies in a society, is it possible to apply the law of value to the whole? In my judgment, when a society articulated in this way is dominated by the capitalist market (which means that the capitalist mode of production is dominant), the concepts of wages, profit, and ground rent can—and should—be applied to the economy. This, as I shall attempt to show, does not imply that these categories explain the internal dynamic of the peasant economy.

That wages are not paid on the typical peasant farm (or are paid only occasionally) is undeniable. But this does not mean that family labor power is not compensated in some way. Here one departs from the analysis of a peasant simple commodity economy, that is, one in which the greatest part of the production is sold to the capitalist market.[15] The way the labor is compensated acquires, through the latter, a monetary character even when parallel elements of subsistence consumption persist. What is it that keeps us from considering this monetary compensation as wages? The fact that, objectively, the worker is simultaneously the owner (or usufructuary) of the means of production (the land, the tools, etc.). Marx referred directly to the problem in these terms:

What is, then, the situation of the independent craftsmen or peasants who do not employ workers and who therefore do not produce as capitalists? . . . They are *producers of commodities* . . . to me they appear to be sellers of commodities, not sellers of labor, and consequently this relation has nothing to do with the distinction between *productive* and *unproductive labor* that depends entirely on whether the labor is exchanged for money as money, or for money as capital. Thus, they belong neither to the category of *productive workers* nor to that of *unproductive workers*, although they produce commodities. But their production does not enter into the capitalist mode of production.[16]

Here, the problem is posed clearly: the peasant economy is not a type of capitalist *production*; rather, it is a matter of an economy *articulated* with the capitalist mode of production: "We are confronted with a characteristic feature of a society in which a definite mode of production predominates, although not all productive relations may have been subordinated to it."[17] Marx says further on in the same text:

The independent peasant or the artisan is divided into two persons. As owner of the means of production, he is a capitalist; as a worker, he is his own wage laborer. Consequently, as a capitalist he pays himself his wage and extracts his profit from his capital; that is, he exploits himself as a wage laborer and pays himself, with the surplus value, the tribute that labor owes to capital. It is possible that he may also be paying himself a third share as landlord (ground rent).[18]

It should be quite clear that this type of analysis is only valid for a peasant economy integrated into the capitalist system. Nevertheless, the interesting aspect of this interpretation is that it enables one to understand the insertion or articulation of one mode of production within another, dominant one. From this perspective, peasant labor is compensated in a peculiar way, which Marx defines in *Capital*: the self-conferred wage.

In the text quoted above, Marx was departing from the explicit assumption that the peasant sold his goods for their value and that therefore he was generating surplus value. In *Capital* he addresses directly the problem of the compensation of labor, of the "wage that [the peasant] pays himself, after deducting his actual expenses."[19] This self-compensation is at times reduced to the "strictly physical limit":

It is not necessary for the market price to rise either up to the value of his product or to its price of production. This is one of the reasons why the price of corn in countries where small-scale ownership predominates is lower than in countries of the capitalist mode of production. A portion of the surplus labour of the peasants working under the least favourable conditions is presented to society for nothing and does not contribute toward governing the price of production or forming value.[20]

The question whether peasant labor does or does not have value is not one of exclusively theoretical interest. Determining whether the pay that peasant labor receives is located above or below its value will enable one to understand the peasant's class position and his place within a system of domination. Nevertheless, what will be the value of the peasant's labor, as distinct from its *price* (which is what he himself assigns to it)? Will there be a difference here between *value* and *price?*

We know that the magnitude of the value of an object is the socially necessary labor time to produce it. In order to be able to determine the magnitude of the value of a commodity produced by a peasant, it is indispensable to know the value of the labor power incorporated into the commodity. Now, the value of the labor power is the value of the means of subsistence necessary to ensure its possessor's subsistence: "In a given country, at a given period, the average amount of the means of subsistence necessary for the worker is a known *datum.*"[21] In another section Marx says, "The individual commodity counts here only as an average sample of its kind."[22] It would not be correct to measure the value of the peasant's labor power solely as a function of *its* productive capacity; it is obvious that in a capitalist country this is below the average and that, seemingly, the magnitude of the value ought to be greater. But this is not so: if a peasant invests triple the time in producing a ton of wheat that a day laborer does on a capitalist farm, that fact does not make the value of his labor power vary: "The same labour, therefore, performed for the same length of time always yields the same amounts of value, independently of any variations in productivity."[23] The change in productive capacity, which increases the labor's yield in a capitalist agricultural enterprise, "also brings about a reduction in the value of this increased total amount, if it cuts down the total amount of labour-time necessary to produce the use-values."[24]

That is, the determining factor is always the socially necessary labor time, and the productive capacity of the labor influences the value through such labor time in an inverse relation (the greater the capacity of labor, the lower the total value, *provided that* the necessary labor time invested varies). The problem, then, consists in knowing the number of hours that the peasant invests in production. Once this datum is obtained, by discounting to the market price of the commodities the cost of constant capital, we will know the price that such labor has acquired in the society; but this is a price that fluctuates with respect to each product and that varies constantly in accordance with the fluctuations in supply and demand. In reality, this price of labor power varies enormously because it includes within it the profit, theoretical or real (i.e., positive or negative), to which the peasant, as owner of the means of production, has a right.

But the value of the labor power is, as noted, determined by a fixed factor (not by the laws of supply and demand); this fixed factor crystallizes socially in the average wage for simple labor. That is, the particular circumstances of an era and a country generate conditions such that an average value of labor power appears, one that is applied on a national scale: "In contrast, therefore, with the case of other commodities, the determination of the value of labour-power contains a historical and moral element."[25] It was for this reason that Marx spoke of the value of peasant labor power, for in a society dominated by the capitalist mode of production, everything that has a relation with the market acquires an exchange value. The peasant's peculiarity is that he does not offer the market his labor power, but his produce. But this does not save him from becoming ensnared in the capitalist social dynamic.

Now we can pose a collateral problem: if peasant labor power has value and generates surplus value, could we say that we are dealing with productive labor? In fact, it is possible to answer either affirmatively or negatively. If we look at the peasant unit of production from the perspective that it contains, in a single person, a capitalist relation of production, then we will be able to affirm that within it there is productive labor. But the relation that the peasant sets up with the market is a relation between the seller of a commodity and a buyer; from this point of view, there is not productive labor. Thus, Marx concludes that from the perspective of the capitalist mode of production, peasants are producers of commodities whom it is not possible to characterize as unproductive or productive;[26] that is, they belong to another mode of production. Nevertheless, this mode of production sets up a distribution relation with the capitalist mode that obscures a relation of production. For this reason the problem of the value of peasant labor and the commodity that it produces has great significance. It must be recalled that this value is not an abstract substance but the concrete expression of a relationship among human beings. Applied to the peasant economy, the law of value enables us to discover relations of exploitation between the peasants on one side and the bourgeoisie on the other.

These relations of exploitation impose a peculiar dynamic upon the peasantry: they lead it toward its own extinction. The essence of these relations is an unequal exchange (or an exchange of nonequivalents) that derives from a difference between the magnitude of the value of commodities and their price: when the peasant sells his commodity at a price lower than its value, he is carrying out a nonequivalent exchange transaction. This mechanism of value transfer is one of the most profound sources of the structural impossibility of the peasant economy's coexistence with the capitalist system without its *tending* to disappear and to be destroyed (or tending to become, in the minority of cases, a capitalist enterprise):

The possibility, therefore, of a quantitative incongruity between price and magnitude of value, i.e., the possibility that the price may diverge from the magnitude of value, is inherent in the price-form itself. This is not a defect, but, on the contrary, it makes this form the adequate one for a mode of production whose laws can only assert themselves as blindly operating averages between constant irregularities.[27]

This feature is the one that Marx explains later, in the third volume of *Capital*, by means of the category of average rate of profit. However, there are "disturbing incidental circumstances which are irrelevant to the actual course of the process" that create exchanges of nonequivalents in a different sense from the one signified by the "haphazard" deviation of prices around the average value.[28] In the first volume Marx investigates "the *process of capitalist production*, taken by itself, . . . in which connection all secondary influences external to this process were left out of account."[29] The third volume, on the other hand, attempts to "discover and present the concrete forms which grow out of the process of capital's movement considered as a whole."[30]

Among the concrete "influences" and "secondary influences" that cause variations in the conditions of free competition presupposed in the analysis of the deviations between values and prices that appears in the first volume of *Capital*, we find the existence of modes of production or of remnants of old relations of production at the core of capitalist society. When these situations create *monopoly* conditions, the possibility that the divergence between prices and values may be frozen and that it may remain fixed as a norm arises. In such cases the transfers of value that are generated for that reason also become norms.

The best-known monopoly phenomenon is that of the private ownership of land. In this case, the landholders require that the commodity price regularly be set above value (and value above the cost of production). The difference constitutes *ground rent*. This phenomenon responds, undoubtedly, to the persistence of superstructural conditions inherited from other eras (latifundio, private property, etc.) that require the capitalist system to adapt.

The unequal exchange with the peasant economy develops from another type of monopoly: the one that the bourgeoisie exercises over the capitalist market. Here I am referring not only to the existence of monopoly prices, typical of the imperialist epoch, but also to the monopoly that every bourgeoisie naturally exercises over its market, in the face of a noncapitalist class of sellers of commodities (the peasants).

This last situation is quite similar, by virtue of its internal mechanism, to the unequal exchange relation on a worldwide scale described by Arghiri Emmanuel.[31] One can—and should—make the same observation that Christian Palloix has made: the unequal exchange that Emmanuel analyzes does not, as he suggests, place the workers of the underdeveloped countries in opposition to those in the developed countries (in the sense that the latter would benefit from imperialist plundering). Similarly, industrial workers do not exploit the peasants in the sense that the former would benefit from so-called "internal colonialism." On an international level, "it is a question of the dependence of one bourgeois class with respect to another bourgeois class."[32]

The monopoly situations in agriculture (with respect to land and the market) also place social groups in opposition to one another *to the extent that they belong to the bourgeoisie:* capitalists and landowners, capitalists and peasants.[33] In the latter case, the situation is quite complex: the peasant transfers value because *as owner of the means of production* he enters the market under disadvantageous conditions. There he is plundered, according to the situation, of part of his profit or his entire profit, and, frequently, a part of his wage as well. In this last case, the conditions that the capitalist market imposes upon him force the peasant into "self-exploitation" to such a degree that it reaches the "strictly physical limit." All these misfortunes befall the peasant, not because he is his own wage laborer, but because he is his own boss. Of course, if he were to enter into a relation involving the direct sale of his labor power (rather than the sale of agricultural products), he would not improve his situation; however, his proletarian condition would enable him to recognize the reasons for his poverty more easily.

One thing must be kept clear: *neither ground rent nor unequal exchange generates value.* That is, in and of themselves, they do not represent a relation of exploitation. In reality, they form a distribution relation and as such do not contribute to the formation of value: "However much we twist and turn, the final conclusion remains the same. If equivalents are exchanged, no surplus-value results, and if nonequivalents are exchanged, we still have no surplus-value. Circulation, or the exchange of commodities, creates no value."[34]

This is illustrated in an often-repeated anecdote of two jewelers who begin a daily mutual unequal exchange operation.[35] The two jewelers, whom we may call Garza and Legorreta, have shops on the same block. After buying a fine pearl necklace for 100,000 pesos, Garza boasts about his bargain to Legorreta, who immediately insists that Garza sell him the necklace. "I've promised my wife Laura beautiful pearls just like these. She'd love this necklace. I'll give you 110,000 pesos for it." Garza allows himself to be persuaded. At lunch, he proudly explains the deal to his wife María: "This morning I bought a necklace for 100,000 pesos, and then I turned around and sold it to Legorreta for 110,000 pesos—a profit of 10,000 pesos in a few minutes." His wife's response was scathing. "Don't you realize that if Legorreta bought the necklace from you for 110,000 pesos, it had to be because he knew that it's worth much more. Get it back, you fool!" Garza rushes to his competitor's shop. "Legorreta, if you want to keep on being my friend, sell the necklace back to me. María got terribly angry at me about it. Here, take 120,000 pesos, but give me the necklace." Legorreta gives in and that evening tells his wife the story. "Early today Garza came to sell me a necklace for 110,000 pesos, and this afternoon he bought it back for 120,000. I earned 10,000 pesos without so much as lifting a finger." Laura explodes: "Don't you realize that if Garza came back to you, it had to be because he knew that the necklace was worth much more? Get it back, you fool!" The next morning, Legorreta spreads out 130,000 pesos on Garza's counter and repurchases the necklace. The following day Garza buys it back for 140,000 pesos, and so it goes.

Some time later, the necklace has sold for 300,000 pesos and happens to be in Garza's hands. Legorreta arrives, puts down 310,000 pesos, and demands the pearls. "There is no necklace anymore," Garza tells him. "Just as I was closing last night, an American came in. I offered to sell him the pearls for 375,000 pesos, and he took it." Legorreta was distraught. "You sold our necklace! Each of us was happily, contentedly earning 10,000 pesos a day with those pearls. And you sold them! Our means of support!"

This story humorously imagines enrichment by transfer, without the intervention of production. The two jewelers were simply distributing on a daily basis the surplus value that had been created in another, quite distant place, perhaps Japan or Venezuela. This same thing is what happens, in essence, with unequal exchange and ground rent: "If a commodity is sold above or below its value, there is simply a different distribution of the surplus-value, and . . . this distribution, the altered ratio in which various persons partake of the surplus-value, in no way affects either the magnitude or the character of the surplus-value itself."[36]

In effect, the ground rent is not created by the landholder (nor by private ownership); rather, it is produced by the agricultural laborer, appropriated by the capitalist, and then transferred from the latter into the hands of the landholder. The unequal exchange seems to generate an amount of value, but in reality it does not come from the exchange itself: it is the profit that the owner of the productive unit would pocket if he himself were not the worker. Here, surplus labor has been generated in the day laborer–capitalist relation that is contained within the single person of the peasant. In this process of self-exploitation, the "bourgeois" has been incapable of retaining the profit extracted from himself as "proletarian"; nor has he even been able, generally, to function at a wage level equal to that in the society that surrounds him.

The benefit of the unequal exchange with the peasants forms part of the very profits that all capitalists obtain in a given society; it does not even appear as an additional profit that a specific sector appropriates for itself, as occurs in the case of ground rent.[37] That additional profit, which does not even have a name or a particular beneficiary, originates in the work of the peasant to the extent that he is a proletarian, and it is "presented to society for nothing" to the extent that the peasant is also a petty bourgeois who ingenuously presents himself with his commodity in the capitalist market.

From the viewpoint of the capitalist mode of production, the fruit of this unequal exchange takes the form of absolute surplus value. Under these conditions, the superexploitation (i.e., the paying of labor power below the average rate) forms the bases for an extraction of surpluses that, apparently, operates at the level of circulation. But this apparent "anomaly" in the operation of the law of value can only occur when commodity circulation forms a corridor that crosses a structural boundary, that is, when the commodity link constitutes a bond between *different* relations of production, between different modes of production. Thus, from the viewpoint of the capitalist mode of production, the superexploitation has an essentially sectorial, transitory, and conjunctural nature, even when, in underdeveloped countries, such junctures and transitions appear to be fixed and crystallized over a long period of time. The mechanisms of superexploitation cannot form the basis of any society in which the capitalist mode of production is dominant, but they make it possible to understand the articulation of some of its socioeconomic sectors.

Given these conditions, how is it possible to define simple commodity relations as a mode of production? It would seem, given their structural linkage with another mode of production, to be a matter of a theoretical reconstruction that generates an abstract and ahistorical concept, which is shown to be contradictory when opposed to the definition of mode of production that I have utilized to this point (i.e., as a concrete concept). However, it is necessary to underscore (as I did with regard to the capitalist mode of production) that the concept simultaneously encapsulates the structure as well as the historicity, its own characteristics as well as its articulation with other relations of production (past or future).

The double nature of the peasant and artisan economy constitutes its specificity as a mode of production; this double nature is expressed in the fact that the capitalist and the worker are fused into a single person: the direct producer. The duality results from the fact that while the peasant and the craftsman are exploited by capital (by way of the market), they themselves are the direct agents of such exploitation to the extent that they work under noncapitalist conditions of production. Every mode of production contains within its interior traces of old modes of production and the foreshadowing of the future mode. These traces and foreshadowings are not "impurities" or "distortions" of the mode of production; on the contrary, they form a part of its concrete, specific character. Just as capitalism contains the feudal past and proclaims the socialist future, the simple commodity mode of production contains its origin in the natural economy and proclaims its ruin in the petty bourgeois nature of the direct producer tied to the market.

In addition, every mode of production should contain (and generate in the superstructure) the conditions for its reproduction, for its permanency. The peasant and artisan economy is capable of reproducing the means of production that it needs, unless it is in an advanced state of deterioration. Within their incipient division of labor, the peasants and craftsmen are able to manufacture their own work tools (plow, looms, etc.). Of course, the absorption of this mode of production into the internal capitalist market causes slow destruction of the capacity for reproducing its own means of production, which are replaced by industrial products. Nevertheless, in the first phase, it is a question of substitution at the same or a similar level; that is, the work tools produced *outside* the simple commodity economy—to the extent that it still subsists—are not perceptibly superior to the ones made traditionally. (A mass-produced Egyptian plow can even be worse than one made by a craftsman.) In these cases, the backwardness of the peasant economy permits only the *substitution* of means of production under a certain technological shadow (thus the failures of the so-called green revolution in the backward sectors of agriculture). Moreover, the reproduction of labor power occurs right in the interior of the simple commodity economy, both from the viewpoint of training and teaching of work methods and from the viewpoint of its physical reproduction.

A more complex problem is reproduction of the relations of production. Every society must ensure that the labor power accepts the established social and political order that permits its exploitation. This "acceptance" of the relations of production is normally ensured by the repressive apparatus of the state and by the political structures of mediation. But in the case of a secondary mode of production not based on class—thus, one without its own state apparatus—it is not possible to locate the explanation of the reproduction of relations of production at the level of the state. It is true that at certain historic junctures, quite common in underdeveloped countries, the capitalist state finds itself faced with the need to support reproduction of noncapitalist forms of production. But this is only part of the explanation.

In the capitalist mode of production, the greater the exploitation, the greater the reproduction of proletarian labor power; however, in the simple commodity mode of production the spread and intensification of exploitation do not reproduce the peasantry or craftsmen as such but turn them into wage laborers. Thus, the intensification of the class struggle between capital and direct workers results in either the destruction of the peasant or craftsman as a class (if the results of the struggle are favorable to capital) or, in the exceptional case, the reproduction of the simple commodity mode of production (if the struggle is favorable to direct workers).

Accordingly, the secret of the reproduction of the simple commodity relations of production is found in the same conditions under which exploitation occurs: upon establishing *formal subordination*, capital generates the ideological and political mechanisms that continue shaping the special resistance of the peasant masses to their own annihilation. The wars and frequent peasant uprisings are proof of how the simple commodity mode of production is capable of resisting in order to attempt to reproduce itself. But in a more ordinary way, it is precisely the political structures of mediation that, located at a systemwide level, contribute to the survival of simple commodity relations of production. Nevertheless, the political results of those same peasant movements show that over the long term and gradually, the simple commodity mode of production will disappear under the onslaught of capital.

The proletariat, in its struggle against the bourgeoisie, usually does not seek to halt capitalist development, even at spontaneous levels of the struggle; in fact, its struggle is one of the principal springboards of such development (e.g., in the process of increasingly greater generation of relative surplus value). In turn, direct workers focus their struggle by starting out from precapitalist positions, in such a way that the struggle itself constitutes a mechanism for generation of the ideology necessary to preserve and reproduce noncapitalist relations of production.

It should be noted here that the contradiction between the "internal" elements and the "external" articulation of a mode of production is revealed as the specifically concrete and determinative factor. All the complexity of a society and all the articulations among different economic relations are expressed in the modes of production that form its base; but all the rich multiplicity of the determinations of the totality will be expressed synthetically only in the dominant mode of production.

The Dynamism of the Capitalist Agrarian Sector

For a long time, traditional economics has attempted to demonstrate that the small agricultural operation presents the best opportunities for economic development; the object of these efforts has been, and continues to be, to demonstrate the "beneficent" and "popular" character of agricultural capitalism, trying to hide the true process of concentration of land and capital that it spawns. John Stuart Mill was undoubtedly one of the most enthusiastic apologists for the efficiency of small peasant units; he, like so many others, did little more than give theoretical support to the "farmer" path to capitalism and generate the ideology necessary to the segment of the bourgeoisie (and petty bourgeoisie) that promotes that path.

In the face of all the evidence of the dynamism and efficiency of the large capitalist farm operations, some economists assert that it is the *minifundios* (small farmsteads) that are the most efficient.[38] Thus, the theoreticians of Mexican agrarian reform have traditionally refused to acknowledge the inefficiency of the ejido and the minifundio. To do so would be to accept that agrarian reform has favored the development of a system of exploitation and that it has opened the way to capitalism. Sergio Reyes Osorio, for example, tries to prove the efficiency of the ejidos and minifundios on the basis of calculating it as a ratio between the product and the inputs used.[39] Thus, the ejido sector contributed 35 percent of the total net agricultural production in 1960, but to do so it had available only 27 percent of the capital in agriculture. Furthermore, as Reyes Osorio goes on to explain, non-ejido plots of more than five hectares contributed 58 percent of the net agricultural output, notwithstanding having available 63 percent of the land value and 66 percent of the sector's total capital (exclusive of the value of land and livestock). The non-ejido properties of fewer than five hectares contributed 7 percent of the net agricultural product, even though they had available only 3 percent of the total land value; that meant that the use they made of their scarce resources was much more efficient than that of the other two systems of land tenure. From the perspective of output, it can be assumed that for each peso of the total inputs utilized (land, capital, wage labor, fertilizers, etc.), properties of more than five hectares yielded 1.88 in product; the ejidos, 2.35; and the smaller properties, 2.88. Our agrarian theoretician concludes: "In reality, the great disparity in earnings observed in the agricultural sector is not the fruit of the inefficiency of productive resources."

Unfortunately for Reyes Osorio, he forgot to include in the budget line for "inputs" the value of the labor power of the peasant and *ejidatario* himself. If this is taken into account, the famous efficiency turns into superexploitation; if the data are manipulated in a nonscientific way, calculating the peasant's income as profit and not as wages (i.e., as an input, as variable capital), it is easy to make the miserable Mexican peasant family economy pass for efficient. As Lenin wrote, "The existence of small peasants in every capitalist society is not explained by the technical superiority of small production in agriculture, but by the fact that they reduce their needs to a level below that of wage laborers and make an incomparably greater effort in their work than do the latter."[40]

The source of this juggling, which makes the *minifundista* appear efficient, is the calculations of the economist Salomón Eckstein, who sets up a ratio between total product (TP) and total inputs (TI).[41] For 1960, this relation, presented in the form of an index, is the following:

	TP/TI
More than 5 hectares	1.89
Fewer than 5 hectares	2.76
Ejidos	2.35

The calculation of inputs omits the value of the peasant's labor power, which is justified in this way:

> In view of the fact that for the agricultural sector as a whole only land and capital are actually scarce, given the high rural unemployment and underemployment, it seems to us more prudent in calculating efficiency to ignore the third factor, which is the labor of the head of the operation and his unremunerated family members. This does not mean that his importance as promoter and source of the entire production process is being taken away from him, but that, given his abundant character (in the strict economic sense), it is not appropriate to impute some value to him as if one were dealing with a scarce input.[42]

The feebleness of the argument, inspired by marginalism, is manifestly obvious: peasant labor is not a "scarce" commodity, because there is unemployment and underemployment in the countryside. Given the high urban unemployment, the labor of the wage laborer would not be scarce either, would it? The difference between the wage laborer and the peasant is that the former's labor is compensated directly in money, while the latter is remunerated for his labor through the market in which he sells his products, or else by direct subsistence consumption of such products.

To proceed in rigorously logical fashion, Eckstein's calculation ought to have eliminated the agricultural and livestock products that are not sold; the latter go toward covering the peasant's "wages." Furthermore, in order to inflate further the total output of the ejidatarios and minifundistas, he attributed to them the entire value of the animal products from the "settlements," even though, according to the census, it is not known to which sector they properly belong.

If we calculate the index TP/TI $(Pm / C + V)$, imputing a value to peasant labor power (250 days per year at minimum wage), we obtain a very different result:

	TP/TI
More than 5 hectares	1.8
Fewer than 5 hectares	0.7
Ejidos	1.3

It can now be seen that it is the minifundios that have the lowest index of efficiency. The very study cited here sets up another criticism of the computation of peasant labor as an input: the index of employment does not exceed, on the average, some 100–150 days per year. Let us accept this reasoning and calculate upon the basis of 125 days per year:

	TP/TI
More than 5 hectares	1.9
Fewer than 5 hectares	1.1
Ejidos	1.6

The large operations still appear to be the most efficient. The central problem, nevertheless, lies in the error of taking the "abundance" of a factor as a basis for considering it in its economic function. This subjective assessment diverts attention away from the essence of the problem: the specific manner in which the peasant is compensated for his labor. The rural bourgeoisie obtain income from *profit* and *ground rent*, day laborers receive *wages*, but what do the peasants get? Eckstein and Reyes Osorio's solution is to pretend that they receive *profits* (and higher rates of profit than other sectors), and in that way they hide the phenomenon of exploitation. From the perspective of this position, the minifundista peasant's problem is not *structural*, given that the basic necessary mechanisms (efficiency, etc.) are available to him; rather, the problem is one of distribution of resources (land, credit, etc.). What they do not point out is that the unequal division and distribution of resources is an effect of the inefficiency of the minifundio in its integration into the global capitalist system. In other words, the structural relation of the small peasant economy with the large capitalist enterprise inevitably involves the disintegration, pauperization, and proletarianization of the former. The situation of Mexican agriculture shows the clear, fresh tracks of the process of capitalist development: its dynamism inevitably destroys every prior economy. In the extraordinary development of one sector of agriculture, one recognizes without a doubt the powerful thrust of capital.

Agriculture and Industry

In what way is Mexican agriculture inserted into the society of the nation? What relations are set up by agriculture and industry? The subject is a broad and complex one, and a great deal has been written on it. Here I shall limit myself to posing some problems that seem relevant for the analysis of class structure.

The relationship between agriculture and industry revolves around a more general subject: the relationship between the countryside and the city. In Latin America, the discussion of this problem has generated a curious theory that attempts to understand the features of "underdevelopment." One of its exponents in Mexico has been Pablo González Casanova, in his well-known book *La democracia en México*.[43] Closely tied to this interpretation are the theses of *marginalism,* upon which I shall also comment here.

The line of reasoning followed by the theory of internal colonialism is the following: Mexico is an underdeveloped country, with a distorted, dependent economy, in which the class structure typical of a capitalist system has not emerged with the strength necessary to determine the social structure. The determinative factors in this situation are imperialism and internal colonialism; confronting imperialism are assembled "national" and "democratic" forces that postpone the need to attain class unity. Internal colonialism, which sets the indigenous world against the *mestizo,* rural Mexico against urban centers, and agricultural underdevelopment against industrial development, impedes the pure expression of the class struggle. Basically, this explanation of reality interprets the situation in terms quite similar to those of the propositions of Weber (and some representatives of classic German sociology): social stratification passes from one era in which the *estates* predominate into another in which *classes* attain their maximum expression. Mexico supposedly has not yet reached the second era.

The relationships between agriculture and industry, between city and countryside, and between the rural population and the urban are interpreted within this conception. The result of this interpretation proves to be extremely confused and contradictory. For example, it is said that the progress of the "colonial" urban-industrial sector is achieved thanks to exploitation of the "colonized" rural and agricultural sector. On the other hand, it is said that the progress of the metropolises does not require the growth of a rural internal market; on the contrary, the backwardness of the rural sector is what sustains the industrial-urban sector's progress.

This explanation hides the core of the problem: it obscures the real fact that the wealth of one sector is attained, not at the expense of another sector, but on the basis of the *exploitation of the working classes.* Objective reality demonstrates that the bourgeoisie (rural or urban) exploits the proletariat (agricultural or industrial), and it is the latter that is the true source of the wealth that is being concentrated. Now, in a manner parallel to the process of exploitation and concentration, the capital that is accumulated circulates in society in a specific fashion; however, these streams of wealth (of surplus labor) do not represent, strictly speaking, forms of exploitation. Streams flowing between agriculture and the rest of the economy demonstrate that the agricultural sector transfers significant amounts to business and industry. A recent calculation establishes that in Mexico between 1942 and 1960, taking into account solely the price mechanism, the banking sector, and the treasury, the agricultural sector has transferred more than 3 billion pesos to the rest of the economy.[44] This sum, which on an annual average does not turn out to be very large, was considerable only in the years 1948 and 1951, in which the transfer came to represent, respectively, 16 percent and 15 percent of annual agricultural output. Even given that this figure is a partial one, for it does not take into account the balance of payments or private loans, the transfer of value over eighteen years is not so significant if it is compared with the billions of pesos of earnings that the industrial sector generates yearly. Moreover, in 1960 only the sector of properties larger than 5 hectares generated earnings of more than 6 billion pesos (see table 5, below). Thus, the "progress" of industrial capitalism is not based on the exploitation of agriculture; rather, it uses it as a lever for its own growth. The transfers of value from agriculture to industry have as their basis the low organic composition of capital in the former.

The underdevelopment and distortions of the Mexican economy, however, generate singular situations. While it is true that the development of industrial capital (domestic or foreign) requires that the internal market be expanded, it seems that this market (to the extent that one refers to the demand for consumer goods) is developing at a rate that is beyond the needs of an industry whose capacity is only partially utilized, owing to the obstacles imposed by dependency and underdevelopment. That is, the rate of dissolution of the traditional relations of production in farming, which proletarianizes the peasantry and enriches the rural bourgeoisie, is more rapid than the rate of industrialization. This aspect of the problem makes it possible to see that the process of primitive accumulation— generator of "free" labor, driving force behind land concentration, sponsor of the accumulation of commercial, usurious profit—creates a rural internal market excessively large for a weak industry and thrusts into the labor market thousands of persons who cannot be absorbed by the economy. However, it is a question of an interior market distorted by processes of *nonproletarian pauperization*, which can hardly become a prop for industrial development; hence the need for the Mexican government to take economic policy measures that will control this situation and that will, to a certain extent, slow down the process of disintegration of noncapitalist relations in agriculture.

This unequal development drives a large number of people out of agriculture and creates a mass of unemployed and underemployed persons. In fact, a good part of the peasant population remains tied to the land, but under such conditions of misery and pauperism that they can scarcely be classified as farmers. This population has been called the *marginal mass*.[45] The concept of marginality has been another of the ways of comprehending one aspect of the relation between agriculture and industry. Here, the duality is no longer seen in terms of colony and metropolis; rather, it is seen now in terms of marginal sector and developed sector. The most

24

serious argument on the concept of marginality, one founded on a Marxist analysis, is that of José Nun, who, in fact, limits himself to showing that the greatest part of the "superpopulation" characteristic of the Latin American countries does not have a function as an "industrial army of reserve."[46] The marginal mass is the "afunctional" or "dysfunctional" part of the superpopulation, for it is totally superfluous even as a labor reserve. It is quite true that this population is "marginal" or "superfluous" to monopolistic industrial capital (and part of it to industrial capital in general) in the dependent countries. This situation is qualitatively different from the classic process of the rise of a superpopulation of rural origin that forms a reserve army for an impetuously growing industry. Nevertheless, the fact that the unemployed from the countryside, the pauperized small farmers, and the out-of-work who swarm in the streets do not conform to the classic portrait of the labor reserve does not mean that they have no function in the system. The confusion lies in looking at the superpopulation exclusively in relation to the system of monopoly capitalism, for the Mexican reality ought to be explained in terms of the global situation of subcapitalism and dependency (in which monopoly capital is only one part, although obviously quite an important one). The situation of the underemployed, unemployed, and pauperized mass of the rural zones is not to be found "on the margin" of the socioeconomic structure and should be explained in terms of *social class*.[47]

The portion of the population that fills the function of a *reserve* is found—with respect to its location as a class—in a *transitional* situation, and in this sense it plays a well-defined role: regulating the price of labor, with the goal of keeping the rates of exploitation high. In turn, the so-called superpopulation (or, according to Nun, the marginal mass), made up of day laborers and minifundista peasants, does not have that *transitional* character. The fact that underemployment (100 days worked per year, on average) dominates in these sectors does not mean that they must be categorized as a class in transition. Moreover, it is apparent that they do not fulfill the typical function of an industrial army of reserve. This segment of the population forms well-defined *social classes*, but ones with traits that distinguish them from the social classes that populated the European countryside a century or two ago. The social classes of the Mexican and Latin American countryside have their own peculiar qualities, which derive in part from the situation that I have labeled *permanent primitive accumulation*.

The concept of marginality creates a great deal of confusion by lumping together, as a single amorphous mass, the poor sector of rural and urban society. In doing so, it obscures the class-based mechanisms that establish norms for the behavior of social groups in the Mexican countryside. An example of this is the assertion—quite widespread in Latin America—that the poor Latin American peasantry has interests antagonistic to those of the urban working class, given that its struggle to redistribute the land (agrarian reform) and to obtain better sales terms causes an increase in food prices in the cities. It is further argued that peasants have the same interests as any landowner and that the workers benefit from the exploitation of the peasant that occurs on the basis of the mechanisms of internal colonialism.

All these confusions arise from failing to take basic class mechanisms into consideration. The increase in prices of agricultural products benefits essentially the agrarian bourgeoisie, but it affects the industrial bourgeoisie that consumes those products as a raw material. The working class is affected only passingly, for over time the increase in the cost of living will prompt the capitalist (pressured by strikes, etc.) to raise wages (his investment in variable capital). On the other hand, to put the minifundista peasant on the same level as the large landholder is to ignore the enormous differences in mode of production that separate them, putting to the foreground a purely formal legal relation instead. Lastly, to suppose that the worker benefits from internal colonialism is completely absurd. The benefits that every city dweller enjoys with respect to the rural population come from the wrenching effects of the first great social division of labor: the one that separated the countryside from the city.

The relation between agriculture and industry cannot be viewed outside the situation of Mexico's dependency with respect to capitalist developed countries. It is not only that structural distortions and imbalances are caused by this situation; in addition, a close connection exists between the agro-exporting sector (cotton, coffee, sugar) and the economy of the developed countries (principally the United States).

Samir Amín makes the following revealing statement:

> Each time the capitalist mode of production enters into relations with the precapitalist modes of production that it subordinates, transfers of value from the latter toward the former appear; these represent mechanisms of *primitive accumulation*. These mechanisms are not found, then, only in the prehistory of capitalism: they are also contemporary. It is these renewed but persistent forms of primitive accumulation for the benefit of the center that constitute the domain of the theory of accumulation on a worldwide scale.[48]

This transfer of values from the backward countries to the developed ones has its origin principally in the inequalities in the organic composition of capital. In fact, what occurs is that surplus value is transferred from the hands of the capitalists of the underdeveloped countries to the capitalists of the developed countries, which causes, as Palloix says, "the dependency of one bourgeois class before another bourgeois class, in which the former is cut off from a surplus profit that it could have available for the accumulation of capital if there were no imperialist relations."[49] To this one must add the direct extraction of surplus value, by means of foreign capital investment in Mexico. However, in agriculture, relations with imperialism are carried out essentially through the marketplace in which the indicated transfers of value occur. Here, in this process of unequal exchange, the low organic composition of agricultural capital in Mexico brings with it the transfer, which is possible only because in this case the prices of the products are set by the international market. Unlike what occurs—at least theoretically—in the domestic agricultural market, where prices are fixed in accordance with the conditions offered by the worst lands worked (which makes the existence of ground rent possible in all cases), in the relation with the international market the average rate of profit is applied, thus obligating those who produce under conditions of underdevelopment to give up the ground rent and sometimes even part of the surplus value to the capitalists of the developed countries.

In summary, capitalism in agriculture suffers from several illnesses and imbalances; but what is most serious is that it develops "healthily," agricultural supply grows, and the entrepreneurial economy expands. The real disease is capitalism's "robust health." There are no medicines to cure it: the remedy cannot be anything other than the revolutionary destruction of the entire diseased social body. The reformist medicine that strengthens its robust health in fact only spreads the disease.

Methodological Note

If what we are seeking is the concrete study of concrete situations, I believe that the appropriate path for understanding the nature of the class struggle in the countryside in the underdeveloped countries is through analysis of the structure of the modes and forms of production and of their articulation. No one can deny that from the moment capitalism dominates the entire social structure in the Third World, the presence of what Lenin called "nonproletarian masses" is, up to our own day, a fact of extraordinary political and economic importance. In the modern and contemporary history of the subcapitalist countries, as the dominance of capital spreads, the economic base of the nonproletarian masses increasingly takes on a simple commodity character and is stripped of the types of extraeconomic coercion that had been manifested in the form of slavery, serfdom, ethnic castes, and the like.

It would be a crude simplification to explain the existence of nonproletarian masses basically through the dependency linkage of the underdeveloped peripheral countries with the capitalist metropolises. The phenomenon of dependency essentially explains the characteristics of the accumulation of capital, the imbalances in the growth of productive forces, the terms of the exchange between nations, and so forth. But the peculiar subordination of a nation on the periphery to the international capitalist system is not automatically internalized in the relations of production that characterize the economic base. On a *first* level of analysis, the features of dependency, among others, appear—with their own expression—in the contradictions typical of the whole of a country's economic structure (monopolistic concentration, foreign capital, etc.). Nevertheless, this analytical first step (level of "economic formation") still does not provide us the basis for understanding class structure. One example of the difficulty of jumping from this level to that of class analysis is the theory of marginality. As we have seen, this theory holds that the population that is not useful to the monopoly capitalist sector escapes from the class structure and is defined as marginal population. (Only the bourgeoisie, the working class, and the industrial army of reserve are the objects of class analysis.)

A *second* methodological step is necessary: study of the contradictions that result from the relation between modes and forms of production. On this level, the problems of unequal exchange (within the nation), transfers of value, ground rent, and so on, appear. At this level of analysis, the *qualitative* differences between the relations of production have a very important role, and studying them enables one to understand the nature of the forms of exploitation, of the obstacles to development, and so on. However, it is also dangerous to leap directly from this level to analysis of the class struggle. An example of a similar leap is the theory of internal colonialism, which superimposes the contradictions between two (or more) modes of production on the class contradictions properly speaking (which thus remain hidden, distorted, or erased).

The *third* methodological step seems inevitable: it is necessary to discover the contradictions *within* each mode of production in order to locate there, in their essential container, the contradictions of class. On this level, the theory of value, the unity of productive forces and relations of production, and so on, must be dealt with. Nevertheless, this third step will lead us successfully to concrete study of concrete reality only if, throughout the process, the links uncovered in the two previous methodological steps have been preserved. Otherwise, the use of the concept of mode of production will become the abstract exposition of a "pure" model to which, apparently, one would give movement by imagining it in a "combinator" with other modes of production; in reality, we would not have advanced beyond the second methodological step described above. That is, as previously indicated, the study of the contradictions in the interior of a mode of production should reflect both its articulation with other modes of production and the characteristics of the entirety of the economic structure. But, at the same time, this focus permits the concrete location of the class struggle in the context of production.

To conclude, I would like to give examples of these methodological steps in a summary fashion along with some concepts used in the study of Mexican agrarian structure. A first concept useful in analysis of the *totality* of the agrarian sector is that of *permanent primitive accumulation,* which denotes the way in which capital is surrounded by noncapitalist modes and forms of production under such conditions of dependency on imperialism that the monopoly sector of the economy becomes a fundamental factor. This is a question, not of true *primitive* accumulation, but of a situation in which the monopoly sector controls and generates the relation of accumulation with noncapitalist modes of production. Up to this point, a first step, which takes into account what I call a *subcapitalist* agrarian structure.

This same concept of permanent primitive accumulation compels us— that is its virtue—to pose the problem on a second level. Here, there will be an attempt to analyze the *articulation* of modes of production itself, for which we can use the concept of *formal subordination,* which I have discussed previously. Its use involves the *self-exploitation–absolute surplus value binomial,* that is, a relation of *unequal exchange* among modes of production.

The multiplicity of determinations implicit in the previous steps brings us to the necessity of synthesizing them in studies of the *capitalist mode of production* and the *simple commodity mode of production,* which reveal the features of the class structure in the countryside: *bourgeoisie-proletariat-peasantry.* Nevertheless, the struggle between these classes is not understood in the least if it is not explained as a result of a process of investigation that has passed through the previous stages of analysis and accumulated the discoveries made through the tools (concepts) specific to each level.

I ought to finish this note by saying that strictly speaking, the moment when economic analysis reaches the point of considering the class struggle is precisely when it begins the true global process of synthesis: the understanding of the state. In countries in which the agrarian sector of the economy is dominant (or quite important) and is characterized by situations of permanent primitive accumulation, articulation of modes of production, formal subordination of labor to capital, unequal exchange, and so forth, the nondemocratic political structures of mediation occupy a revealing place in the configuration of the state, although they appear in quite varied forms and conditions in accordance with specific historic determinations.

Chapter 2

The Mexican Path

Civilization has made the peasantry its pack animal.
—**Leon Trotsky**
History of the Russian Revolution

I T SEEMS clear that Mexican agriculture at the end of the nineteenth century was developing along a path that can be identified as the Porfirian version of the "Junker road." But the revolution of 1910–17 and, above all, the reforms that commenced, rather too tardily, in the 1930s cut this development short. The elimination of traditional *latifundista* forms and of the systems of exploitation of semi-serf, semi-slave labor (peonage), along with the birth and development of the ejidos and small properties, seems to indicate that the "farmer" road was opening for agriculture in Mexico. However, some peculiarities of the ejido system impeded the process of de-peasantization or, at the least, created considerable obstacles to it: by law, ejido land remained outside the market. Ejido parcels, property of the nation, were conveyed in usufruct and could be neither sold nor rented. Thus, obviously, a retaining wall to halt capitalist development in agriculture was put in place. Of course, that happened only in the ejido sector; the rest of agriculture suffered the consequences of capitalist development. In saying this, I do not want to suggest that there was no capitalist development in the ejido sector, but that it was slowed down. We can ask ourselves the cause of this situation. Was it that the Mexican Revolution had, in effect, an anticapitalist character? Was it a popular revolution that subsequently went astray?

The answer is provided for us by one of the Mexican government's agrarian theoreticians in his dispute with René Dumont. Not long ago, the latter bitterly criticized Mexican agrarian reform from a bourgeois-technocratic point of view. Our theoretician responded:

With the elimination of the ignorant peasants whose property rights would be transferred to those selected for their technological virtues, these somber prospects would, according to Dumont, be counteracted, and in addition, the minifundios

Table 1
Indices of Agricultural Production in
Eight Latin American Countries, 1965
(Base: 1934–38 = 100)

Country	1965
Argentina	133
Brazil	196
Chile	166
Colombia	227
Cuba	153
Mexico	*324*
Peru	193
Uruguay	135

Source: Edmundo Flores, "Cómo funciona el sector agropecuario de México," *Revista del México Agrario* 2, nos. 1 and 2 (1968–69): 35–48.

would be eradicated—the latter, again according to Mr. Dumont, constituting the mortal sin of Mexican agrarian reform, from which he demands acts of attrition and contrition to disavow the democratic heresies that up to now have inspired the redistribution of land and the new forms of property.[1]

Marco Antonio Durán, the theoretician speaking to us, goes on to reveal that the important thing is the so-called "social function of the new forms of property." After a bit of demagoguery, he concludes by revealing the truth:

Among the social functions of landownership must be counted those of a political nature, the simplest and clearest expression of which is that it has produced a tranquility that has aided the struggles for progress. . . . The political functions are complex, for they include *keeping up the peasants' hopes,* while it is possible to create the instruments that will definitively extract them from their poverty, by means of the organizations formed by men who have received land, which, even as they are struggling for the realization of revolutionary goals, *keep up faith and hope among the peasants and avoid outbursts of impatience.*[2]

The function of the ejido and the minifundio can only be understood simultaneously on their economic and political levels: they form a buffer that permits controlling the violence inseparable from the process of rapid expansion of the capitalist sector. Without that, under the conditions in Mexico the capitalist state could not ensure the rural bourgeoisie the rapid economic growth that it has enjoyed. The virtues of the "Mexican path" are apparent upon an examination of the indices presented in table 1.

But let us return to the origin of the Mexican evolutionary process. Some authors rightly point out that economic development in Mexico in the past century followed the paths of primitive accumulation of capital.[3] Indeed, the application of the liberal principles of the Revolution of Ayutla, which led to the "disamortization" law of 1856, which expropriated the properties of the church and the indigenous communities, is a phenomenon that must be understood within the process of primitive capitalist accumulation. This law, which sought to create small property-owning farmers, actually led to latifundista concentration and, above all, thrust the land into the capitalist market. The activity of the notorious surveying companies similarly formed a part of the primitive accumulation. The Yaqui War, which dispossessed the indigenous people of the fertile lands of the Valle del Yaqui, and the war of extermination against the Mayas of Yucatán gave a "colonial" character to this process.

But the process of capitalist accumulation was slowed down by determinative circumstances: dominance of foreign capital and weakness in the concentration of domestic financial capital. Of the two facets of the process of primitive accumulation (separation of the worker from the means of production, and accumulation of capital available for productive investment), only the first was carried out with dynamism (and only partially at that), so that the process remained curtailed, converted into a vicious circle from which only violence could save it.

In fact, during the last years of the nineteenth century and the first decade of the twentieth, the pace of the concentration of land and the plundering of the peasants is astonishing. This accelerated process found no counterpart in the development of agricultural capital, so that immense latifundios were created with extremely low investments of capital. The organic composition of agricultural capital remained quite low; the estate owners preferred superexploitation of labor (even using feudal systems) to carrying out productive investments with their profits. With that, they condemned to death the possibility of "Junker" agricultural development and opened the way for a revolution. Hence the paradox: the pains of primitive capitalist accumulation generated a bourgeois revolution *against the bourgeoisie itself*, in which the dispossessed peasant mass took the part of leading actor (but was not the director).

The violence of a primitive accumulation destabilized by the colonial heritage and the imperialist presence, which was the underlying cause of the Mexican Revolution, explains why the center of the agrarian revolutionary movement (of Emiliano Zapata) was the state of Morelos, where the peasants had been plundered by a developed system of capitalist *haciendas* (estates). In this zone, with its sugarcane plantations and its forty-odd sugar mills, the development of capitalism in agriculture was significant. Since Lázaro Cárdenas's time, the Mexican government, the heir of that revolution, has taken care to *control* the process of capitalist development in agriculture; its own experience shows it that brutal exploitation of the peasantry can unleash a revolution, which these days would surely take on a socialist character.

In conclusion, the "Mexican path" is nothing more than a specific version, adapted to the conditions of a dependent country, of what Lenin termed the "farmer" road of capitalist development of agriculture. (The features of the farmer-ejido road are explained in greater detail in chapter 4.)

The Accumulation of Capital and The Internal Market

Several recent studies of the Mexican agricultural economy emphasize the existence of two agricultural sectors: a small, privileged, capitalist sector that produces largely for export and generates the greatest part of the agricultural output placed in the market; and a populous sector of poor peasants, largely still tied to subsistence consumption, who form the majority of the peasant population.[4] The problem that was posed for the Mexican bourgeoisie once in power (and that still faces it today) was how to attain an increase in agricultural production with the aim of supplying the urban and industrial markets (domestic as well as foreign). To that end, it had to channel surpluses outside the agricultural sector, avoiding the redistribution of those surpluses among the impoverished rural masses but also avoiding "explosions of impatience" among the latter. The only solution was the one outlined in the previous section, and that has resulted in this apparent dualism of the Mexican agrarian structure. This solution would not have surprised Rosa Luxemburg in the least: she suggested that the process of accumulation of capital could only exist as a relation between capital and the noncapitalist environment.[5] Although this statement is debatable with respect to conditions of advanced capitalist development, it certainly reflects the situation of backward countries such as Mexico, where political as well as economic circumstances lock agricultural production into a vicious circle in which the capitalist sector manages to develop only by destroying the noncapitalist sector. Such destruction aggravates the crisis, which requires protecting the noncapitalist sector in some way.

Many of the conflicts experienced by countries dependent on imperialism arise in this way. The economic relation with the metropolises favors the underdeveloped status of such countries, which compels them to remain in a situation that could be classified as *permanent primitive accumulation*. In fact, if one reads Marx's extraordinary analyses of primitive accumulation, it is difficult to stop thinking of the Mexican situation (and that of underdeveloped countries in general); the only difference is that such countries remain over the long term in this condition, in which the succeeding stage—advanced capitalism—does not seem to exist. This is the situation that is behind so-called unequal, combined development.

Now, this condition of permanent primitive accumulation is a dual system in appearance only. In reality, it is a single structure whose constituent parts are not explicable except as a whole. Its constituent parts—the capitalist sector and the noncapitalist—represent two modes of production that together shape a single subcapitalist socioeconomic formation.

The intrinsic tendencies of the development of the capitalist sector—concentration of capital and land, mechanization—inevitably assist in the erosion and destruction of the noncapitalist peasant economy. As a result, large population masses are displaced, which, along with high demographic growth, leads to the existence of an enormous reserve army of unemployed labor. Will this mass manage to form a true popular revolutionary army? The bourgeoisie, which, along with ensuring the reproduction of capital, must ensure the reproduction of the social and political relations that permit the existence of the capitalist system, finds itself obliged to control the process of accumulation. Thus the survival of the inefficient ejido and the minifundio. But in addition, there are strictly economic reasons for the existence of this apparently dual system.

The development of the interior market proves to be a highly important factor not only for comprehending the dynamic of Mexican agriculture but also for understanding its link with the growth and expansion of capitalist industry. In approaching this problem, it would be useful to set out an important premise of the method of analysis. Lenin expressed it clearly:

> What counts in the interior market is not, even in the least, the overall earnings of the producer (by which his prosperity is determined) but exclusively his earnings in *money*. The well-being of the producer does not mean in any way that he possesses money: the peasant who obtains from his plot of land—even though he exploits it within the framework of the natural economy—all the products to supply his needs enjoys well-being but does not possess money; a semi-ruined peasant who takes from his plot only a small part of the grain that he needs and who obtains the rest by means of occasional, supplementary "earnings" does not enjoy well-being but has monetary resources. It is clear, then, that the rationales for the importance of the peasant farms and their commercial profitability have no value at all if they are not based on calculations of the portion of that income in money.[6]

The interpretations of the process of accumulation, growth of the internal market, and profitability ought to be proposed within the framework of the commodity economy. This means, moreover, that the internal agricultural market was growing independently of the well-being of the rural population (and almost always to its detriment). The internal agricultural market is a function of the value of the products of the countryside sold and of the total earnings obtained through wage labor.

Table 2
Value of Agricultural Production and Yields per Hectare,
1940-1970 (in millions of 1960 pesos)

Land Tenure	Total Value of Agricultural Production (a)	Value of Agricultural Production Sold (b)	Total Area Cultivated (thousands of hectares) (c)	Pesos per hectare (a/c) (b/c)		Percentage of Production Sold (% b/a)
1940						
> 5 ha.	1,958	1,090	6,752	290	161	56
< 5 ha.	452	181	1,074	421	169	40
Ejidos	2,458	1,331	7,045	349	189	54
Total	4,868	2,602	17,871	272	146	54
1950						
> 5 ha.	5,820	5,201	9,859	590	528	89
< 5 ha.	943	742	1,280	737	580	79
Ejidos	4,013	2,904	8,791	457	330	72
Total	10,776	8,847	19,929	541	444	82
1960						
> 5 ha.	7,703	6,725	12,219	630	550	87
< 5 ha.	823	551	1,269	649	434	67
Ejidos	5,870	4,543	10,329	568	440	77
Total	14,396	11,818	23,817	604	496	82
1970						
> 5 ha.	6,989	6,167	9,675	722	637	88
< 5 ha.	630	510	710	887	718	81
Ejidos	8,021	6,917	12,753	629	542	86
Total	15,640	13,594	23,138	676	588	87

Sources: Censos agricola, ganadero y ejidal, 1940-70.

In table 2 one can observe the evolution of the value of agricultural products put on the market from 1940 to 1970. It is interesting to note not only the accelerated growth of the value of the production but also some phenomena linked to the form of land tenure and size of the land. The decade 1940–50 witnessed a true leap in the commercialization of agricultural production: the portion sold to the market moved from 54 percent to 82 percent of the total value produced. The leap is particularly evident for privately held lands; the ejido experienced noticeably slow growth in this decade (doubtless the fruit of the antiagrarian policies of presidents Manuel Avila Camacho and Miguel Alemán).

In the following decade (1950–60), the commercialized production of the ejido sector grew more rapidly than that of the private sector, especially if compared with the properties of fewer than five hectares, which reached a point of near-stagnation. Furthermore, between 1940 and 1960 the area cultivated in parcels of fewer than five hectares practically did not increase; and from 1950 to 1960 that area decreased. In 1970, after thousands of small farmers had been ruined, the cultivated area corresponding to smaller fields declined enormously.

One aspect of the evolution of the value of production during these years is particularly interesting: the changes in productivity per hectare with respect to types of land tenure and size of the land. If the *total value* of agricultural production *per hectare* is considered, we note that parcels of fewer than five hectares produce an average value higher than that of the larger properties and ejidos.

Analysis of this type of information (as well as the use of the capital and land factors) has led almost all economists who have treated the topic to affirm that small units of production are more efficient and more productive than large ones. This interpretation started originally with Salomón Eckstein,[7] and it has been repeated by so many people that it has come to seem like a commonplace. Such an interpretation does not correspond to reality for several reasons, some of which I will examine here, although a more detailed analysis of the problem is reserved for another section of this book.

The criterion of "productivity" (or efficiency) cannot be applied in the abstract. From the perspective of both the formation of an internal market and the process of the accumulation of capital, it is not possible to consider only the total value of agricultural production. The portion of the production not sold can neither generate an internal market nor be a direct base for a process of accumulation. Therefore, considering it for the purpose of calculating the efficiency, profitability, or productivity of agriculture in an essentially capitalist country does not make sense. On observing the data on the value of agricultural production *sold,* one draws conclusions different from the preceding ones:

1. In 1940 the average value of the production sold per hectare was similar in the three sectors (with the ejido occupying first place).
2. In 1950 the ejido sector receded definitively and held the position for lowest value per hectare, while the small plots barely exceeded the larger parcels.
3. In 1960 the larger parcels generated the highest value per hectare and significantly exceeded the other two sectors.
4. In 1970, because of the effects of the agricultural crisis, the small plots again occupied first place.

Although one cannot mechanically consider parcels of more than five hectares representative of the capitalist sector in agriculture, it is apparent that the tendencies shown above are caused by the greater dynamism of capitalist agriculture, which is the sector that has access to the largest tracts of land. In conclusion, from the perspective of agricultural production, the concentration of land in large units of production is what generates an internal market most rapidly. This last point is revealed with even greater clarity if we pause to note the indices of growth of the average value of commercial production per hectare: if we take the value for 1940 as equal to 100, in 1960 the parcels of more than five hectares were producing 2,037, while the smaller plots were producing 1,550, and the ejidos, 1,419.

It is quite interesting to stop to examine what happened in 1970, a year in which the census registered the terrible devastation of the grave agricultural crisis. That year plots of fewer than five hectares again took over first place with respect to production sold per hectare. But that occurred at the cost of a brutal reduction in the area cultivated (and total production) that reflects the ruin of thousands of small peasants who found themselves compelled to abandon production. As a consequence, the units of production in the hands of the wealthiest farmers tended to survive, and the most inefficient ones disappeared. Later on, when we examine the structure of the agricultural crisis, I shall explain the peculiarities observed in 1970.

Another angle of the problem is the proletarianization of the peasantry. It leaps to one's attention that the immense majority of the peasants who possess fewer than five hectares of land cannot live exclusively on the value of their production. Even those who have the maximum available (five hectares) will, on the average, only manage to produce around three thousand Mexican pesos annually, an amount insufficient for a family's subsistence. Even a good portion of those who possess more than five hectares are in this position, as are the majority of ejidatarios. The existence of this sector of the peasantry, which finds itself obligated to sell its labor power in order to subsist, represents a factor as important or more important than the sale of agricultural products for the expansion of the internal market. It will suffice to mention that in 1960, 1.24 million peasants were classified as holders of "infrasubsistence plots" (with an average gross family income of fifty to eighty pesos per month); these peasants, representing 50 percent of the total, had to supplement their earnings with wage labor. (Perhaps it would be better to say that they were proletarians who complemented their wages with agriculture.) Furthermore, also in 1960, 820,000 peasants were classified as possessors of "subfamilial plots," producing, on average, little more than what was strictly necessary to feed themselves. They constituted 33 percent of the peasant-

Table 3
Annual Expenditures on Agricultural Day Labor and Percentages with Respect to
Total Cash Expenditures, 1940–1970 (in millions of 1960 pesos)

	1940		1950		1960		1970	
	Expenditures	%	Expenditures	%	Expenditures	%	Expenditures	%
More than 5 ha.	474	58	977	40	1,003	29	1,837	34
Fewer than 5 ha.	—		115	55	136	62	394	26
Ejidos	11	3	131	28	228	18	1,149	37
Total	484	43	1,224	40	1,367	28	3,394	34

Sources: Censos agrícola, ganadero y ejidal, 1940–70.

ry, and obviously a high percentage obtained income in the form of a wage. All of this without even counting the millions of persons who had no land whatsoever![8]

This aspect of the growth of the internal market can be observed from the angle of cash expenditures for wages paid in agriculture. The extremely rapid increase of this monetary distribution can be seen in table 3, where the expenses have been calculated at 1960 prices in order to make it possible to observe their evolution with greater objectivity. The growth was by all lights most accelerated in the period 1940–50; in 1960, around 200 million work days were paid (calculated by taking 6.86 Mexican pesos as the minimum wage). At the same time, it can be seen how the organic composition of capital increased rapidly in the decade 1950–60 (labor went from 40 percent to 28 percent of the total of cash expenditures). Expenditures on wages (variable capital) rose at a slower rate, the result of the Alemán policy of technification and capital investment in agriculture. In 1970 expenditures for wages again rose enormously, although the organic composition of capital declined—the typical combination that occurs in times of crisis: an advance in proletarianization combined with a slowdown in investment (especially that applied to technology). Only on the small properties did the organic composition of capital rise, additional evidence that in this sector only those farmers who were relatively efficient and oriented toward capitalist production would survive the crisis.

The development of Mexican agriculture since the Cardenista years of agrarian reform has been characterized by the rise of a powerful sector of capitalist farmers situated in the middle of a sea of semi-proletarianized and pauperized peasants and of landless day laborers. This situation of advanced decomposition and differentiation of the peasantry has to a certain extent managed to develop and expand the internal market for industry (domestic and foreign). Nevertheless, the process of proletarianization has been consciously slowed down in order to keep rooted to the land a large mass of peasants that neither industry nor agricultural enterprises would be capable of absorbing. A situation of this nature, in which a developed sector and an underdeveloped one coexist, generates factors that are negative as well as positive for the process of the accumulation of capital: the existence of a noncapitalist underdeveloped sector provides capitalist merchants the possibility of obtaining enormous superprofits and provides the capitalist industrialists and agriculturalists a reserve of cheap labor. On the other hand, maintaining this situation restricts the internal market *over the long term* (we have already seen how investments in wages began to decline in the 1950s) and causes at some stage—sooner or later—huge investments of capital in infrastructure projects with the aim of "capitalizing" the backward sector. The economist Jesús Puente Leyva confirms this last point when he concludes that "the tangible expression of public investment in the agricultural sector has been seen to have deteriorated in recent years by virtue of the combined effect of its absolute stagnation and the exaggerated increase in the costs of irrigation projects."[9]

The Problem of Ground Rent

It is necessary to take up again here the problem posed earlier with respect to ground rent, which is at bottom nothing more than the generation and distribution of *superprofits* in agriculture. The concept of ground rent will help us to begin to understand the specific mechanisms of the capitalist development of the Mexican countryside and will initiate us into the complicated themes of the setting of agricultural prices, formation of profit rates, and forms taken by wages in the countryside.

In order to introduce the methodology applied to the analysis of ground rent, I shall perform a calculation of ground rent in corn production. The calculation is based on five types of land, differing from the perspective of fertility, but the capital investments are taken as constant. The example is hypothetical, but everything possible has been done to adjust it to the Mexican reality of 1960. The unit is the production from one hectare, and the calculations are in Mexican pesos.

K = Total invested capital (in this example, $K = C + V$)
C = Constant capital
V = Variable capital
Pr = Production, in Kg/H
AP = Average profit, 10 percent
Pi = Individual price of production

Pg = General price of production
Pm = Market price, 0.70 pesos/Kg
k = Price per Kg
SV = Surplus value
RP = Rate of profit
GRD = Differential ground rent
GRA = Absolute rent

The calculations are carried out in accordance with the following formulas:

$$SV = Pm - (C + V)$$
$$Pi = C + V + AP \text{ (Cost of production: } Cp)$$
$$Pik = \frac{C + V + AP}{Pr}$$
$$Pg = Pik (A) \times Pr$$
$$Pgk = Pik (A)$$
$$Pm = Pmk \times Pr$$
$$RP = \frac{SV}{C + V} \times 100 \text{ or } \frac{SV}{K} \times 100$$
$$GRD = Pg - Pi$$
$$GRA = Pm - Pi = SV - AP \text{ (Total rent: } GRT)$$

The first thing that jumps into view, and departs from Marx's classic model, is that lands A and B produce negative absolute rent,[10] and land C does not produce absolute rent at all. That is so because both land A and land B produce negative surplus value and in the case of land C, the surplus value is equal to the average profit rate. All this is owing to the fact that the market price (Pm) is not equal to the individual price of production on the worst land (Pik [A]). How is this phenomenon possible? In a pure capitalist economy it would not occur, but lands of types A and B are exploited in Mexico because they are not exploited under capitalist conditions, notwithstanding that they are surrounded by and subjected to the capitalist market.

The analysis is a simplification, but it corresponds to reality. Of course, the low fertility of the land is not the only factor that causes the minifundios and a good portion of the ejidos to operate under loss conditions. In the noncapitalist peasant sector, the organic composition of capital is extremely low (lack of irrigation, archaic technology, etc.), and the conditions for moving the product to the centers of consumption are worse (high costs of transportation, middlemen, etc.).

The foregoing calculations are based on a Kautskyan interpretation of ground rent; this interpretation is undoubtedly the most functional one, but it brings with it important theoretical errors. The *differential ground*

Table 4
Ground Rent in Corn Production

Land	C	V	Pr (Kg/ha.)	Pi	Pik	Pg	Pgk	Pm	Pmk	SV	RP (%)	GRD	GRA	AP (10%)
A	136	500	500	700	1.40	700	1.40	250	0.70	-286	4.5	0	-350	64
B	136	500	750	700	1.07	1,050	1.40	525	0.70	-111	17.5	350	-175	64
C	136	500	1,000	700	0.70	1,400	1.40	700	0.70	64	10.0	700	0	64
D	136	500	1,250	700	0.56	1,750	1.40	875	0.70	239	37.5	1,050	175	64
E	136	500	1,500	700	0.47	2,100	1.40	1,050	0.70	414	65.0	1,400	350	64
Total	680	2,500	5,000	3,500	0.70	7,000	1.40	3,500	0.70	320	10.0	3,500	0	320

rent (GRD) is a relative quantity that is expressed in the difference between the market price (Pm) and individual value (Vi). In turn, *absolute rent* (GRA) is a fixed quantity that is expressed in the difference between the individual value (Vi) and the price of production (Pp). The *total rent* (GRT), therefore, will be the sum of both, and it will be expressed by the difference between the market price (Pm) and the cost of production (Cp).

The foregoing discussion does not appear to be reflected in Kautsky's analysis; the theoretical problem that it does not clarify is the distinction between the cost of production and individual value. It is a matter, basically, of the difference between *average profit* and *surplus value*. Thus, we will have:

$$Pp = C + V + AP \text{ (equal to } Pi)$$
$$Vi = C + V + SV$$

Moreover, the market price is different from the foregoing and is calculated with the concept of *profit:*

$$Pm = C + V + P$$

The difficulty of working with these three concepts (surplus value, profit, and average profit) has made Kautsky's calculation theoretically erroneous. Without taking into account the difference between surplus value and its transfigured forms (profits), it is not possible to distinguish between absolute rent and differential ground rent. This is what happens in the example of corn, where the calculation of absolute rent is carried out under the false assumption that $Pm - Pi = SV - AP$, which is true only if the surplus value is calculated by starting from the selling price in the market (which is what we did above), and not according to an average rate of surplus value existing throughout the economic system. (Marx almost always uses the rate of 100 percent.) In reality, the absolute rent calculated above *is the total rent,* since the individual price (which is identical to the price of production, $C + V + AP$) has been discounted to the market price.

The calculation performed for differential ground rent is not correct either, but it has the interesting feature of functioning as an *indicator* of the differences in productivity on the different types of land: the figures reflect the range of difference (from 0 to 3,500) between land A and land E. Thus, the true formulae would be the following:

$$GRA = Vi - Pp = SV - AP$$
$$GRD = Pm - Vi = P - SV$$
$$GRT = Pm - Pp = P - AP$$

But the difficulty of defining individual value empirically has prevented us from distinguishing the types of ground rent. Kautsky's method enables

Table 5

Political Economy of Agrarian Structure in Mexico, 1940–1970 (in millions of 1960 pesos)

Land Tenure	K	C	V	C/V	Pi	Pm	SV	Pg	D	GRt	AP	RP
1940												
> 5 ha.	12,898	1,169.3	935.5	1.2	3,394.0	2,337.0	232.2	5,466.3	2,072.3	-1,057.0	1,289.8	1.8
< 5 ha.	4,506	244.0	1,445.8	0.2	2,141.6	916.0	-773.8	2,141.6	0.0	-1,225.6	450.6	-17.1
Ejidos	9,024	1,102.4	2,179.0	0.5	4,185.0	3,223.0	-58.4	7,537.3	3,352.0	-962.0	902.4	-0.6
1950												
> 5 ha.	33,732	3,727.2	1,509.4	2.5	8,612.0	7,836.5	2,600.0	14,610.3	5,998.3	-775.5	3,373.2	7.7
< 5 ha.	2,711	811.0	1,213.4	0.7	2,295.0	1,233.0	-791.4	2,295.0	0.0	-1,062.0	271.1	-29.2
Ejidos	20,159	1,593.5	1,859.0	0.9	5,467.0	5,499.0	2,046.5	10,237.5	4,770.5	32.0	2,015.9	10.2
1960												
> 5 ha.	55,401	6,006.0	1,634.0	3.7	13,180.0	13,761.0	6,121.0	22,915.0	9,735.0	581.0	5,540.0	11.0
< 5 ha.	3,750	520.0	1,423.0	0.4	2,318.0	1,392.0	-551.0	2,318.0	0.0	-926.0	375.0	-14.7
Ejidos	29,059	3,171.0	2,763.0	1.2	8,840.0	7,513.0	1,579.0	12,510.0	3,670.0	-1,327.0	2,906.0	5.4
1970												
> 5 ha.	53,240	6,855.0	4,769.0	1.44	12,786.0	12,920.0	1,296.0	20,484.0	7,698.0	134.0	5,324.0	2.4
< 5 ha.	8,811	1,811.0	2,382.0	0.76	4,613.0	2,909.0	-1,284.0	4,613.0	0.0	-1,704.0	881.1	-14.6
Ejidos	48,998	4,795.0	9,256.4	0.52	15,456.0	9,733.0	-4,318.0	15,431.0	-25.0	-5,723.0	4,899.8	-8.8

Sources: Censos agrícola, ganadero y ejidal, 1940–70. Amounts have been deflated to 1960 pesos using the Banco de México implicit price index.

Notes:

K	= Total invested capital
C	= Constant capital
V	= Variable capital
C/V	= Organic composition of capital
Pi	= Individual price of production
Pm	= Market price (value of production)
SV	= Surplus value
Pg	= General price of production
D	= Index of differential productivity (fewer than 5 ha. = 0)
GRt	= Total ground rent
AP	= Average profit
RP	= Rate of profit (SV/K × 100)

one to differentiate them, but at the cost of a theoretical error. It seems convenient, for the moment, to be limited to dealing with the concept of *total rent*. Note that the formula *GRT* is the one that was in fact applied in the table for corn in order to calculate the *GRA*, since the $SV = P$ and $Pi = Cp$ (see table 4).[11]

To apply this sort of analysis to the information available for Mexico is extremely complicated, above all because the statistical data are confused and inadequately classified. Nevertheless, I wanted to present an example of application of the theory of ground rent on a national scale; obviously, it will not be possible to use the concept of "production per hectare" or "unit of production." The first concept (which represents the fertility of the soil) will be replaced by calculating the general price (*Pg*) as a function of the value of the production in the market (*Pm*), since that fact is an expression of fertility. Thus, the formula for the general price will be:

$$Pg = \frac{Pm \times Pi \text{ of the worst lands}}{Pm \text{ of the worst lands}}$$

(On the worst lands $Pi = Pg$).

The "units" that will be selected are the three sectors into which all information from the agricultural censuses in Mexico appears to be classified: parcels of more than five hectares, parcels of fewer than five hectares, and ejidos. In the calculations of the amount of constant capital invested in the agricultural cycle (*C*), we have followed the data provided by the Centro de Investigaciones Agrarias (Center for Agrarian Research [CDIA]);[12] that is, within *C* are included cash expenditures, 5 percent of the value of the land, 10 percent of the fixed capital, and 10 percent of the value of the livestock. Variable capital (*V*) was calculated on the basis of total expenditures on day labor wages, adding an imputed salary to the head of each operation (on a base rate of 250 days of minimum wage). The calculation of the production in the marketplace (*Pm*) was completed by taking into account the total value of the agricultural, livestock, and forestry production, but census information on animal products "in the villages" was excluded because it involved ambiguous, confused data, resulting in a slight increase in the rates of earnings.[13]

The formulas used in the previous calculation were applied to this information; the result is presented in table 5. Table 5 concentrates, as it were, on the features of the development of capitalism in Mexican agriculture. The leap in production that occurred in the 1940s was significant, especially for the ejidos and the larger parcels. The 1950s were also characterized by rapid growth of production, but the sector of parcels of more than five hectares stands out definitively.

The calculation of differential ground rent has been replaced here by an index D (calculated using the first GRD formula), which measures the differences in productivity in relation to the land taken here as equivalent to the worst (fewer than five hectares $= 0$). This index shows that over the course of twenty years the large units of production decidedly took the lead. Furthermore, the process of polarization that had been generated proved palpable: the gap between large units and small ones continued to grow by leaps and bounds.

As I have already noted, the presence of negative ground rents is quite significant; it reveals the existence of a large number of noncapitalist units of production. Thus, not only is the appropriation of large amounts of *superprofits* confirmed but one observes that there are important flows of *transfer* of value between sectors. In 1960, for example, sector 3 (of properties of more than five hectares) produced a value (Pi) of 13,180 million pesos, while in fact it appropriated for itself 13,751 million pesos. The superprofit that it obtained originated in part from the possession of better lands, in part from its monopoly of the land, and, finally, in part from the transfer of value from sector 1, which, in spite of having produced (Pi) 2,318 million pesos, earned a value (Pm) of 1,293 million Mexican pesos.

One of the most important conclusions that can be drawn from the analysis of ground rent in Mexico is that the noncapitalist small peasant economy (ejido or otherwise) is perfectly integrated into the capitalist system and that its features cannot be understood without the use of the conceptual tools created for the study of any capitalist economy (wages, profit, and ground rent), although it is necessary to adapt them to the specific conditions in question.

Chapter 3

The Modes of Production

Methodology

FROM the preceding chapter, one obtains a general vision of Mexican agrarian structure and concludes that it is indispensable to develop a concrete methodology for the analysis of the agrarian systems of production. When they have not resulted in arid descriptions, traditional studies have applied the methodology of marginalist economic analysis. On the other hand, Marxist analysis runs into difficulties upon confronting a situation in which an enormous segment of the agrarian structure produces under noncapitalist conditions.

Witold Kula has recently presented the problem with great clarity, for which reason I permit myself to quote him at length:

> The economic analysis of the pre- or semi-capitalist peasant farm as a type of "enterprise" has an enormous importance. It is a burning issue for us, men of the twentieth century, since the majority of the world's population belongs to developing countries and lives right in the heart of small, rural, family-style farms, with few ties to the market and working, above all, for subsistence.
>
> Traditional methods of enterprise analysis have frequently been applied to this type of operation. We know, generally, what conclusions to expect from them. Let us cite a surprising example: the study of 600 farms, conducted in 1937–38 in 21 villages in India, showed that these farms were reporting an average annual income of 88 rupees, if income is calculated in accordance with market prices and without taking into account the cost of family labor or interest on capital. But if we include in the budget the cost of this labor established according to the current salaries of day laborers in the region, and we add 3 percent interest, then these farms appear to be operating decidedly at a deficit (annual deficit of 90 rupees). . . .

Traditional science does not see major difficulties here. It would respond that the average peasant does not count the expenses of family labor or the interest on capital, given that these notions are foreign to him and that he does not know that a proper budget ought to incorporate these two factors. It would not see more than one way of incorporating them: by referring to market prices, as they are implemented in the region at that precise moment. These farms would truly be operating at a loss for the peasant.

This conclusion, according to which half of the human species today works at a productive activity with a constant deficit, is, nevertheless, a form of *reductio ad absurdum*. And it would be equally absurd to state that all the feudal manors and all the peasant farms of Poland, during the four centuries of its existence, have constantly operated at a loss.

But apart from its absurdity in fact, this method can be criticized according to the criteria of traditional science itself. If to begin a productive activity it is necessary to have, let us say, a quantity A kilograms of raw material, plus a number B of days of labor, and the "entrepreneur" has A kilograms of raw material but B + X days of labor, without any other possibility of using this superfluous labor, then *all* the labor employed must be considered to be equal to zero. In this sense, we can say that the peasant applies marginal theory perfectly.[1]

The essence of the problem is set forth here, but the correct solution is not. Let us see what we are told by an economic science that is not exactly traditional. In *The New Economic Changes in Peasant Life*, Lenin states: "In the lower groups, the peasants do not cover the basic necessities of their famil[ies] by means of farming their land. If a calculation of farm expenditures were made, we would find that the operation of these farms *is carried out at a deficit*."[2] Why does Lenin make this statement? Clearly, it is because he considered that

the system of economic-social relations (agricultural and communal) among the peasantry shows us the existence of all the contradictions common to any commodity economy and to any capitalism. . . . those contradictions show us clearly and irrefutably that the system of economic relations in the "community's" village does not in any way represent a special type of economy ("popular production," etc.), but a common petty bourgeois type.[3]

What happens is that the concept of *deficit* proves inadequate to embrace the core of the problem, for it gives only a pallid idea of the complexity of the social relations that play a part in the peasant economy. The essence of this "deficit" lies in the *valuation* of peasant labor and in the fundamentally commercial character of the peasant "enterprise," which finds itself submerged in the dominant capitalist system. Lenin pointed out that "not taking into account one's work within the capitalist social system means surrendering the labor itself for free (to the merchant or to another capitalist), means working for an incomplete remuneration of labor power, means reducing the level of consumption below the norm."[4] Elsewhere Lenin fleshed out his idea in this way:

> The existence of small peasants in every capitalist society is not explained by the technical superiority of small production in agriculture, but by the fact that [these peasants] reduce their needs to a level inferior to that of wage laborers and exert themselves in their work incomparably more than the latter do.[5]

Upon studying peasant smallholding ownership, Marx indicated clearly that in it

> the governing market price of the product only reaches its value under extraordinary conditions; this value, however, will stand as a rule above the price of production, on account of the preponderant element of living labour, even though the excess of the value above the price of production will be limited again by the low composition also of non-agricultural capital in countries where a smallholding economy prevails.[6]

The limit is not, then, the average profit (as it would be in the case of a capitalist) but "the wage that [the peasant] pays himself." Thus Marx concludes that a "portion of the surplus labour performed by those peasants working under the least favourable conditions, is presented to society for nothing and does not contribute towards governing the price of production or forming value."[7] Accordingly, the famous "deficit" is a reality: it hides a "self-attributed wage," an "unequal exchange," forms of "self-exploitation," and "transfers of value," to use concepts that will be explained further on. But it simply cannot be said that peasant labor has no value.

Subject to further elaboration on the subject, I shall now attempt to translate the ideas outlined here into a concrete, practical methodology. The analysis that is proposed next was developed by me during a research project in the Valle del Mezquital; there, a certain number of units of agricultural production were studied in great detail, with the aim of testing a method of, and proposing a set of formulas for, interpreting systems of agricultural production.[8]

Detailed data on the inputs and the production of the agricultural units were obtained. The data were classified in the following way:

Cm = Expenditures in *constant capital* paid out in money, including cost of seeds, machinery, fuel, and fertilizers and cash payment of ground rent, water fees, etc.

D = Imputed constant capital; depreciation of machinery and tools, etc.

C = Total constant capital spent in the annual cycle

Rc = Imputed ground rent, in accordance with the rents paid in the region

Rm = Ground rent actually paid

Vw = Variable capital paid in money (wages)

Vc = Imputed variable capital, in accordance with regional wages for the type of work performed, and calculated in accordance with the number of work days actually employed in the agricultural cycle in question

P = Value of total production, at current prices in the marketplace

Pc = Value of production not sold (consumed), at current prices in the marketplace

K = Total capital invested

On the basis of this information, one proceeds to calculate the "profit" of the units of production. The first type of profit considers monetary flows exclusively:

$$Pr_1 = P - Pc - (Cm + Vw)$$

This formula reflects the conditions that the agricultural unit meets in confronting the capitalist market; if it yields a negative result, the farm faces a situation that pushes it toward selling or renting out land. To this calculation must be added the depreciation of constant capital, for otherwise only the farmer's short-term situation is reflected. Although this depreciation is not a cash expenditure in the agricultural cycle under consideration, over the long or medium term the farmer will have to spend that amount in order to replace fixed capital used. The following formula is adapted for this consideration:

$$Pr_2 = P - Pc - (Cm + Vw + D)$$

To this point, formulas that attempt to reflect the conditions indispensable for the farm's subsistence have been used. If the imputed value of family labor is added in, one will have an idea of the problem discussed above:

$$Pr_3 = P - Pc - (Cm + Vw + D + Vc)$$

In order to calculate the profitability of the capitalist enterprise, it is next necessary to add the imputed rent:

$$Pr_4 = P - Pc - (Cm + Vw + D + Vc + Rc)$$

When the result of Pr_4 reaches the average rate of profit, we are looking at a capitalist landowner who is also appropriating ground rent. However, in order to understand the subsistence of noncapitalist economic units, it is necessary to take into account subsistence consumption and to eliminate the calculation for family labor:

$$Pr_5 = P - (Cm + Vw + D) = Pr_2 + Pc$$

But to measure the amount of unremunerated living labor, one uses the following formula:

$$Pr_6 = P - (Cm + Vw + Vc + D) = Pr_5 - Vc$$

Application of this set of formulas to regional and national data will serve as a basis for the study of systems of production in the Mexican countryside. The figures are brought together in tables 6 and 7. The calculations have been tested in more than one hundred units of production from the Valle del Mezquital (Hidalgo). The cases were analyzed in great detail, and to the extent possible, the errors characteristic of this type of survey of peasants have been eliminated. In every case, the data on imputed ground rent, imputed wages, and depreciation were calculated with exact data from the region and from the unit of production itself. The imputed wages, for example, were based on the wages that the unit of production itself paid; "technicians'" salaries were assigned to the rich farmers, in accordance with regional norms. The depreciation (imputed constant capital) was calculated tool by tool, machine by machine, taking as a basis the actual age and cost. Profits were figured in accordance with the formulas already set forth; the rates of profit were figured over K (total capital invested):

$$\frac{Pr}{K} \times 100$$

Table 7 includes a column representing the organic composition of capital $(C/V \times 100)$.

The regional results for the Valle del Mezquital are not included in this book, although the analysis of the economic mechanisms of the modes of production done here was based in great part on that regional study. Tables 6 and 7 were calculated using the same methods, but with information on a national scale obtained in 723 direct surveys conducted by the CDIA.[9] To the extent possible, the information was adjusted to the needs of our calculations; however, that was not possible in every case. The concept Rm also includes payment for irrigation as well as ground rent; the rates and ratios used in that study for ground rent, imputed wages, depreciation, and so forth, were respected, which undoubtedly causes some variations with respect to our method. Furthermore, the social strata were ordered in a different manner.

The national-level data are not presented on a case-by-case basis; each "type" (numbered from 1 to 21) represents the average of all the units of production according to land tenure and CDIA stratum (from I to V). These strata are based upon a classification in accordance with the total value of the production.[10]

The four strata into which we divide the information correspond to the following definitions:

Stratum A: Impoverished, ruined, or semi-ruined farmers, with incomes from agriculture that only rarely exceed four thousand pesos per year

(Pr_5), who work under monetary deficit conditions, have high rates of subsistence consumption, and support themselves essentially by wage labor or petty commerce.

Stratum B: Middle-level, typically simple commodity farmers with incomes that afford them subsistence but do not permit any savings.

Stratum C: Well-to-do farmers in a transition situation.

Stratum D: Capitalist farmers.

These strata represent a *provisional* division for purposes of analysis. The data in tables 6 and 7 (especially for profits) permitted categorizing them in this manner.

Some Features of
the Developed Capitalist Sector

One notes immediately that the sector of units of agricultural production that has a clearly capitalist character is extremely small. If we use the 1960 census data to locate what in tables 6 and 7 was called stratum D (which is the only one that has overtly capitalist traits), we find that these units represent barely 0.5 percent of all units of production; they represent what the CDIA study calls *large multifamily farms.*[11]

In 1960, this sector was made up of only twelve thousand farmers; notwithstanding their reduced number, these enterprises *generated 32 percent of the total value of domestic agricultural production.* As an effect of the polarization and expansion of capitalist relations of production, in 1970 this sector increased to around fifty thousand enterprises and climbed to almost 2 percent of the total units of production (according to data from CEPAL, 1982). I shall now attempt to outline its essential features:

1. *The profit created derives from the exploitation of wage laborers.* The capitalist farms studied in the Mezquital use, on average, more than twelve man-years of wage labor; the data on a national scale yield a figure of around forty man-years of wage labor. The capitalist farms are characterized by the predominant use of day laborers, and the profit that their owners obtain is the *surplus value* that is extracted from those laborers. The rates for surplus value are, on the average, about 71 percent for the national-level data and about 185 percent for the Mezquital. Table 8 presents in detail the surplus value rates, along with profit and organic composition of capital. As can be seen, the rates of exploitation—quite high in general—have a wide range of fluctuation (from 50 percent to 348 percent). The most noteworthy phenomenon is that there is a close correlation between the rates of surplus value and of profit. In fact, everything seems to indicate that the high rates of profit are attained by increasing the rate of exploitation of day laborers. That is, the "efficiency" and "profita-

Table 6
Composition of Capital and Agricultural Production

Number	K	Rm	Rc	C	Cm	D	Vw	Vc	V	Pc	P	Land Tenure	Stratum	Soil
Stratum A														
1	26,983	220	542	8,924	7,648	514	75	2,730	2,805	205	4,061	Ejido enterprise	II	Irrigation
2	20,875	61	609	2,921	1,458	793	369	1,387	1,756	436	1,396	Ejido	I	Dry farming
3	25,994	290	606	2,686	637	1,153	851	2,316	3,167	3,197	3,937	Private property	II	Dry farming
4	16,400	20	730	1,110	290	70	60	1,120	1,180	430	580	Ejido	I	Irrigation
5	7,726	5	169	699	216	309	84	721	805	317	571	Private property	I	Dry farming
6	28,747	125	880	2,704	806	893	529	3,387	3,916	2,357	3,267	Ejido	II	Dry farming
7	23,579	294	459	2,467	1,128	585	422	2,835	3,257	2,168	4,188	Private property	II	Irrigation
8	26,225	81	878	2,893	1,354	580	602	2,488	3,090	1,416	3,949	Ejido	II	Irrigation
Average	22,066	137	609	3,050	1,692	612	374	2,123	2,497	1,316	2,742			
Stratum B														
9	53,975	711	1,199	4,516	1,242	1,364	1,880	3,442	5,322	4,879	10,953	Private property	III	Dry farming
10	48,711	412	1,109	5,744	2,343	1,880	1,583	4,973	6,556	4,667	12,505	Ejido	III	Dry farming
11	56,902	500	1,516	8,351	4,400	1,935	1,778	4,424	6,202	3,336	14,695	Ejido	III	Irrigation
12	39,670	191	625	11,958	9,136	2,006	1,243	2,810	4,053	1,793	13,776	Ejido enterprise	III	Irrigation
13	82,229	1,363	1,636	13,573	7,176	3,398	3,065	6,195	9,260	3,300	16,648	Private property	III	Dry farming
Average	56,311	635	1,217	8,288	4,859	2,117	1,910	4,369	6,279	3,595	13,715			

Stratum C

14	160,158	3,707	1,997	32,980	12,669		2,979	5,465	8,444	9,352	45,887	Ejido	IV	Dry farming
15	320,477	76	9,616	31,547	9,049		8,379	8,916	17,295	15,141	59,420	Private property	IV	Dry farming
16	274,120	4,012	4,407	58,080	18,623		11,912	4,758	16,670	18,239	65,163	Private property	IV	Irrigation
17	157,899	71	1,414	31,340	15,321		5,767	9,100	14,867	34,572	72,203	Ejido enterprise	IV	Irrigation
18	150,341	3,058	3,554	35,564	24,185		7,273	6,225	13,498	5,373	55,202	Ejido	IV	Irrigation
Average	212,598	2,185	4,198	37,902	19,591	11,928	7,262	6,893	14,155	16,535	59,575			

Stratum D

19	2,528,564	30,376	34,416	668,047	419,702	183,553	150,105	8,581	158,686	234,982	1,107,888	Private property	V	Irrigation
20	607,997	66,801	—	364,431	262,448	35,182	173,651	6,797	180,448	372	628,914	Tenants	V	Irrigation
21	680,810	24,189	4,133	186,271	124,191	33,758	45,380	12,450	57,830	28,207	357,068	Ejido	V	Irrigation
Average	1,272,457	40,455	12,850	406,249	268,780	84,164	123,045	9,276	132,321	87,854	697,957			

Source: Calculations based on CDIA data, *Estructura agraria y desarrollo agrícola en México*, 3 vols. (Mexico City, 1970).

Notes:

K = The sum of the value of the land (table III-33, p. 515) + Rm + Cm + V + fixed capital, plantations, irrigation equipment, machinery, and livestock (table III-39a, p. 524). For renters, land value is not added in.

Rm = Ground rent + water fees (table III-50a, p. 541)

Rc = Imputed rent (ibid.)

Cm = Money capital (ibid.); does not include Rm

D = Imputed capital (ibid.)

Vw = Wages (ibid.)

Vc = Imputed labor (ibid.)

Pc = Production consumed (ibid.)

P = Total production (ibid.)

Table 7

Types of Profit and Organic Composition of Capital

Stratum	Profits						Profit Rates						C/V
	P_1	P_2	P_3	P_4	P_5	P_6	P_1/K	P_2/K	P_3/K	P_4/K	P_5/K	P_6/K	
Stratum A													
1	-4,087	-4,601	-7,331	-7,873	-4,396	-7,126	-15.1	-17.1	-27.2	-29.2	-16.3	-26.3	3.2
2	-928	-1,721	-3,108	-3,717	-1,285	-2,672	-4.4	-8.2	-14.9	-17.8	-6.6	-12.8	1.7
3	-1,038	-2,191	-4,507	-5,113	1,006	-1,310	-4.0	-8.4	-17.3	-19.7	3.9	-5.0	0.9
4	-220	-290	-1,410	-2,140	140	-980	-1.3	-1.8	-8.6	-13.1	0.8	-6.0	0.9
5	-51	-360	-1,081	-1,250	-43	-764	-0.7	-4.7	-14.0	-16.2	-0.6	-9.9	0.9
6	-550	-1,443	-4,830	-5,710	914	-2,473	-1.9	-5.0	-16.8	-19.9	3.2	-8.6	0.7
7	176	-409	-3,244	-3,703	1,759	-1,076	0.8	-1.7	-13.8	-15.7	7.5	-4.6	0.8
8	496	-84	-2,572	-3,450	1,332	-1,156	1.9	-0.3	-9.8	-13.2	5.1	-4.4	0.9
Average	-775	-1,387	-3,510	-4,119	-71	-2,194	-3.1	-5.9	-15.3	-18.1	-0.4	-9.7	1.2
Stratum B													
9	2,241	877	-2,565	-3,764	5,756	2,314	4.2	1.6	-4.8	-7.0	10.7	4.3	0.9
10	3,500	1,620	-3,353	-4,462	6,287	1,314	7.2	3.3	-6.9	-9.2	12.9	2.7	0.9
11	4,681	2,746	-1,678	-3,194	6,082	1,658	8.2	4.8	-2.9	-5.6	10.7	2.9	1.4
12	1,404	-597	-3,407	-4,032	1,196	-1,614	3.6	-1.5	-8.6	-10.2	3.0	-4.1	2.9
13	1,744	-1,654	-7,849	-9,485	1,646	-4,549	2.1	-2.0	-9.5	-11.5	2.0	-5.5	1.5
Average	2,714	597	-3,772	-4,989	4,192	-177	5.1	1.2	-6.5	-8.7	7.9	0.0	1.5

Stratum C												
14	15,242	2,573	-2,892	-4,889	11,925	6,460	9.5	1.6	1.8	-3.1	7.5	4.0	3.9
15	23,018	13,969	5,053	-4,563	29,110	20,194	7.2	4.4	1.6	-1.4	9.1	6.3	1.8
16	-38	-18,661	-23,419	-27,826	-422	-5,180	-0.0	-6.8	-8.5	-10.2	-0.2	-1.9	3.5
17	16,472	1,938	-7,162	-8,576	36,510	27,410	10.4	1.2	-4.5	-5.4	23.0	17.4	2.1
18	15,313	10,546	4,321	767	15,919	9,694	10.2	7.0	2.9	0.5	10.6	6.5	2.6
Average	14,001	2,073	-4,820	-9,018	18,608	11,715	7.5	1.5	-2.1	-3.1	10.0	6.5	2.8
Stratum D												
19	272,723	89,170	80,589	46,173	324,152	315,571	10.8	3.5	3.2	1.8	12.8	12.5	4.2
20	125,642	90,460	83,663	83,663	90,832	84,035	20.7	14.9	13.8	13.8	14.9	13.8	2.0
21	135,101	101,343	88,893	84,760	129,550	117,100	19.8	14.9	13.1	12.4	19.0	17.2	3.2
Average	177,822	93,658	84,382	71,532	181,512	172,236	17.1	11.1	10.0	9.3	15.2	14.5	3.1

Source: Calculations based on table 6.

bility" of agrarian enterprises have as their basis a *superexploitation* of wage labor.

2. *Capitalist-sector agricultural enterprises have a higher organic composition of capital than do those in the noncapitalist sector.* In fact, in the national-level data, the relation between variable capital and constant capital indicates that investments in land, technology, seeds, and so on, are high in stratum D. Nonetheless, the C/V ratio shows a very symptomatic behavior: although the tendency is not a marked one in the data from the tables for the capitalist sector, an inverse correlation is observed between the increase in the rate of profit and the increase in the organic composition of capital. That is, as the organic composition of capital rises, the rate of profit declines. Combined with the information on rates of exploitation, this indicates that by increasing the investment in constant capital, the agrarian capitalist attains elevated rates of exploitation that permit him to counteract the profit rate's tendency to fall.

3. *The high rates of profit, fruit of superexploitation, take the form of superprofit.* That is, the opportunity for capitalist farmers to appropriate high profits derives from the existence of direct usufruct of the land (private property or ejido). When the farmer is simultaneously the owner or ejidatario, he does not pay any rent at all for the land, and in fact he reserves the value of the ground rent for himself as extraordinary profit. This can be seen quite clearly when the economic unit is subjected to rigorously capitalist accounting (Pr_4), in which the imputed value of ground rent is taken into consideration. Section 19 of the national-level tables (6 and 7) yields a profit rate below 9 percent, which could be taken as an average rate for the entire system (or at least as the interest that would be obtained from bonds or mortgage certificates). The capitalists who obtain low profit rates (Pr_4) compared with the average rate surmount their inefficiency by appropriating the ground rent. This does not happen with tenant farmers (section 20 of tables 6 and 7), for whom rent is not a theory but an amount they have to pay in cash; they represent the "pure," "classic" image of the agrarian capitalist. Thus, high profits and superexploitation of labor often conceal inefficiency that manages to hide itself by means of ground rent, by means of monopoly of the land.

4. *In Mexico, one observes the existence of two groups of units of capitalist production: one is highly efficient and obtains high profit rates; the other is not very efficient and has low rates of profit.* Undoubtedly, this situation is a result of a prior historical condition, typical of the second half of the nineteenth century: the existence, in the countryside, of an agrarian bourgeoisie and of a traditional latifundista sector. The latifundios did not function like landholders in an advanced capitalist system, but they did not represent a sector defined by feudal relations of production, either. *Latifundismo*, today just as it was one hundred years

Table 8
Comparison of Surplus Value Rates on Capitalist Farms

Types of Farm	Pr_2/V (%)	Pr_2 (%)	C/V
Mexico			
Owners	56	3.5	4.2
Tenants	50	14.9	2.0
Ejidatarios	175	14.9	3.2
Mezquital			
1	152	7.0	3.5
2	42	9.2	2.2
3	120	17.5	1.6
4	67	6.3	2.5
5	206	12.2	5.9
6	348	21.9	5.5
7	308	32.2	2.5

Sources: On Mexico, see table 7; data for Mezquital are based on personal research in 1972.

ago, with all the feudal overtones that one could want, is basically the expression of a distorted capitalist mode of production; its peculiar trait is a significant concentration of land with a low concentration of capital.

These days it is difficult to speak of latifundismo, not because large concentrations of land do not exist but because agrarian reform essentially eliminated the system both economically and politically. But the elimination of the majority of the large haciendas did not end the economic imbalance or the structural distortions that were the base of the latifundista system. Heir of these conditions, the Mexican agrarian bourgeoisie today contemplates the existence at its core of an important sector sufficiently inefficient to provoke agricultural crises like the one that the country has been experiencing since the late 1970s, one that is connected with the global economic crisis of the early 1980s.

This situation is clear in the tables we are analyzing. Not only in stratum D do we find cases with low productivity and low rates of profit. We have placed in other lower strata units of production that in terms of both the amount of investment and their relatively abundant use of wage labor would be capable of generating capitalist profits. The most noteworthy example is that of the ejido enterprises, whose survival is explained—in many cases—only by the fact that they are subsidized by official credit banks.

5. *The inefficiency of a group of agricultural units is intimately connected to low investment in constant money capital.* This reflects meager use of improved seed, fertilizers, insecticides, and modern machinery. In cases

of inefficiency, the relation between total capital and the money capital invested, excluding ground rent, yields low ratios.[12] If, on the other hand, we examine the relation between investments in seed, fertilizers, insecticides, machinery, and so on, and expenditures for wages, we will obtain a ratio that reveals a significant imbalance: the meager utilization of modern technology is compensated for with abundant labor. This last ratio expresses the organic composition of money capital used in the annual cycle. In other words, in the capitalist sector, one observes a tendency according to which as investments in constant capital (excluding ground rent) increase and, therefore, as the organic composition of capital rises, the rate of profit climbs. This means that by eliminating the land factor, a tendency that is the inverse of the one noted in subsection 2 occurs, one that ends up confirming the Marxist thesis according to which monopoly of the land represents an obstacle to the development of capitalism in agriculture.

6. *Land ownership (private or ejido) is a hindrance to investment of capital in agriculture.* This is an important theoretical aspect: at first glance, it might seem that the fact that the capitalist is simultaneously the owner of the land facilitates the development of capital and the obtaining of extraordinary profits that could be reinvested. However, as Marx points out, this situation exists purely *by chance,* which is to say that it may occur or not (it may even occur very often, as in Mexico), depending upon sociohistorical conditions. The capitalist-owner "can treat the land as a simple natural element and let his decision be determined exclusively by considering the valorization of his capital."[13] However, if, as happened in Mexico, the demand for wheat rose as a result of imposition of guarantee prices higher than world prices as part of the import substitution policy, then things would change. As Marx says: "If an increased demand for corn requires the cultivation of a greater extent of type A land than is to be found in the hands of self-farming proprietors, i.e., if one part of it has to be leased in order to be cultivated at all, this hypothetical abolition of the barrier landed property places to the investment of capital immediately disappears."[14] Thus, in Mexico, all the irrigation districts are inundated with capitalist tenant farmers.

The internal contradictions of the capitalist sector revolve around the fact that the possibility of obtaining superprofits (e.g., ground rent) benefits the rural bourgeoisie in the short term but in the long term generates forms of parasitism and inefficiency that pose obstacles to the growth of the business of the rural bourgeoisie itself. The immediate solution is the superexploitation of day laborers, as a result of which the already high rates of displacement of labor from agriculture end up being accelerated.

Features of the Simple Commodity Economy

The strata that can be defined roughly as simple commodity (typically peasant) strata represented around 367,000 farms and 16 percent of the total units of production in Mexico in 1960. They generate 47 percent of the country's total agricultural production. They comprise strata B and C in the tables and what the CDIA considers *family and medium multifamily* farms. The latter stratum (C, of well-to-do peasants) is small: 67,000 units (3 percent of the total number of farms), but it generates 22 percent of the total production. This means that the greater part of the simple commodity units (the remainder, 13 percent of the total units) generates only 25 percent of the total yield. In reality, this calculation essentially follows the *form* of production; but one must take into account that many units of production that are simple commodity *in form* are actually integrated into capitalist agro-commercial or agro-industrial units. This means that the figures and percentages on production for these strata are considerably inflated.

In 1970, according to a CEPAL study (1982), the number of well-to-do peasants rose significantly and the number of average peasants decreased. Those well-to-do produced 26 percent of the total value of the agricultural production, while the average peasants generated barely 15 percent. Although these data do not include the value of livestock production, by comparing them with the data for 1960, we can discern the fact that the effects of the crisis not only cut down peasant production but also accentuate the process of polarization and differentiation.

Let us consider some of its internal features:

1. *The peasant units of production rely on the use of unremunerated family labor.* The simple commodity system of production has as its basic unit the family cell. The entire family, from the smallest children to the adults, contributes in a greater or lesser degree to the agricultural and livestock production. The peasant does not have variable capital in cash available except in tiny quantities. He has no alternative except to make use of the only labor power that has no exchange value for him: his own labor, that of his relatives, and, on special occasions, the collective effort of the community. To the extent that the possibilities of communal effort are being exhausted, for the intrusion of commodity relations erodes and obstructs them, the peasant finds himself compelled to use wage labor in certain periods of the year (for the preparation of the land and, above all, for the harvest). In fact, these days, a peasant can only very rarely avoid hiring day laborers, as can be seen in column Vw of table 6. At the level of the well-to-do peasants, there are even instances of those who invest

more wage labor in the land than labor of their own. However, these peasants are not yet able to stop investing their own efforts in the farm, for their incomes would drop considerably. This situation poses an important problem: does the peasant who uses wage labor maintain a relation of exploitation with the day laborer? Does the peasant extract surplus labor from the day laborer? We will attempt to answer these questions below when we turn to simple commodity "profit."

2. *The peasants produce fundamentally for the market.* This trait, along with the use of unremunerated family labor, is what gives these units of production their simple commodity character. Despite the fact that these small farmers live in considerable poverty, as a group they generate a very high proportion of the commodities that are placed in the market. I have already pointed out that almost half the value of domestic production originates from these strata. Of course, a part of that is consumed for subsistence; but only approximately one-quarter of the production is consumed by the peasant family economy itself. Of the cases recorded in the tables, none consumes more than half for subsistence. Subsistence consumption, at the heart of the simple commodity economy, is a *complement* of income. Its existence nevertheless enables one to understand the peasant economy's great resistance to the most adverse market conditions, as well as the rooting of the producer to his land.

3. *In the simple commodity economy, profit and variable capital form one unit.* If the profits of the peasant units are calculated by imputing a value to family labor power, in the majority of cases one observes, as already mentioned, a deficit or very low profits. What does this situation reveal? If one examines the calculation of commercial profit without discounting imputed ground rent $[Pr_3 = P - Pc - (Cm + D + Vw + Vc)]$, one discovers that in the majority of cases, the peasant does not even receive the entire value of the family labor power. That is, not only does he fail to make profits but he does not even receive his whole "wage." Even if one adds in the value of production consumed for subsistence (Pr_6), the situation does not essentially change. What happens is that the peasant operates with a different formula: he does not take into account the value of his own labor. He operates with what we are calling profit (Pr_5). But in reality, this situation hides an important fact: profit and wages get confused; that is, *there is no profit.* In the cases in which a positive rate of profit appears (in Pr_3 and Pr_6), the amount is so small that it can barely be taken into consideration. Only among some well-to-do peasants does the profit prove meaningful, without ever reaching, in any event, the capitalist farmers' rates.

Often the amount earned by the peasant (taking into account subsistence consumption as well) is less than the sum of the rent of the land that he possesses and the value of his labor. This explains the typical situation in the irrigation districts, where the small peasant prefers to rent his land to a capitalist entrepreneur and to work for him as a wage laborer—on the peasant's own parcel!

We have previously seen that in every case, on a small scale, the peasants use wage labor. However, the economic mechanisms of the simple commodity system hinder them from obtaining surplus value from the day laborers: there being no *profit*, the peasant obtains no surplus labor. Only in the few cases in which a profit appears does the peasant extract surplus labor from the day laborer, but the rates of exploitation are extremely low, except among well-to-do peasants (without ever becoming, in any event, as high as those among the capitalists). We could conclude that the peasant appropriates surplus labor (in very small quantities) only when the profit rate Pr_6 is positive. In general terms, then, peasant profit is nothing more than a self-attributed wage.

4. *The peasant simple commodity economy does not contribute to the setting of product prices: prices are determined by the capitalist market.* Reality shows that the peasants' simple commodity production limits its objectives to the obtaining of a necessary wage and that it does not seek profits, not only because the internal dynamic and the conditions of the productive unit prevent it but also because in Mexico the market has a capitalist character. This means that as a general rule, the prices of agricultural products are set in accordance with the production costs of capitalist farmers. As is palpably demonstrated in tables 6 and 7, those costs of production are much higher in the peasant sector than in the capitalist sector.

This is the tendency under conditions of perfect competition, but for various important items, the existence of monopoly conditions or the state's setting of guarantee prices changes things. This is the case, for example, with the prices of coffee and cotton—key products in the Mexican economy—which are set by the international market; in these instances, the price fluctuations can affect even sectors of the agrarian bourgeoisie. On the other hand, the government supports corn prices at artificially high levels in an attempt to halt the deterioration of the economy of millions of peasants. However, not even in the case of corn do official prices manage to permit profits among the peasants.[15]

The Mexican economy could not tolerate the functioning of a market for agricultural products in which the noncapitalist sector participated on a massive scale in setting prices. The high prices would cause disturbances in industry, difficulties in foreign trade, and impoverishment of wage laborers in the cities. Such a situation, which would be the peasant utopia, would halt the country's economic development.

5. *The simple commodity sector is experiencing a process of de-peasantization and decomposition, which manifests itself in a polarization of the*

social groups among farmers. The adverse market conditions, the impossibility of savings and accumulation in the majority of cases, the lack of credit, the poor quality of the soil or its impoverishment, and the competition from capitalist farms are causing a permanent crisis in the peasant economy that results in stagnation, dissolution, or ruin. Although this tendency is slowed down by multiple political factors and economic mechanisms (which we have defined briefly as a situation of *permanent primitive accumulation*), it has left deep imprints on the situation of the simple commodity sector and on the social composition of the peasantry. The most noteworthy is the polarization in the form of a broad spectrum of the peasant farms; another, no less important, is the rapid decline of the percentage of peasant population.

For example, the normal profits (Pr_5) of the peasants in strata B and C typically fluctuate from five thousand pesos to more than thirty-five thousand pesos annually, that is, a ratio of 1:7. This means that there is the same distance between the extremes that there can be in the city between what a servant earns and a bureaucrat's income. On the other hand, it could be said that this process of polarization is slow. This can be appreciated in the figures in table 9 (in which strata III and IV represent what we consider the simple commodity sector).

The table shows that during the 1950s the proportions among the strata changed little. During those years there were obviously displacements of population toward the cities, which becomes apparent in the fact that in ten years only 11,000 new units of production appeared. Stratum IV (of well-to-do peasants) increased considerably, while stratum III grew slowly. It is evident that the simple commodity sector was polarized: a small sector with higher incomes was able to multiply (it was the only group that more than doubled in size), while the poor majority has not grown significantly. But in the sixties more important changes took place: the number of units of production increased by more than 100,000 (undoubtedly owing to the distributions of ejido land), and the polarization process was notably accentuated.

6. *One observes the existence of two groups of simple commodity units of production: a stratum of average peasants and a stratum of well-to-do peasants.* The polarization mentioned above has resulted in two sectors with distinct dynamics and traits of their own. While the average sector has no possibility of saving, the well-to-do sector generates a little capital that can be productively reinvested. While the average sector has no profit, the other obtains small rates of profit, gained from a greater use of wage labor. The average peasant tends, slowly but inexorably, toward proletarianization. The dynamic of the well-to-do peasants, on the other hand, tends toward "kulakization," toward becoming bourgeois.

Table 9
Polarization of Peasant Farms, 1950–1970

		Number of Farmers[b]			Percentage		
Stratum[a]		1950	1960	1970	1950	1960	1970
I	Infrasubsistence	1,312	1,241	1,423	53.8	50.7	55.7
II	Subfamilial (subsistence + stationary)	800	821	580	32.8	33.5	22.7
III	Familial (surplus)	289	307	210	11.9	12.5	8.2
IV	Average multifamilial (transitional)	28	67	297	1.2	2.8	11.6
V	Large multifamilial (entrepreneurs)	8	12	47	0.3	0.5	1.8
	Total	1,437	2,448	2,557	100.0	100.0	100.0

Sources: For 1950 and 1960, CDIA, *Estructura agraria y desarrollo agrícola en México;* for 1970, CEPAL, *Economía campesina y agricultura empresarial: tipología de productores del agro mexicano* (Mexico City: Siglo XXI Editores, 1982).

[a]The CEPAL strata for 1970 are not the same ones used by the CDIA. In parentheses are indicated the equivalent designations for those appearing in this table, which are only approximate.

[b]In thousands.

Forms of Exploitation of the Small Peasant

One point that I am most interested in emphasizing is that the exploitation of the small peasant derives essentially from his *structural* relation with the capitalist economy. The *base* for the exploitation is not the unequal distribution of land but the deep-seated mechanisms that cause this inequality and that accentuate it day in and day out. To assume that the fundamental problem has its roots in the unequal distribution of land leads to the populist fiction according to which it is necessary to push for land distribution in order to strengthen the small peasant economy.

Reality shows clearly that to the extent that an agrarian structure is dominated by the capitalist market, the inevitable tendency will be toward an increasingly marked differentiation of the peasantry, toward the proletarianization and pauperization of the lower strata of the peasantry. The noncapitalist peasant sector finds itself dominated by the capitalist market, and as we have seen, it is not in a position to influence farm prices. As I have pointed out, the individual price of production is lower in the capitalist sector, which is the one that determines prices. Thus, the small peasant finds himself forced to limit his aspirations to obtaining, at the most, the necessary wage. To repeat the observation made previously, Marx emphasized this phenomenon in explaining that in the peasant smallholding economy,

> the governing marketprice of the product only reaches its value under extraordinary conditions; this value, however, will stand as a rule above the price of production, on account of the preponderant element of living labour, even though the excess of the value above the price of production will be limited again by the low composition also of non-agricultural capital in countries where a smallholding economy prevails.[16]

Accordingly, among the peasants the limit is not the average profit but "the wage that [the small producer] pays himself." Thus, as I have noted earlier, Marx concludes that a "portion of the surplus labour performed by those peasants working under the least favourable conditions is presented to society for nothing and does not contribute towards governing the price of production or forming value."[17]

But to which segment of society does the peasant present a fraction of his labor? Or does he give it, instead, to society as a whole? ("Who [is] then the gentleman?") And if the latter is true, does the working class actually benefit from this "gift"? It is evident that the poor peasant is interested in higher prices for agricultural products, for which reason he is *apparently* in agreement with the rural bourgeoisie; however, he is also affecting the interests of the urban working class and the industrial bourgeoisie. Both these latter groups, which consume foods and raw materials that come from the countryside, would be in open opposition to all groups of agricultural producers, rich and poor alike.

This is nothing more than the expression of imbalances and contradictions in the capitalist system as a whole, but in reality it cannot be interpreted on the level of a *relation of exploitation among social classes.* What we find is a manifestation of the opposition between sectors (ultimately, the countryside and the city), which creates friction (at times quite significant) between the rural classes and the urban. The struggle between landholders and entrepreneurs, which was apparent in nineteenth-century England in the conflicts over the Corn Laws, is an example of that.

We ought to remember that, in fact, it suits the industrial bourgeoisie to keep the prices of agricultural goods low, for with such low prices it can manage to keep investments in constant and variable capital low as well:

1. It is interested in keeping the prices of raw materials low (circulating constant capital).
2. It is interested in keeping wages low. The paying of a wage is payment for the value of labor power, the value of which—like that of any other commodity—is determined by its cost of production. The latter is what it costs to support the worker as such and to train him for that job, that is, the price of the necessities of life and education. Thus, the industrial bourgeoisie is interested in keeping the prices of the basic foods that the workers consume low (variable capital).

For all these reasons, it is false to say that the worker "exploits" the peasant by demanding low prices. The one interested in keeping prices low is the capitalist, who does not want to be compelled to adjust wages to the new standard of living. If prices rise, the cost of living will climb, and sooner or later he will have to increase wages. Nevertheless, all this does not occur automatically, and, thus, the interests of workers and peasants can periodically come into opposition. Furthermore, the industrial bourgeoisie can adopt a different attitude toward the prices of agricultural products destined for export, toward those that do not directly affect their interests.

Thus, the industrial bourgeoisie benefits from the terms of the exchange between agriculture and industry; this can even reach the point of removing from some (inefficient) sectors of the agrarian bourgeoisie a portion of their profits. But the industrial bourgeoisie is totally in agreement with its rural counterpart on setting prices of farm products on the basis of the conditions imposed by the capitalist agrarian sector, and not in accordance with the costs of production on peasant farms. Thus, it is the bourgeoisie as a whole that benefits from peasant surplus labor "presented to society for nothing."

In fact, in Mexico, given the enormous weight of the peasant sector, the state has in some cases favored an increase in prices to a point above the production costs of the most developed capitalist sector. Furthermore, the existence of a significant inefficient capitalist sector (with higher costs) has also pushed prices upward. This situation has in fact contributed to encouraging the development of a small group of well-to-do peasants by accelerating the process of kulakization.

The mechanism of extraction of the peasant's surplus labor is driven by the dominant capitalist system. For this reason, the exploitation of the peasant has a *structural* character; that is, it is caused by the very laws of operation of the dominant capitalist structure. We have said that it is the bourgeoisie as a whole that is the beneficiary of the peasant's exploitation. Nevertheless, at the level of mechanisms of transfer of surplus labor to which we are referring, *it is above all the industrial (and financial) bourgeoisie that obtains the peasantry's excess labor.*

Given that peasant surplus labor is transferred through the market, "consumers" are the ones who take advantage of it. These "consumers" are largely the domestic or foreign industrial sectors, which absorb the raw materials and food products. We have already explained how it is not the industrial working class that benefits but the bourgeoisie. In reality, the urban bourgeoisie is appropriating a part of the profits that the agrarian sector generates; but just as "profit" is confused with compensating family labor in the peasant economy, in this case it is apparent that the industrial bourgeoisie keeps a part of the peasant's labor. In exchange, the rural bourgeoisie only relinquishes (in those cases where there is a transfer) a part of its profits. Thus, the antagonism between the peasantry and the industrial bourgeoisie is evident; their interests are definitively antagonistic.

The peasantry's struggle to raise prices affects urban enterprises but finds support among the rural bourgeoisie, especially in the inefficient sector of that bourgeoisie, for given that its prices of production are high, it is the one that has the most interest in obtaining greater profits. On the other hand, to the extent that the advanced, efficient sector of the rural bourgeoisie obtains in excess of the average rate of profit (and ground rent as well, when the bourgeoisie are landholders), it exerts less pressure than do other rural sectors for an increase in agricultural prices. Moreover, it is firmly tied to financial capital—on which it often depends—and therefore it represents an ally much closer to the urban entrepreneurial sector. Of course, the rural bourgeoisie as a whole also attains benefits from the exploitation of the peasantry, but through indirect mechanisms, given that it does not consume the peasant output. The general situation of the agrarian structure permits the rural bourgeoisie to obtain significant superprofits, thanks especially, although not exclusively, to the mechanisms of differential rent. That is, to the extent that small peasants farm the worst lands or that they find themselves compelled to produce under the worst economic conditions (with extremely low organic composition of capital, slow cycles of capital turnover, etc.), the levels attained by the differential rent that the capitalist farmers receive tend to rise.

It is not in the least surprising, then, that it is the industrial bourgeoisie that is the most interested in eliminating the peasant economy: although it is the principal beneficiary of its exploitation, the bulk of its earnings come from the surplus value extracted from the industrial proletariat; to the industrial bourgeoisie, the peasant surplus that it appropriates represents merely a few insignificant crumbs. On the other hand, these crumbs can cost it very dearly politically, for the peasantry forms a contingent that can create explosive conditions if income levels drop excessively. It is not only as a class segment that the industrial bourgeoisie is interested in the annihilation of the peasantry: in fact, this class interest reflects the tendency of all capitalist systems to proletarianize the peasantry in order to expand the internal market. This logic of the dominant mode of production is expressed in the type of exploitation to which the peasant is subjected: *unlike the exploitation of the worker, the exploitation of the peasant does not tend to reproduce the conditions for extraction of surplus labor.* On the contrary, it tends to make the peasants disappear, to transform them into an authentic extraction of surplus value; that is, it tends *to proletarianize the peasantry.*

The unequal exchange that the capitalist market imposes is not the only means by which the small peasant is exploited, although it is undoubtedly the most structural, inherent in the framework of the capitalist mode of production. Parallel to these mechanisms of exploitation, and as a typical consequence of economic backwardness and of what we have called permanent primitive accumulation, merchant and usurer capital plays a frontline role in Mexican rural zones. In the agrarian structure, the bourgeoisie of merchants, moneylenders, and middlemen is the most parasitic stratum in the countryside. Not only does the poor peasant face a market that is hostile and alien to him but in the majority of cases he cannot interact with it directly. He finds himself forced to sell his production to *acaparadores* (buyers of goods or produce, some with monopsony power, often referred to as hoarders) and middlemen, to whom he becomes progressively indebted, having to pay interest rates of a usurious nature. The problem with merchant and usurer capital is that to the extent that it develops independently, it manages to slow down the process of capitalist development itself. In Mexico, as in other backward, dependent countries, the group of merchants, moneylenders, and middlemen that slips into the network of relations of the urban sector with the rural comes to take on a massive character. Alongside the major rural merchants and moneylenders swarm numerous petty merchants who, with increasing difficulties, compete with the former for a few crumbs of commercial profit. "The independent development of merchant capital is found in an inverse relation to the degree of development of capitalist *production;* the more rigorous the development of merchant and usurer capital, the weaker that of industrial capital."[18]

The existence of middlemen and their mode of operating is quite significant. The clearest case is that of cotton, a key export product.[19] Cotton and coffee are the most sensitive items in the Mexican balance of trade. In these cases, the process of unequal exchange directly connects Mexican agrarian structure with imperialism; the price decreases for cotton and coffee that took place in 1967 produced a loss of 1,270 million pesos in export income. (In that year, the total value of Mexican exports was 737 million pesos.) But the problem does not stop here: Mexican producers do not sell their cotton directly to the international markets; rather, they sell it through Anderson Clayton, Hohenberg International, MacFadden, and other companies, all of them U.S. companies that corner the cotton output. In addition, these foreign firms provide credit, seed, and fertilizers to the farmers.

It is important to reiterate that the two forms of exploitation that have been mentioned—unequal exchange and merchant capital from money-lenders and middlemen—are not two isolated phenomena separated from one another: they are two sides of the same coin. The traits of merchant capital in the Mexican countryside relate to the degree of development attained by agricultural production; that is, they are a reflection of the existence of a simple commodity economy. Usury is a type of "secondary exploitation, which proceeds alongside the original exploitation that takes place directly within the production process itself."[20] By way of contrast with the mechanisms of unequal exchange, which exist thanks to *the very conditions of peasant production,* usury and trade take advantage of these conditions. Referring to the system of small producers, Marx said that "usury, just like trade, exploits a given mode of production, but does not create it; both relate to the mode of production from outside."[21] Thus, although the two mechanisms do not always appear separately, it is of great importance to distinguish between the appropriation of excess rural labor on the part of industrial capital and the appropriation of commercial profits by usurious merchant capital. "Usurer's capital," says Marx, "as the characteristic form of interest-bearing capital, corresponds to the predominance of petty production, of peasants and small master craftsmen working for themselves."[22]

The merchant and the moneylender also appropriate a part of peasant labor, but the disappearance of usurious merchant capital does not put an end to the exploitation of the small peasant: only the *parasitic form* of the extraction of surplus labor ends; the *structural exploitation* imposed by the modern capitalist market continues. In Mexico, both forms coexist; indeed, one of the traits of underdevelopment is precisely this curious symbiosis between the two forms of exploitation. The moneylender and the banker fraternally divide the products of peasant effort, but fundamentally, they represent two opposite tendencies: the moneylender will attain greater profits to the extent that the system of simple commodity production is maintained; the banker, in contrast, will be enriched to the extent that capitalist production prospers.[23] "A difference between two modes of social production and the social arrangements corresponding to them is involved here."[24] Primitive merchant capital—moneylender, middleman, and acaparador—is based on *plunder* and remains isolated from production. But the development of agriculture itself causes the merchants to continue investing in production, little by little, and to continue turning the peasants into workers. The most noteworthy examples of this last phenomenon are the merchant–tenant farmers of La Merced (the great market-stomach of Mexico City), who have penetrated many agricultural zones in the center of the country.

But as long as a sector of noncapitalist direct producers subsists, no matter how modern the market system may be, unequal exchange mechanisms will be established. The latter are inherent in the commercial relation between noncapitalist modes of production and the capitalist system. This complex situation does not generate the decomposition of the peasantry either overtly or without pitfalls; the presence of acaparadores, middlemen, unscrupulous merchants and moneylenders, who condemn thousands of peasants to misery, leads to a process of *nonproletarian pauperization*, which represents the lowest, most backward form of differentiation of the peasantry.

Pauperized Peasants and Semi-proletariat

Lastly, in 1960 and in 1970 there were more than two million peasants in Mexico with income derived from their own land so low that it can be said that, for them, agriculture was nothing more than a supplement. They are the peasants who appear in our tables as stratum A and whom the Center for Agrarian Research identifies as "infrasubsistence" and "subfamilial." In 1960, they represented 83 percent of the total number of producers but produced barely 21 percent of the total value of production. To give a better idea of this sector, it is useful to note that the majority of these peasants (the ones categorized as "infrasubsistence" by reason of producing less than five thousand pesos annually) only generated 4 percent of the total value of production in 1960, while they represented 50 percent of the total number of producers.

One can observe the following characteristics of these groups:

1. *The lowest strata of the peasantry carry on an agriculture with high rates of subsistence-consumption.* As a norm, the value of the production consumed by the laborer's family itself exceeds 50 percent of the total output. The products put on the market represent insignificant amounts, so that the transfers of value via unequal exchange are quite small. *As farmers,* they contribute little to national agricultural production, and accordingly, they generate a weak internal market. Because of the meager amounts that they receive in cash and because they make use of virtually no commercial inputs, these productive units mean very little for the

country's agricultural economy. The benefits that these farms yield for the peasant family are so feeble that even taking into account what they consume for themselves, they do not manage to maintain the family at even the lowest levels of subsistence. In every case, agricultural activity is accompanied by other remunerative activities. In the majority of cases, the amount of family labor that the farm absorbs is quite small.

2. *The agricultural activity of the pauperized peasants and the semi-proletariat has a marked tendency to result in cash losses.* This is one of the most significant aspects of these strata of the rural population. Not only do they face losses because of the uncompensated labor invested in the farm (just like the poor peasants in strata B and C) but they also have cash monetary losses. This means not only that they do not receive the entire value of their labor but that they have to lay out a certain amount of cash in order to be able to produce. (The P_1 profit rates, in cash, are negative [see tables 6 and 7].) Here, obviously, we are encountering an essentially antieconomic situation.

3. *The constant monetary losses make the pauperized and semi-proletarianized peasant population an easy victim of usurer capital.* In fact, in order to be able to face this situation, these peasants normally resort, by different methods, to moneylending merchants. These methods range from systematically obtaining goods on credit in the stores to selling crops *al tiempo* (in advance) at extremely low prices. It is at this level that the phenomenon of the *nonproletarian pauperization of the peasant* occurs: the merchant who makes a loan with high interest rates in exchange for a future crop encourages the rooting of the peasant to a piece of land that will never produce profits for him but will increasingly tie him to the moneylender. By means of subsistence consumption and usurious loans, the peasant manages to maintain himself in this miserable condition, without tearing himself loose from his sliver of land or moving away from his community or village. Nevertheless, he lives in the worst of situations: he loses money in cash, he transfers away a great part of the value of his labor, and in addition—as if that were not enough—he pays high rates of interest to the moneylender.

4. *In reality, for the lowest strata of the peasantry, agriculture is a secondary, supplementary activity.* In fact, the major part of their income derives from wage labor as day or incidental laborers, the practice of some trade or craft, petty commerce, work as servants, and so forth. Upon analyzing these units of production, one discovers almost invariably that they *are* subsidized, that is, that as isolated units they represent, in effect, an inexplicable antieconomic phenomenon. They can operate only in conjunction with other remunerative activity that will absorb the monetary losses from agricultural production. Thus we are confronted with the fact that agriculture is sustained by petty commerce, money from daughters

who work as servants in the city, day labor, profits from crafts, or earnings from the practice of a trade.

Just as the peasant does not calculate the value of his own labor, he does not separate agricultural activity from his other jobs or trades. The real unit is formed by the family economy, which is oriented toward obtaining whatever is needed in order to survive. Thus, even though the peasant is actually losing money with agriculture, and is subsidizing it with income derived from other activity, the family economy as a whole is kept afloat, although not without resorting to usury as a means of stabilizing it. However, this still does not enable one to understand why the family economy permits at its very core an activity that produces losses. The functioning of deficit agriculture within a larger unit explains how the loss is covered but not why it occurs.

5. *The agricultural activity of the impoverished and semi-proletarianized peasants is a form of acquiring food apparently at low prices.* It is not possible to explain the monetary losses by attributing them to the peasant's ignorance or stupidity. In reality, his existence obeys a powerful logic: with a certain amount of labor invested and a more or less small amount of money, he obtains a volume of food (almost always corn and beans) the market price of which is greater than the monetary loss that its production causes. It is true that if the labor invested is taken into account, the cost of these foods is in fact higher than it would be in the marketplace; but the producer here does not valorize his labor. If the tables on composition of capital and profits (stratum A) are examined, it will be seen that in almost all cases, the monetary loss does not exceed the price of the production consumed for subsistence: the exceptions comprise credit societies and some ejidos (cases 1 and 2 of tables 6 and 7), which obviously receive a state subsidy.

In this way, the peasant obtains food for relatively small sums of money; he pays in cash only a fraction of the price of such foods in the marketplace. This "discount" fluctuates, in our data, between 10 percent and 90 percent of the price. For the peasant, this system also functions as a stabilizer of his family economy: if for some reason (e.g., illness) he needs cash, he can sell a larger portion of his crop; of course, this will have negative repercussions in his economy over the long term, but for the moment he can get himself out of a jam. The scarcity and insecurity of paying work compel him to resort to this mechanism. In conclusion, one cannot properly call these producers "farmers"; their principal activity is something else: the cultivation of the smallholding conceals a peculiar form of acquisition of food at a "low" price.

6. *In the lowest stratum, we can distinguish two levels: the pauperized peasants and the semi-proletarians.* Although these two strata do not appear to be totally differentiated, we can establish that the *rural semi-*

proletariat is made up of individuals who support themselves fundamentally from their work as day laborers or workers but keep up the work on their plot of land as a supplementary activity. They are characterized as semi-proletarians not only because they still maintain ties to the soil as a means of production but also because their position as wage laborers is not at all stable. The ones we call *pauperized peasants* are those who are not being proletarianized in the process of decomposition of the peasantry and are basically living off so-called tertiary activities: petty commerce, services, and so on. For them as well, agriculture is a secondary activity. The boundaries between these two strata are not in the least precise. Their existence is a reflection of the two tendencies in the depeasantization process previously mentioned.

Modes of Production and
Subcapitalist Agrarian Structure

Transfers and Exploitation

In order to outline the structure of social classes, it is essential to make some brief comments on problems noted previously; in fact, it will be necessary to begin to systematize and reorder the foregoing analyses to advance toward a synthesis of the situation. The functioning of the modes of production has been presented; next, I shall attempt to amplify the explanation of the bonds that link the different modes of production and the contradictions that characterize the functioning and evolution of the Mexican agrarian structure.

The use of the concept *mode of production* is indispensable for understanding these contradictions because the latter must be placed on three levels: (1) the contradictions *within the interior* of each mode of production; (2) the contradictions that result from the relations *among* different modes of production; and (3) the contradictions characteristic of the structure *as a whole*. As can be seen, this concept is a basic tool for analysis. I shall define the mode of production of material goods as the *unity* of the productive forces and the relations of production, a unity that determines the characteristics and the dynamic of the society. A mode of production is not simply a set of productive forces and concentrated relations of production; it comprises a specific type of relations of production *united and perfectly congruent* with certain levels and features of the productive forces.[25]

In the foregoing pages, contradictions of the first type have appeared, that is, those that are characteristic of the two modes of production considered: the simple commodity mode of production and the capitalist mode.

But even in introducing these first contradictions, the discussion of the other two levels of contradictions has already begun, for two reasons: first, because the "internal" contradictions of the simple commodity economy originate in its relation with the capitalist mode of production; and second, because the contradictions of the capitalist mode of production, to the extent that it is the dominant one, form the basis of the contradictions of the entire agrarian structure. This section will be devoted principally to discussing these structural contradictions as well as those that are based on the articulation of the two modes of production.

The articulation between the simple commodity economy and the capitalist mode of production is qualitatively different from other types of articulation, because neither mode represents the *remnants* of a once-dominant mode of production in the process of disappearing. For example, during the transition from feudalism to capitalism and during the first phase of capitalist development, the feudal mode of development represents the *ancien régime;* in Mexico, however, the simple commodity mode of production is, despite its precapitalist character, a creation of the *new regime.* Not only this: in addition, the peasant simple commodity economy's own secondary nature gives a singular character to this articulation. This is quite important, because the fact that the simple commodity economy is both structurally and by definition prevented from becoming the dominant mode of production means that some of its *internal* contradictions derive from its articulation with another mode of production. In sum, the simple commodity mode of production in Mexico is totally dependent on the model of capitalist evolution that has been imposed since the late 1930s, a model that, paradoxically, became simultaneously the procreator and the executioner of the peasant economy.

The most important internal contradiction of the simple commodity economy manifests itself in the atomization of the economy into millions of units of production that block the introduction of more advanced productive forces, which can only be employed on the basis of concentration of production. This contradiction determines the high costs of production of commodities (in comparison with costs in the capitalist mode of production), and consequently, the relation of *unequal exchange* arises between the two modes of production. But the contradiction that is at the base of this unequal exchange no longer has an *internal* character; rather, it can only be explained by the link between the two modes of production. Technically speaking, this unequal exchange prompted by the price mechanism is only a *transfer* of values between two sectors; but the fact that it occurs in the form of a levy by the dominant mode of production enables one to affirm that one is dealing with a form of *exploitation* (extraction of surplus labor).

The articulation occurs here through relations of exploitation; in contrast, the articulation between the feudal system and capitalism is manifested essentially through the *transfer* of value from the capitalist to the landholder in the form of ground rent.[26] The articulation in this latter case appears as a relation between two exploitative classes, in which the parasitic class of precapitalist origin takes on a remora-like role in compelling the capitalist to transfer part of the profit to it; but there is no relation of exploitation between them.

In contrast, between the peasantry and the bourgeoisie there is indeed a relation of exploitation, notwithstanding which the former, to the extent that they are owners of land, simultaneously play the part of landholders. This is a typical situation in countries in which, as in Mexico, the bourgeoisie found itself obliged to build a noncapitalist peasant system in order to protect its power, and to ally itself with the peasantry in order to destroy the political power of the latifundistas. In these situations, the bourgeoisie inherits from the latifundistas the uncomfortable task of eliminating the peasantry, and the peasants, for their part, inherit from the landholders the no less uncomfortable role of representatives of the private ownership of land and monopoly of the soil (and with that, therefore, the right to appropriate ground rent). Theoretically, the articulation between capitalism and the peasant economy implies transfers in two directions: from the peasant to the bourgeois via unequal exchange, and from the bourgeois to the peasant via ground rent. This latter flow occurs only in the irrigation districts, where the peasant rents out his land. Although individually the peasant who receives rent is not situated like a landlord, the peasantry as a whole fulfills that function.

Nevertheless, it is important to underscore that from the *quantitative* perspective, these transfers have very little economic importance. The bourgeoisie does not live off the unequal exchange, just as the peasant does not feed himself with the ground rent; these flows have more significance for the one paying them than for the one receiving them: for the peasant, the unequal exchange can even be his ruin, and for the bourgeoisie, ground rent can become a serious obstacle to capital investment in agriculture. That is, the existence of these transfers and the characteristics of their mechanisms enable us to discover the forms of articulation of two modes of production, and the real basis for the possible alliances of social sectors and social classes.

Finally, it is necessary to point out that between these two modes of production there is a key common element: the commodity character of the economy. Everything said here, including this last remark, indicates clearly that the articulation between these two modes of production forms a single *structure* decidedly dominated by capitalism.[27] The relations between the two systems are so close and so interdependent that the contraditions of each one are expressed in the interior of the other. This particular structural overlap is the one that has been called an instance of *subcapitalism.*

Monopoly Capitalism and
Permanent Primitive Accumulation

Various studies have shown the dynamism of the accumulation of capital in Mexican agriculture, even as they have taken note of the obstacles it faces.[28] Next one must ask oneself, What form does this process of accumulation of capital assume? Is one dealing with an accumulation that multiplies capitalists (as some have supposed) and that tends to turn the peasants into bourgeois? Or is there instead a process of *concentration* and *centralization* of capital that leads to a situation with a monopoly structure? This last alternative seems to be the one that corresponds to reality.

On one hand, it must be emphasized that an important part of agricultural production (especially that in the ejido sector) is controlled by the state by means of the combination of banking institutions, control organizations, and warehousing systems.[29] This complex forms a species of state monopoly capitalism of one sector of agriculture, operating with degrees of inefficiency that vary from case to case. One must also add a sector of *agro-industrial enterprises,* some *agro-commercial enterprises,* and the group of governmental agencies in charge of major infrastructure projects (especially for irrigation).[30] The state sector does not merely take charge of financing, control, construction, and distribution in accordance with a strictly capitalistic logic. From the moment the government is charged with maintaining political equilibrium as well, the state sector of the agricultural economy includes a type of operations that implies subsidies to noncapitalist units, distributions of earnings to placate the impatience of the rural population, and so forth. Thus, the nature of this system as an agricultural capitalism monopolized by the state must be colored by the fact that with a certain frequency, it will have to make concessions that will affect the dynamism of the accumulation of capital.

It is also possible to recognize a process of monopoly concentration in the private sector in agriculture. It has already been mentioned that there is—within the sector decidedly oriented toward capitalist production—a group of enterprises that are characterized by their efficiency, as well as by the size of the capital managed. These large agricultural enterprises function in a way that makes it difficult to understand them as isolated units, given that they are closely linked to banking, business, and industry. It is possible to state that a monopolistic concentration of large private agro-industrial and agro-commercial enterprises closely tied to financial capital (itself inseparable from imperialist capital) is developing and showing strength in the country. It comprises not only the large livestock owners and farmers but also the large food product and alcoholic beverage enterprises. The paper, cardboard, cellulose, soap, and rubber industries, and so forth, are also linked to agriculture. Moreover, the big merchants at La Merced market and the groups that control gigantic chains for distribution and sales of foods in markets or the export companies are added in.[31]

The strong tendencies toward centralization and concentration of capital are crystallizing in important sectors of agricultural production, where the monopoly situation has advanced quite far. An interesting example is that of barley, the cultivation of which is largely controlled by an intermediary enterprise created by the large brewing companies; the intermediary enterprise distributes seed and credit and corners the harvests by means of purchase contracts. A similar situation holds sway in tobacco production; which is in the hands of financing and purchasing companies owned by the cigarette monopolies; but the state took the monopoly for the purchase and financing of tobacco cultivation into its own hands by creating the Tabamex company. Wheat cultivation has also been tied to the flour industry, and there, too, monopoly conditions are developing. The sugarcane and hemp crops represent agro-industrial units where production is in the hands of private monopolies or the state. The financing and purchasing of cotton place that crop in the hands of capitalist interests as well.

In many of the cases cited, what occurs is the organization of a monopolistic enterprise that clusters together peasants as well as capitalist farmers by means of financing. In the cultivation of hemp, sugarcane, and tobacco, the credit and purchase contracts often create a situation in which the farmer, under the simple commodity structure of his production, is turned into a species of wage laborer for a large enterprise. In other cases (commonly in the production of wheat, barley, and garden vegetables), the farmer sets up a very peculiar relation with the large finance company: that of a small agricultural *maquiladora* enterprise. In those instances in which the state controls production, the farmers may also be organized into cooperatives (as in Sinaloa).

From the viewpoint of the large monopoly conglomerates (private or state), we can see the following principal types of agricultural enterprises:

1. *The large agro-industrial enterprise*, the nucleus of which is formed by a factory (e.g., a sugar refinery or paper mill) that finances the production of the raw material it needs by means of credit and purchase contracts for small peasants. In this way, the peasants become, in fact, proletarians disguised as petty bourgeoisie.
2. *The large agro-commercial enterprise*, in which the nucleus is formed

by an intermediary commercial enterprise that takes charge of financing, purchasing, or distributing the product (tobacco, cotton, coffee, wheat). The farmer may already occupy either the position of worker, as in the previous example, or that of petty bourgeois in real functions as administrator of the large enterprise; in this last case, he becomes a type of small entrepreneur totally dependent on the intermediate financing enterprise, which is generally owned by the large cigarette or cotton firms (a situation quite similar to that of the maquiladora industry that has developed in the northern border zone, which relies on contracts and financing from large U.S. enterprises).

3. *The large agricultural enterprise,* relatively autonomous, based on the leasing of lands or on illegal concentration of property. The financing derives from the enterprise's own accumulation and from bank loans. This type of enterprise represents the majority of large-scale capitalist units of production: it is characteristic of the irrigation districts, in the production of fruits, garden vegetables, fodder, and oil-producing plants, and in livestock raising.

4. *The cooperative ejido enterprise,* financed by the government's credit apparatus. Whether these enterprises group together into cooperatives for production or for sales, in the majority of cases they are bureaucratized enterprises that function with a deficit and must therefore be subsidized.

Two facts must be taken into account in order to be able to determine the significance of monopoly concentration in agriculture. First, these large enterprises are surrounded by thousands of relatively independent small and medium-sized capitalist agricultural enterprises. Moreover, they are submerged in a mass of poor peasants, whom they use only partially (whether directly as wage laborers or indirectly by integrating them by means of financing).

As can be understood, the relation established between the monopoly sector and the huge, impoverished mass of peasants does not reproduce the conditions for the primitive accumulation of capital. In the typical process of primitive accumulation, the monopoly sector did not exist, and the evolution of the agrarian structure took the direction of a free-competition capitalism that could (and needed to) absorb the labor that was being driven out of the countryside. But in Mexico that is not possible, as much because of the monopoly situation as because of underdevelopment, so that the monopoly sector must *control* the relation of accumulation that the development of capitalism maintains with the peasant simple commodity sector. I am calling this controlled relation *permanent primitive accumulation,* and it is the state that is in charge of politically and financially lubricating this peculiar mechanism, which has become the protective retaining wall preventing an overflow that would break down the politicoeconomic equilibrium attained through the maintenance of a simple commodity mode of production.

Thus, the condition of permanent primitive accumulation is nothing more than the particular way in which—in an underdeveloped country's agriculture—the capitalist mode of production is articulated with noncapitalist modes of production, under such a condition of dependency on *imperialism* that the monopoly sector of the economy becomes a fundamental factor—that is, a *subcapitalist* agrarian structure.[32] The combined existence in Mexican agriculture of processes of monopoly concentration and of mechanisms of permanent primitive accumulation represents contradictions characteristic of the whole of the agrarian structure. Although they might have their *basis* in the articulation of two modes of production, contradictions of this type have their explanation only at the level of the overall structure and its relation with the world imperialist economy.

The Mexican agrarian economy finds itself tied to imperialism by the international (foreign) character of the monopolies and by the destination of the output of various crops. Perhaps the case of cotton is the most symptomatic of this double subjection and linkage: its marketing is monopolized by North American firms (Anderson Clayton, Hohenberg International, MacFadden, etc.), which, in addition, take charge of the ginning and grading. The example of cotton shows, furthermore, how a conjunction between the international monopolies and governmental monopoly operates: the national banks for farm and ejido credit themselves sell cotton to these North American companies. One must also mention that a company acquired by the government to market the cotton produced with official credit (Algodonera Comercial Mexicana) did not manage to organize sales abroad directly, so that it has to avail itself of foreign companies to do so.[33] This example shows the articulation of two monopoly systems and the weakness of the state sector in the face of the large U.S. companies. We find a very similar situation in the marketing of strawberries, ixtle, honey, cacao, and so on.

The insertion of the Mexican agricultural economy into the world structure is not the subject of analysis here, for such a discussion would merit a volume especially dedicated to the topic. What I have been most interested in singling out here is the objective reflection that such a relation of dependency generates in the agrarian structure: its *significant monopolistic tendencies,* inserted as basic processes at the core of a complex socioeconomic articulation.

Chapter 4

The Forms of
Land Ownership

THE ANALYSIS and the historical notes that shape this chapter are aimed at proving a central thesis that will serve as a basis for completing this structural portrait of the class struggle in the Mexican countryside. That thesis can be summarized in this way: *all forms of ownership (with the exception of nationalized property, but including communal usufruct as well as private property) represent an obstacle to the development of capitalism in agriculture.* This thesis, which is one of the central ideas of the Marxist interpretation of agrarian development, has often been forgotten or only partially understood.

The types of land ownership do not represent a mere formal legal situation; rather, they represent social and economic relations that generate particular legal forms. Thus, the statement that, for example, private property is an obstacle to capitalist agriculture means that behind the legal form we find noncapitalist social relations that restrain capitalism. But as I shall clarify, these forms of land tenure (communal ownership, individual private ownership) are not an insurmountable obstacle, nor must they disappear to make way for capitalism: it manages to impose itself and creates the conditions necessary to valorize land ownership.

Communal Property

Communal property is the most evident crystallization of social relations that imply a close union between the worker and the natural conditions of production. Not only does it reveal this close union but it also expresses very strong forms of collective cohesiveness and cooperative labor in the heart of communities dominated by relations of production oriented to the consumption of use values.

In Mexico today, barely 5 percent of the land area reported by the census is classified as communal property. But when the Spaniards trod upon this soil for the first time, more than four hundred years ago, they found that this was the dominant form of land tenure.[1] Among the Aztecs, this was expressed in the *calpulli*, a collective form of tenure with individual usufruct of parcels, located in the heart of the *altepetlalli* (village land). In the Aztec communities, each family received a portion of the land, which it held in usufruct in perpetuity and bequeathed to its descendants. However, if the land remained uncultivated for more than two years, it was repossessed by the calpulli and assigned to another family. This was not the only form of land tenure among the Aztecs; there were lands directly controlled by the state. The production of these lands was designated for maintaining the personnel of the *tlatoani* (king), the temples, war expenses, the palace, and so forth.

There has been a great deal of controversy about the nature of another form of tenure called *pillalli* or *tecpillalli*. Some have considered it a type of private property of a feudal nature. These were lands that the tlatoani granted to nobles and warriors as a reward for services rendered. In fact, if the sources are read carefully, it is possible to distinguish two different forms of this "private property": (a) tecpillalli land, assigned to a group called *tectecuhtzin* and to other nobles and functionaries; and (b) pillalli land, belonging to the hereditary nobility. The former (tecpillalli) was nothing more than the expression of a payment of "wages" to state functionaries. This was merely the temporary granting to an individual of the right to collect the tribute that the entire community had to pay to the state. These lands were worked by the so-called *tecallec*, who were communal landholders (*comuneros*) who made beneficial use of their land but who paid tribute to the tectecuhtzin rather than to the tlatoani.

All the types of tenure explained to this point had as a basis the communal beneficial use of the land and were differentiated by the destination of the tribute that the peasants paid. In contrast, the pillalli lands were worked by a type of dependent population totally dispossessed of land: the *mayeques*. The latter did not pay tribute to the tlatoani, but to the *pilli* (noble) owner of the land; the mayeques were sold and inherited along with the land and were on the margin of the community organization (calpulli). In any event, this type of property was firmly tied to the state: it had its origin in a royal grant, the tlatoani sometimes imposed limitations on its sale or inheritance, the pilli had the obligation of serving the sovereign, and so forth.

All these forms of property were perfectly coherent with the tributary

(Asiatic) mode of production that predominated. The latter form never became dominant, nor was it the key to the system: the secret of the Aztec economic structure was the tribute paid by the communities, which owned the land collectively.

An aspect of the Spanish colonization that has attracted significant attention—and that has prompted numerous arguments and controversies—is the Crown's protectionist policy toward the indigenous people, which shaped a singular mode of adaptation of the indigenous forms of ownership to the colonial socioeconomic structure. Nevertheless, it is the conquest of Mexico that marks the beginning of the rapid disappearance of communal forms of property, which succumb before the vigorous onslaught of the processes of primitive accumulation of capital. But what I am interested in explaining at this point is, not how large private property arose, principally at the expense of communal property, but how and under what conditions the latter survived.

The Spanish Crown was concerned with protecting the communal forms of ownership, managing to adapt them to the Spanish systems of land tenure. Gradually, all during the sixteenth century, especially in the second half, a series of royal grants and ordinances was shaping a legal apparatus protective of native ownership that functioned up to the end of the colony. Actually, this protectionist system functioned with relative efficiency only with respect to the property of the villages. However, the property of the indigenous nobility (pillalli or tecpillalli) was seriously affected and, little by little, passed into Spanish hands.[2]

The Crown's orders decreed a *fundo legal* for each village (five hundred meters around, starting from the church door), around which extended the ejido, which encompassed a minimum area of one square league. This area was inalienable and was to be controlled by a village council. Originally, the Castilian ejido was a small area located at the village exit (hence its name); but in New Spain what became the ejido was, in many instances, the land that previously had been known as the altepetlalli, that is, a considerable expanse of land that included zones for farming, forests, and pastures. Nevertheless, the Spaniards did not respect the clan-based internal division of the village lands (the calpulli).[3] At the same time, each village had lands called *propios*, property of a municipal character that was worked in common, worked by rotation, or rented out; its produce was destined for maintaining the local government and paying taxes.[4]

Why was the Spanish state so interested in keeping the indigenous communities alive? The explanation or interpretation that seems most accurate is the one that proposes the coexistence of three distinct modes of production during the colonial period, one of which—the despotic-tributary mode of production—required the preservation of the indigenous communities. The analysis of Enrique Semo offers the greatest insight into the system.[5] I believe that, as Semo astutely suggests, the despotic-communitarian system represents a mode of production that has as its basis a series of mechanisms of surplus transfer by means of ground rent, which reveals the true owner of the land to be the state. But I think that it is necessary to note some limitations of this mode of production. First, the tributary relation here is also a colonial relation inscribed within a global process of primitive accumulation of capital, which makes it very different from a traditional "Asiatic" tributary situation. Second, and because of that same colonial situation, it is necessary to emphasize that the objective of the tribute is the accumulation of capital, although the Spaniards knew how to utilize this accumulated capital only very poorly. Third, this tributary system cuts across social relations of a feudal nature: the systems of tribute and the obligatory rendering of services encompass the New Spanish nobility. It is not a matter of two parallel systems; rather, a single social group is simultaneously immersed in a tributary relation and in a feudal relation.

It is precisely these mechanisms of exploitation of the communities by the Spanish state that enable one to understand the Crown's "indigenist" policy. The colonial bond was founded, in part, on the exploitation of the community: for that very reason, the state was interested in impeding the community's dissolution. "The despotic-tributary mode of production did not disappear by itself. A revolution was necessary to assist it in abandoning the stage of history."[6] This revolution was the War of Independence, which broke the colonial tie with Spain.

The communal property of the indigenous people was, in spite of everything, doomed to disappear; the growth of the semi-feudal economy and the capitalist system could do nothing but destroy the ancient forms. But this growth was extremely slow and plagued by contradictions and internal imbalances. One of the ways in which indigenous property was attacked was through the system of *composiciones*, which, theoretically, were legal proceedings designed to fix property boundaries. But the indigenous people did not understand the necessity of confirming their titles by means of the composición, with the result that the large landowners took advantage of the procedure to confirm legally their possession of land plundered from the communities. In sum, the landholders used innumerable means, lawful and unlawful, to dispossess the indigenous people. The fact is that toward the end of the colonial period, the communities had lost a large portion of their lands. But in spite of all of this, many communities survived; according to an 1810 census, in central Mexico alone there were around four thousand indigenous communities.[7]

The colonial economic and political structure destroyed communal property to a great extent, but it was the liberal republic that gave it the mortal blow that eliminated it. What the semi-feudal system was unable to achieve was accomplished by the bourgeois republic. The basis of the process of disintegration of the communal properties was the interests of the agrarian and industrial bourgeoisie, crystallized in the set of laws on disamortization that culminated in the Lerdo Law of 1856 and the Constitution of 1857.

Shortly after independence was attained, laws concerning the disamortization of lands possessed by "dead hands" (principally the church) were being decreed in various states of the republic. Thus, around 1825 the state of Chihuahua issued a colonization law that ordered distribution of abandoned community land and permitted the sale of communal lands, and in 1833 another law ordered that the lands of indigenous villages be divided up into parcels. In that same year, the distribution of municipalities' lands began in Zacatecas. In 1828, in the states of Occidente and Puebla, the distribution of communal lands was decreed. The state of Mexico followed the same path in 1830. In the state of Jalisco, from 1825 to 1857 many laws were issued with the same thrust: splitting up communal land into parcels and converting it into private property. The federal government itself began its disamortizing activity after 1824 but did not achieve decisive results until the second half of the nineteenth century.[8]

Clearly, the liberal laws on disamortization were principally directed at requiring that church lands be put on the market, for the benefit of tenants who would be able to buy them, with the goal of forming a "rural middle class." However, another of their objectives was undoubtedly to destroy indigenous communal property, which represented a restraint on the penetration of commercial relations into the communities. In the law of June 25, 1856, the Lerdo Law, the expropriation of the rural properties of ecclesiastical and civil corporations was decreed, with a valuation calculated by treating the rents they were paying as equivalent to an annual return of 6 percent. The municipalities were included among those corporations, although the fundos legales and the ejidos were excepted. But the Constitution of 1857, in its Article 27, did include ejidos among the properties that could be expropriated. The inspirer of these reforms, Interior Minister Miguel Lerdo de Tejada, explained in a circular of December 19, 1856, that the indigenous communities had to disappear.[9] The result was, in the words of Eyler N. Simpson, that

the majority of the peasants, who had not the least idea what private property was, were unaccustomed to working under the stimulus of individual initiative, and lacked capital and tools, saw their small parcels absorbed by the large estates or snatched out of their hands by unscrupulous speculators. Thus, a fatal blow was given to one of Mexico's most important and stable agrarian institutions.[10]

The Porfirian dictatorship only furthered and completed the process of total elimination of communal property. The rate of primitive accumulation of capital—one of the basic mechanisms of which is the expropriation of peasants' land—accelerated extraordinarily, although in an erratic fashion. The Porfirio Díaz regime rigorously applied the reform laws against the communities, but in addition, the concentration of land was intensified by an 1894 act regarding the occupation and expropriation of idle land. This law was the basis for the notorious speculative activity of the surveying companies, which continued to snatch land from the villages and communities. Furthermore, violence now played an important part in the process of accumulation: the repression of indigenous rebellions, especially the great uprisings of the Yaquis of Sonora and the Mayas in Yucatán, cleared the way for sanctions that eliminated the indigenous people physically and made it possible to take away their land. By the beginning of the twentieth century, according to Luis Cabrera's estimates, 90 percent of the villages of the Central Mesa owned no land at all.[11]

The reforms flowing from the Revolution of 1910 eliminated all prior legal decrees regarding communal lands, and a system of restitution for the lost lands to the communities was proposed. The Agrarian Code of 1934 established a system of communal properties practically identical to that of the ejidos, the difference being that the communal land could not be split up into parcels. However, in 1958 a regulation establishing the right of title to individually owned parcels was issued.

The restitutions of communal lands have not been a significant factor in the agrarian reform process. The legal difficulties of proving rights to the land claimed compelled many communities to apply for endowment with ejidos. Thus, in 1960 we find only 1,915 tracts of communal property registered (around 9 million hectares in total). More than three-fourths of these tracts (with 84 percent of the total communal land area) were concentrated in eight states. Only in the state of Oaxaca was the importance of communal property comparable to that of ejido property (38 percent of all land area in that state reported in the census was communal property). Furthermore, on the basis of a sampling of the communal land tracts registered by the census in 1960, it has been determined that 74 percent of the land of these communities was occupied by forests and pastures; some 11 percent was arable land, and the remaining 15 percent was nonproductive land.[12]

Thus, after a struggle that lasted several centuries, the development of capitalism managed to eliminate the obstacle that communal land ownership represented. In doing so, it eliminated the social relations that sustained such ownership, destroyed the bonds of collective labor in the indigenous villages, eroded the natural economy, and thrust the indigenous population into the realm of the marketplace and capitalist production.

The destruction of communal property in Mexico followed paths similar to those taken by the process of primitive accumulation in Europe. According to Marx,

> In the history of primitive accumulation, all revolutions are epoch-making that act as levers for the capitalist class in the course of its formation; but this is true above all for those moments when great masses of men are suddenly and forcibly torn from their means of subsistence, and hurled onto the labour-market as free, unprotected and rightless proletarians. The expropriation of the agricultural producer, of the peasant, from the soil, is the basis of the whole process. The history of this expropriation assumes different aspects in different countries, and runs through its various phases in different orders of succession, and at different historical epochs.[13]

In fact, while the Reformation destroyed the large feudal holdings of the church in England during the sixteenth century, in Mexico the clergy were receiving this blow until the second half of the nineteenth century; but the essence of the process was the same. The destruction of communal property in England was astonishingly similar, in its inclusive form, to the situation just described. Consider Marx's analysis:

> Communal property . . . was an old Teutonic institution which lived on under the cover of feudalism. We have seen how its forcible usurpation, generally accompanied by the turning of arable into pasture land, begins at the end of the fifteenth century and extends into the sixteenth. But at that time the process was carried on by means of individual acts of violence against which legislation, for a hundred and fifty years, fought in vain. The advance made by the eighteenth century shows itself in this, that the law itself now becomes the instrument by which the people's land is stolen, although the big farmers made use of their little independent methods as well. The Parliamentary form of the robbery is that of the "Bills for Inclosures of Commons," in other words decrees by which the landowners grant themselves the people's land as private property, decrees of expropriation of the people.[14]

This is only one of the aspects of the process of primitive accumulation; it will be necessary to examine what happened with other forms of property in Mexico in order to clarify why in Mexico—in contrast to what occurred in England—the process did not lead to widespread development of capitalist relations of production in agriculture.

The Large Haciendas

The history of the Mexican haciendas (estates) is the history of a particular form of the development of capitalism in agriculture: what Lenin labeled the "Junker road." That is, the slow process of transformation of large precapitalist units of production the internal economic relations of which continue to evolve without breaking up the productive unit and without violating the forms of ownership (the latifundio). It would be difficult to summarize here the complicated process of the origin and development of the haciendas in Mexico; for that, I direct the reader to the excellent studies by specialists.[15]

Undoubtedly, the economic structure of the haciendas until the middle of the sixteenth century had a precapitalist character; it was starting in 1550, with the extraordinary mining boom, that the economy of the haciendas (especially those in northern Mexico) gradually became a supplier for the mining centers. Notwithstanding this, from their beginnings, the latifundios had a markedly commercial character; in fact, although the private ownership of land was only obtained through *merced real* (royal grant), the process of land concentration was only carried out by means of significant investments of money. Sooner or later, the land grants bestowed upon people with meager resources were hurled into an intense, speculative title market, which effectively cut off the possibilities that small and medium-sized properties might arise.

During the entire sixteenth century and until the early seventeenth century, the large latifundios that were to characterize Mexico's agrarian economic history until 1936–40 were being formed and consolidated. But until 1620 the economy in New Spain was based on mining; from that date, silver production stagnated, and the agrarian economy moved to the foreground, but without the protection of the mining sector. Then the latifundios had to develop with a certain degree of autonomy; the first reaction of the haciendas was an emphatic contraction, which reinforced the natural character of their economy. Only the haciendas connected with supplying the cities managed to reinforce their commodity economy and to continue the process of substitution of production of the communities, which were being destroyed or engulfed by the latifundios. A recent study has characterized this process with great insight:

> The rise and spread of the hacienda in the seventeenth century coincides with two contradictory phenomena: (a) the eclipse of the mining complex, and (b) the crisis of the community-based indigenous economy. This phenomenon is the cause of antagonistic interpretations regarding the origin of the hacienda. While economics scholars from the center see in it progress with respect to the indigenous community, a means of stabilizing the supplying of the cities by increasing productivity, a replacement of supply through tribute by that through commerce, other researchers, with eyes set on the North, identify the hacienda with the weakening of the mining complex and the commodity economy linked to it and a step backward towards autarchy. *The hacienda is an ideal fruit of a society in which feudalism and commodity economy are indissolubly woven together.* It has a double function: that of serving alternatively as autarchical unit and as commercial producer. Throughout the seventeenth through nineteenth centuries, we witness a movement of systole and diastole that makes the hacienda a predominantly commercial unit in periods

of market expansion and decidedly autarchical in periods of contraction. In that double character of the hacienda, present from its beginnings, and in its adaptability to the pulsations of a market subjected to powerful external pressures, resides the secret of its stability.[16]

The hacienda, throughout its history, has brought together very complex relations of production. The slavery, *encomienda*, serfdom, and tribute peculiar to its initial phases were later replaced by or intermingled with sharecropping, tenant farming, and, above all, peonage. The forms of labor within the haciendas made apparent a peculiar situation: even as the process of primitive accumulation of capital in Mexico was achieving great successes in the plundering of land and concentration of property, it was encountering serious difficulties in generating a "free labor force." The indigenous population had been decimated by starvation and illnesses, which caused a scarcity of labor. In spite of everything, part of the population remained rooted in the communities. Moreover, the very process of expansion and contraction of the commodity economy did not permit the haciendas to maintain advanced systems of wage labor, which obliged them to keep the working population in precapitalist conditions of dependency.

When Marx, in *Capital*, explains the conditions of transformation of money into capital, he states that the owner of labor power

> must constantly treat his labour-power as his own property, his own commodity, and he can do this only by placing it at the disposal of the buyer, i.e., handing it over to the buyer for him to consume, for a definite time, temporarily. In this way he manages both to alienate . . . his labour-power and to avoid renouncing his rights of ownership over it.[17]

Marx goes on to contrast this with the Mexican situation:

> In some states, particularly in Mexico . . . , slavery is hidden under the form of peonage. By means of advances repayable in labour, which are handed down from generation to generation, not only the individual worker, but also his family, become in fact the property of other persons and their families. Juárez abolished peonage, but the so-called Emperor Maximilian re-established it by a decree which was aptly denounced in the House of Representatives in Washington as a decree for the reintroduction of slavery into Mexico.[18]

Even during the nineteenth century and the beginnings of the twentieth, the latifundio remained a unit of production into which capitalist wage labor relations, properly speaking, forced their way only with great difficulty. In order to give an idea of what the large property represented in contrast with other forms at the beginnings of the nineteenth century, it is sufficient to cite the figures calculated (in hectares) for 1810 by Miguel Othón de Mendizábal:[19]

Land of indigenous communities, including fundos legales, public land, ejidos, and private indigenous small properties	18,000,000
Land of nonindigenous villages, including land occupied by cities, towns, spring sources, etc., and the small and medium-sized properties of their inhabitants	5,000,000
10,438 haciendas and *ranchos*	70,000,000
Uncultivated land	100,000,000
Total	193,000,000

Once independence had been attained, and continuing until the imposition of the Porfirio Díaz dictatorship, a process of reforms developed. That process had an extraordinary significance for understanding the role that the latifundio played in opposition to the interest of the nascent liberal bourgeoisie. The effects of these reforms on the destruction of communal property have already been examined in the foregoing pages. Here, it will be interesting to examine them from another angle.

As far as agriculture is concerned, the reforms that culminated in the Constitution of 1857 had a specific objective, which was only partially achieved: to *valorize the private ownership of land*, or, stated in terms of that era, to "disamortize" land ownership—that is, to break the monopoly on land in order to permit capital investment that would make the latifundios productive. The law was directed exclusively at lands owned by civil or religious corporations (that was its great limitation). The blow was aimed at the largest latifundista of that time: the church.

The background of interests that motivated a segment of the dominant classes to initiate the disamortization process reveals another aspect of the economic relations hidden under the mantle of latifundista property. Not only did precapitalist forms of labor predominate but, in addition, the economic situation of the latifundio implied an *amortization;* that is, one was dealing with a dead capital investment, which produced meager earnings. In sum, the large properties of the church represented, above all, a restraint on productive capital investment. Evidence that the disamortization laws were seen as a tool for extending capitalism to agriculture is the so-called Three Years' War, which pitted the large estate owners, supported by the clergy, against the liberals, led by Juárez.

The result of the Liberal Reform was, in effect, to disamortize the church's large properties and to place the land belonging to religious orders on the market. But the ecclesiastical latifundios were acquired by large private estate owners or by individuals with sufficient resources to become the new latifundistas. The petty and middle-level rural bourgeoisie (the "mestizos"), who had encouraged the Juárez reforms, did not benefit from the sales of the ecclesiastical estates, which passed undivided into the hands of new landholders. In a certain sense, it could be said that the ecclesiastical haciendas passed from one set of "dead hands" into another.

It is necessary to clarify here that the aim of this analysis is to study, not the hacienda as an economic unit, but the function of latifundista property and the social relations implicit in this legal relationship. Thus, when it is stated that the latifundio had as a base precapitalist relations of production and labor, one does not want to ignore the obvious fact that many haciendas attained high levels of efficiency and developed relatively modern forms of labor (on the basis of the free labor of nonresident peons). In fact, it was precisely this capitalist development in agriculture that, ultimately, put the very existence of the traditional latifundio in doubt. Nevertheless, this situation was also affected by the old struggle that pitted the latifundistas against the church. In the end, as has been said, the large property holders, and not the petty and middle-level bourgeoisie, were the ones who benefited from the liberal reforms.

In this sense, the argument advanced by Andrés Molina Enríquez at the beginning of the century is essentially correct: he contended that the large property, the hacienda, represented an amortization:

> In it is invested capital that under normal conditions can not produce anything but a yield lower than other investments do, even though it is in the form of a secure, perpetual, and fixed rent. That it is not a truly interesting investment is shown by the fact that it does not attract foreign capital: the investments of American capital in grain haciendas are almost nil. Their true spirit is shaped by the gentry and the rent.[20]

On the typical Porfirian hacienda, the landholder was seeking an equilibrium that would ensure more or less stable production. Once this was achieved, the hacienda was turned over to the administrators. From them was demanded the established rent, which was passed down from father to son, independently of what might happen internally in the complex world of the large hacienda. Within the latifundio, the most diverse situations could develop—from forms of semi-slavery, serfdom, or varied kinds of sharecropping to modern lease agreements with small capitalist *rancheros*. However, to a large extent, the estate owner was indifferent to all of this; for him, the hacienda was a perpetual rent and, at times, a place for a seignorial excursion. This is the connection that was expressed in the latifundista property relation.

Despite this, during the long Porfirian dictatorship, two fundamental processes were occurring: (1) in the economy of many haciendas, the capitalist system was clearly continuing to develop; and (2) the feverish activity of the surveying companies supported by the state, along with other factors, was accelerating considerably the process of land concentration. Joined together, these two factors would be one of the engines of the enormous popular restiveness that exploded violently in 1910. The large latifundios showed their inefficiency ("amortization") not only as capitalist enterprises but also as feudal-style units. The hacienda, the "Junker road" from feudalism to capitalism, was paralyzed halfway there; the development of an agrarian capitalism founded on the large property was aborted by the revolution of 1910–17.

The large landholding had been situated as an obstacle to capitalism's development; yet, it was not its size that formed a barrier but the *private* nature of the ownership. Because of the relations of production dominant in the majority of the haciendas, the latter became private enclaves into which capital had no possibility of penetrating productively. Save in those cases, increasingly numerous but never reaching a majority, in which the landholder was simultaneously an efficient capitalist entrepreneur, capital investment in agricultural production was hindered by a private property in the hands of inefficient latifundistas.

Just as the Juarista bourgeoisie in the mid-nineteenth century had eliminated the great obstacle that communal and ecclesiastical property represented, during the first half of the twentieth century the revolutionary bourgeoisie finished off the great Porfirian latifundios: the Revolution of 1910 established the bases for the Cardenista reforms of the 1930s to carry out this historic task of capitalist development. The first revolutionary governments began the struggle against latifundismo timidly. Carranza distributed barely 132,000 hectares; Obregón, almost a million; and Calles, more than 3 million. Between 1915 and 1934, 10 million hectares were distributed to around 1 million ejidatarios, but it was Cárdenas who gave a huge impetus to expropriations of the latifundios: between 1935 and 1940, almost 18 million hectares were distributed among 772,000 ejidatarios. The effects of these distributions on the tenure of non-ejido land (almost in its entirety private property) are shown in table 10.

The overall distribution of non-ejido land by size groups does not signify more than a slight decrease in properties of more than 1,000 hectares between 1930 and 1940. But the real effects on private property must also be measured by the changes that occurred in the distribution of cultivated land and exploited land: while in 1930 the average land cultivated on non-ejido tracts was 16.3 hectares, in 1940 the average fell to 6.4; in 1930, the average area exploited on non-ejido tracts was 189.6 hectares, and in 1940 it was 81.9 hectares.[21] Latifundismo received a harsh blow, but in 1940 the census still registered just over 300 properties of more than 40,000 hectares, occupying a total area of 31 million hectares. However, the latifundistas as a class segment were displaced from power and ceased to be the center of the Mexican agricultural economy.

The "Junker," or latifundista, road of capitalist development was elim-

Table 10
Effects of Land Distribution on Tenure of Non-Ejido Land, 1930 and 1940

| | 1930 | | 1940 | |
Property Size	Number of Tracts (%)	Area (%)	Number of Tracts (%)	Area (%)
0–5 ha.	69.2	0.8	76.2	1.1
5–50 ha.	21.5	2.8	16.6	3.6
51–100 ha.	2.9	1.7	2.6	2.4
101–500 ha.	4.0	7.1	3.3	9.0
501–1,000 ha.	0.9	4.8	0.5	4.4
More than 1,000 ha.	1.5	82.8	0.8	79.5

Source: *Censos agrícola, ganadero y ejidal*, 1930–40.

inated by the Revolution of 1910. It was not the great concentration of land that impeded development. As has been mentioned, it was the inefficient, backward and/or precapitalist character of the relations of production that were deteriorating behind the private monopoly of land in the hands of the Porfirian estate owners.

Small Private Property

During the colonial era, a stratum of small independent farmers with visions of development was able to spring up only with great difficulty. The large haciendas prevented the small-property-owning ranchers from proliferating. According to François Chevalier, "the small *rancho*, free of all rent, is a relatively recent phenomenon, from the end of the eighteenth century and especially from the nineteenth."[22] Nevertheless, we find the origins of the small property owner in the era of the Conquest. Not all the grants that the *conquistadores* received were for great tracts of land; grants of small areas, called *peonías*, were made to Spanish soldiers who decided to become colonists. "The majority of them married Indian women and established themselves on their farms to work them with their own hands. Their children were *mestizos*, and their lands represented a form of agricultural property that is a precursor of what is now known in Mexico as the *rancho*."[23]

But by 1810 this type of small property did not include even 5 percent of the land area occupied. According to the data calculated by Othón de Mendizábal and cited above, only 5 million hectares pertained to nonindigenous village lands (including the area occupied by cities, villages, and spring sources) and to the small and medium properties (in contrast to 70 million for the haciendas and ranchos and 18 million for communal lands).

The reform laws had as an explicit objective encouraging the rise of a "middle class" of small property holders, but as has been explained, the church's great haciendas passed undivided into hands of large landholders, into the hands of those Molina Enríquez called *criollos nuevos* ("new Creoles"). Mestizo ranchers, who were proponents of the disamortization laws, gained nothing from the law of June 25, 1856. They lacked the resources necessary to pay the property-transfer taxes and the cost of the land. A decree from October 9, 1856, tried to get around this difficulty:

> The decree . . . seems at first glance well on the way to favoring the mestizos, whom it refers to as a *clase nemesterosa* (indigent class): it suppressed the sales tax and the expenses of paperwork for the disamortization of the small properties; but . . . where were they? By looking and looking, the mestizos found those of the civil corporations and, among them, those of the municipalities.[24]

That is, the development of the small ranchos occurred at the expense of indigenous communal property, giving an impetus to a class of small agrarian capitalists rather than to the formation of independent small peasants.

Colonization programs have also represented a form of development of the small property. After 1823 a province was created in Tehuantepec to offer soldiers from the army a chance to become farmers. Subsequently, in 1824, uncultivated land in the northern part of the country was opened to colonization, prompting the arrival of North American colonists; however, the result was the secession of Texas and its annexation to the United States. During the Porfiriato, significant foreign colonies were founded: between 1885 and 1900, Mormons settled in northwestern Chihuahua and northern Sonora, and Mennonites established colonies in the Valle de San Antonio, Chihuahua, and in Durango. A colony of Molokange Russians, natives of southern Russia, was established in 1905 in the Valle de Guadalupe, Baja California.[25]

The significance of the rural small property holders, relying on independent labor, can be measured with the population censuses beginning in 1895 (see table 11). But it was Cardenista agrarian reform that was the true creator and promoter of the small property in its typical form: the minifundio. Table 12 shows how the number of private properties of fewer than five hectares grew from 1930 to 1970. However, during the 1950s the small properties began to decrease in number. By 1970 there were, strictly speaking, only 577,000 private small property owners, if colonists, squatters, sharecroppers, and tenant farmers are excluded from the figure for "non-ejido" tracts given by the census.

The small private property—like the latifundio—is also the legal expres-

Table 11
Growth of Independent Rural Small Property Owners,
1895–1921

Year	Property Owners
1895	282,906
1900	576,120
1910	410,345
1921	639,461

Source: José Calixto Rangel Contla, *La pequeña burguesía en la sociedad mexicana, 1895 a 1960* (Mexico City: Instituto de Investigaciones Sociales [UNAM], 1972).

Table 12
Growth of Private Properties of Fewer than
Five Hectares, 1930–1970

Year	Number of Tracts (in thousands)
1930	545.1
1940	928.5
1950	1,004.9
1960	899.1
1970	880.9

Source: *Censos agrícola, ganadero y ejidal*, 1930–70.

sion of relations of production that block the development of capitalism. In this case, one is dealing with the peasant's independent labor on his own land. But, as distinct from the case of communal property, in this instance the land is not subject to restraints that prevent its sale (or its rental) in such a way that the economic ruin of the small producer can lead to his parcel's being put on the market. This form of property does not, therefore, represent such a vigorous obstacle to capitalist development as does property that, by being linked to patrimonial, seignorial, or communal relations, does not represent an exchange value. This is why when capitalism is introduced to agriculture by the revolutionary path (the "farmer" road), it destroys the communal and seignorial forms of property and opens the way for the peasant private small property. Subsequently, capitalist development's own laws will take charge of dissolving the peasantry in a process of polarization. But the important thing is that peasant property can be sold and rented, in such a way that the land can be concentrated again (on new bases), thus permitting the concentration of capital.

In this sense the Revolution of 1910 and agrarian reform opened for capitalism the "farmer" road to its development. The destruction of the latifundios was achieved not only with the distribution of ejido lands but also, to a great extent, through the proliferation of the private small property. Thus, the Mexican bourgeoisie buried one enemy, the latifundista, but created another, equally dangerous one: the minifundista peasant. These days we find the bourgeoisie engaged in an all-out struggle against him.

The Ejido

With agrarian reform, the Mexican bourgeoisie created yet another, even more dangerous enemy, a brother of the minifundista property owner: the ejidatario. But this is a question of an enemy from the economic point of view; politically, the ejidatario has been one of the supports that has made it possible to legitimize the power of the bourgeoisie. Nevertheless, today capitalist development in agriculture is itself beginning to erode this legitimization. In any case, here we are interested in the economic problem: how is ejido property situated in the context of capitalist production? Examining this problem will enable us to understand the peculiarities of the Mexican version of the "farmer" road.

It has been said that the formation of the ejido, as a fruit of the Revolution of 1910, has represented the triumph of communal ownership. If one examines the problem with detachment, this turns out to be a falsehood: *the ejido is not a form of communal property*; rather, it is a disguised form of small private property, or minifundio. Mexican legislation does not define what an ejido is, but from the legal application of that legislation we are able to derive some fundamental traits:

1. Above all, the ejido is the product of a legal process called *dotación* (endowment); the lands are received by a population nucleus. At its origin, then, there is no purchase: the lands are obtained for free, and they derive from expropriated haciendas, state lands, and so on.
2. The beneficial use of the ejido is subject to a large number of restrictions and limitations that attempt to reproduce the traits of communal property: the only persons eligible for endowment are those who have resided in the locality for at least six months prior to the date of application, those who customarily work the land personally, those who

do not own an area of private land greater than or equal to the unit of endowment, those who are Mexicans by birth, those who do not have capital greater than 2,500 pesos invested in industry or business or agricultural capital greater than 5,000 pesos, and so forth. Moreover, the sale and leasing of ejido land are generally prohibited. Inheritance of the ejido parcel is subject to special regulations.

3. Ejido property is set within a framework of a complex of state and parastate institutions that also impose conditions upon it: a rigid system of ejido authorities exists in each population nucleus and is strictly supervised by the Department of Agrarian Affairs and Colonization and by the official banks that have granted credit. In addition, all ejidatarios are organized by the Confederación Nacional Campesina (the CNC), which is affiliated with the official party, the Partido Revolucionario Institucional (the PRI).

In fact, the ejido is a form that intermingles various types of property: state or nationalized, corporate, communal and private. The ejido is, in principle, property of the nation but is granted to a community of peasants in usufruct. It acquires a corporate character through the imposition of rules of organization and control on the ejido population nucleus. But the law also establishes a series of rules that, when rigorously applied, have produced the so-called collective ejidos, thus imparting the feel of communal property. Its character as peasant private property derives from the individual usufruct of the ejido parcel in the majority of cases and from decrees that permit inheriting the land. The whole set of characteristics produces in reality, and in the majority of cases, a disguised form of corporatized private small property.

The ejido is a creation of the Revolution of 1910, subsequently made concrete by the state, which converted it into a cell within its complicated corporate bureaucratic system. The ejido is a reflection of the intricate labyrinth of alliances and contradictions among different classes and class segments that are structured in the core of the state that emanated from the Mexican Revolution. The great peasant demand is expressed in the granting of individual usufruct of parcels; with that same act, moreover, a goal of the modern, efficient bourgeoisie is met: breaking the back of the latifundio. The embryos of a state capitalism give the ejido its form as nationalized property and even its communal or collective aspect; the latter was also promoted by socialist political groups of a populist stripe. The corporatization responded, above all, to a political need of the group in power: to ensure control of the peasant masses and to block a possible assault from the conservative, reactionary sectors, cutting them off from the possibility of once again concentrating great areas of land in a barely productive, inefficient way.

Thus, along with the parallel process of proliferation of private minifundios, the distribution of ejido lands has represented the "farmer" type of development of capitalism in agriculture, but with concrete characteristics that give a singular content to the Mexican process. Its typically "farmer" aspect materializes in the creation of thousands of individual peasant small units of production; but this type of property put restraints on the possibilities of a renewed concentration of land, indispensable for the rise of a modern agriculture. In effect, by prohibiting the sale and leasing of ejido land, the agrarian law automatically placed a considerable portion of the productive land area outside the dynamic of the capitalist market. Today's bourgeoisie pays very dearly for the bourgeois populist radicalism of the thirties; of course, it won something invaluable: the famous political stability of the Mexican system.

The ejido contains in its heart the original sin of a weak bourgeoisie that had no remedy in the revolutionary process but to ally itself with, and to make serious concessions to, the impoverished peasantry. Although defeated by the Carrancista bourgeoisie, the peasant revolutionary movement left a profound imprint on the process of agrarian reform. Almost twenty years after the conclusion of the revolution, the country found itself at a crossroads: either profound reforms in the agrarian structure would have to be undertaken or the bourgeois sector that had recently come to power would run the risk of confronting an explosive peasant movement. The Cárdenas government decided to carry out agrarian reform in depth and thus avoided the need for the now-empowered revolutionary bourgeoisie to play, two decades after its triumph, the role of liquidator of the peasant movement.

Various experts on agrarian problems who have placed their experience at the service of the bourgeoisie have become aware of the restraints that ejido property imposes on capitalist development. For example, Ramón Fernández y Fernández, in his proposal for resolving the problem of the "inflexibility of ejido tenure," says:

> I believe that internally, within the ejido, without destroying the ejido unit that is a nucleus of democracy and social solidarity, germ of cooperative developments, without destroying the ejido, sales should be permitted, with the approval of the General Assembly of Ejidatarios and supervision of the agrarian authorities—let us not say the sale of the parcel because, in the end, I am not recommending a system of totally private property—but the sale of the beneficial use of and improvements to the parcel. . . . If, without destroying the ejido unit, we permit the sale of the usufruct and improvements to the parcel, we attain a spontaneous, automatic selection of ejidatarios. . . . Otherwise, the drunkard will stay there, stuck to his half-hectare, and the hard-working, enterprising person who is alongside him will also stay there for his whole life, stuck to the half-hectare, which is not only unjust, but contrary to the goals of development. . . . In the second place, we are destroying,

Table 13
Percentages of Exploited and Cultivated Land Found in Ejidos,
1930–1970

Year	Percentage of Area Exploited in the Ejidos	Percentage of Area Cultivated in the Ejidos
1930	7.5[a]	13.4[a]
1940	22.5	47.4
1950	26.7	44.1
1960	26.3	43.4
1970	44.8	55.1

Source: Censos agrícola, ganadero y ejidal, 1960–70.
Note: [a] Tracts of more than 1 ha.

automatically as well, ejido minifundismo by permitting, by means of these sales, parcel concentration up to whatever limit we may set.[26]

Deep down, and from the point of view of the economic interests of the bourgeoisie, Fernández y Fernández is right. The data in table 13 give a quantitative idea of the growing magnitude of the obstacle that ejido lands can represent. Since 1940 almost one-quarter of the country's exploited land and around half of the total area of farmland has been *by law* outside the capitalist real estate market. In 1970 the proportions were much greater. The size of the ejido parcels is itself suited to a very small-scale type of exploitation (see table 14). In contrast, the lands in private ownership present much higher averages, although they show a tendency toward a decrease (see table 15).

Like other forms of land tenure, the ejido crystallizes a specific type of relations of production. In this case, it is a matter of noncapitalist, simple commodity relations, generated by the political and economic needs of the revolutionary bourgeoisie. The ejido—like private property—contains an internal contradiction: the monopoly of land face to face with the monopoly of capital.

The Lease

Is there any type of land tenure that does not enter into contradictions with capitalist economic development in agriculture? In order to answer this, it will be necessary to note, first, how capital manages to leap over the barrier of the land monopoly. In a developed capitalist system, the

Table 14
Average Land Area Exploited and Cultivated per Ejidatario, 1930-1970

Year	Average Area Exploited per Ejidatario (ha.)	Average Area Cultivated per Ejidatario (ha.)
1930	15.5	3.6
1940	18.1	4.4
1950	25.1	5.7
1960	27.9	6.4
1970	26.0	6.9

Source: Censos agrícola, ganadero y ejidal, 1930-70.

Table 15
Average Land Area Exploited and Cultivated per Owner of More than Five Hectares, 1930-1970

Year	Average Area Exploited per Owner of More Than 5 Hectares	Average Area Cultivated per Owner of More Than 5 Hectares
1930	421.6	49.5
1940	340.0	23.2
1950	291.8	44.6
1960	275.6	44.0
1970	149.7	29.9

Source: Censos agrícola, ganadero y ejidal, 1930-70.

typical way is ground rent; only by means of the rental can capital leap across the boundaries of the monopoly of the land. Nevertheless, ground rent first appeared in the history of Mexico, as in Europe, as a precapitalist relation. Its most primitive form was tribute, characteristic of the despotic-tributary system imposed by the Aztec empire in the pre-Hispanic epoch and subsequently by the Spanish Crown, as a form of colonial domination; these forms have already been referred to in the discussion of communal ownership.

Another way in which ground rent appeared in a primitive form, but with feudal traits, was in the form of sharecropping. During the colonial period, sharecropping represented an important mechanism for procuring labor on haciendas; parallel to the system of cash advances and perpetual debt, the estate owner often gave those lands the hacienda had annexed to itself to the indigenous people for sharecropping. These sharecroppers were called *terrazgueros* (tenant farmers), although there is a certain confusion with respect to the features of this system; other texts employ *terrazgo* (rent paid for farmland) and *tributo* (tribute) as synonyms. Apparently, during the first years of the colony, the terrazgueros' work was a continuation of the pre-Hispanic tributary relation that linked together *caciques* (nobles) and mayeques, with the difference that the Indian cacique had been replaced by the estate owner. Gradually, this relation was defined as a clear instance of sharecropping; already by the end of the sixteenth century, the Jesuits were recommending (in some cases) distribution of lands to the Indians *a medias* (by halves). "In fact, by conceding some little pieces of land to the indigenous people, the owners of the first haciendas were trying above all to root them to the locale with the aim of having sufficient labor available for their own crops."[27] This form of linking the indigenous peasants to the hacienda led to development of the perpetual poll tax of one peso per year, characteristic in the eighteenth century, that the tenants paid on many haciendas.

Sharecropping subsists even today, but it has lost its feudal content. In the majority of cases, one is dealing with a relationship among peasants; it is a matter of a reproduction, in the heart of the peasant simple commodity economy, of forms of exploitation of feudal origin. Here, they seem like complicated mechanisms of exploitation of the poor, landless peasants by the wealthier ones, but also like a disguised, distorted system of mutual aid and collective labor.

The rise of small units of production on the periphery of the large haciendas began slowly; these were the ranchos, which seem to have originated at the end of the seventeenth century. The history of this unit of production known as the rancho is of great interest but, unfortunately, remains largely obscure. During the sixteenth century, the term was used to refer to a hut *(jacal)* built for temporary use by shepherds; but at the close of the seventeenth century, according to Chevalier, the word "referred, completely naturally, to the installation of a third party on land that did not belong to him, and, hence, to the land itself, the more modest farm that formed part of a large property."[28] We find here, undoubtedly, the genesis of the tenant farmer, who, unlike the sharecropper, obtained relative independence with respect to the hacienda: The similarities between this tenant-farming ranchero and the English bailiff of the sixteenth century are noteworthy.[29]

The rancheros' political presence was important during the Juárez reform era. It has already been pointed out that they were the ones who exerted the greatest pressure for affecting church land, although the disamortization process left only crumbs for them: some of the communal lands the indigenous people found themselves obligated to sell. Like the small property owner, the small tenant farmer had few opportunities for developing himself during the nineteenth century; the latifundista system blocked the expansion and accumulation of his meager capital. These rancheros, many of them tenant farmers, were, at the beginning of the twentieth century, the most powerful leading political force of the revolutionary agrarian movement. Like small capitalists, many of them, still only slightly differentiated from the peasants, properly speaking, saw the latifundio as an implacable enemy. Here, the contradiction between private property and capital was expressed in an extraordinarily acute fashion.

In order to demonstrate that the estate owner–tenant farmer conflict had enormous importance at the beginning of the century, I will cite one of the most clear-thinking experts on the agrarian problem of that era (1908): Andrés Molina Enríquez. The following paragraph is, in essence, a weighing of the possibilities that the contradiction between landholders and capitalist tenant farmers in the Mexican countryside would be resolved in the English way:

> Of course, one must set aside the solution that would occur to everyone, that the estate owners, through long-term leasing of fractions, or through permanent voluntary partitioning that would not be responding to a special stimulus, would remedy the incongruities of the large property of which they are owners. *Rentals of fractions that are commonly called "ranchos"* are in use and produce insignificant results . . . . In fact, the evil in the spread of long-term rentals of fractions or ranchos would not be so much on the part of the landlords from the haciendas as on the part of the renters and tenant farmers, who tend to be the mestizos, on account of their extreme poverty. In fact, the rental agreements are completely precarious for the tenants. *An estate owner would need to lose, above all, the feeling of dominance that is preponderant in him in order to divest himself spontaneously of the right to dismiss his tenants at his will.* The obligation to respect leases for several years is, then, on his part impossible; the estate owner will always judge it to be contrary to his interests, and he will get around it, even though the laws impose it upon him, as long as the large property does not disappear. . . . But even admitting that he might decide to enter rental agreements for various fractions or ranchos on his hacienda for ten, twenty, or thirty years, he would be unable to get anyone except persons with meager resources as tenants or renters, given that, because of the enormous gulf that there has always been between the large property and the small, no middle class capable in terms of resources of doing useful work on the scale that a greater division of the large property would require has been formed in the farming population; and with *persons with resources as minimal as are those of the current tenants,* he would gain little, the tenants would gain little, and the country would gain little.[30]

In sum, two factors were preventing a nonrevolutionary solution: (1) the economic inability of the larval-state capitalist tenants, the rancheros, to increase their capital; and (2) the backward character of the relations of production on the haciendas, which prevented the spread of the lease as a form of penetration of capital into agriculture.

This contradiction reveals the bourgeois character of the agrarian revolution of 1910. The rancheros were expressing, although only in embryonic form, the absolute necessity of capital's breaking with the predominant form of private ownership. The statistics for 1910 indicate that there were 8,431 haciendas and 48,633 ranchos.[31] It is difficult to know how many of these ranchos were rented properties, but they had to represent a rather large proportion; recent studies have discovered, moreover, that a good number of the ranchos were actually leased fractions within the haciendas.[32] I believe that in many cases the hacienda administrator himself could be considered a *sui generis* tenant. In the numerous cases in which the absentee landlord limited himself to demanding a set rent from his administrator and was totally disengaged from production, the latter undoubtedly pocketed a part of the profits (the difference between the real profit and the rent paid) along with his salary. Nevertheless, in these cases, the amount of the ground rent and the seignorial ties that linked the latifundista to his estate prevented the dynamic growth of capitalist production.

The Revolution of 1910 and the Cárdenas reforms broke down the traditional obstacles to capitalist tenant farming, but they put other, new ones in place: the ejido "protected" by the Agrarian Code against the possibilities of use of wage labor and rental. But these days, capitalist development in the countryside, represented no longer by weak rancheros but by a powerful entrepreneurial bourgeoisie, clashes openly with the ejido, which represents an annoying impediment to the free circulation, investment, and concentration of capital. It is not surprising that the Federal Agrarian Reform Act (1971) hides, under various cloaks of legal artifice, an attempt to adapt the legislation to the development of capitalism in the countryside. The prior Agrarian Code established the (legal) impossibility of renting ejido land, thereby condemning this sector to the vices of *minifundismo*. It is apparent that the prohibition against renting (combined with the fact that private banks did not consider ejidatarios to be subjects for credit) curtailed the possibilities of the ejido's development.

As is well known, the phenomenon of illegal leasing is extremely common in all the ejidos situated in irrigation districts or in zones of high fertility. The ejidatario does not have sufficient capital or the opportunity to obtain such a lease; however, there is no lack of capitalists who are disposed to lease several parcels in order to set up an enterprise and to employ the ejidatarios themselves as wage laborers. The proportions that this phenomenon reaches are considerable. For example, in the Valle del Yaqui, in 1961, 63 percent of the ejido area was leased; and in 1965, 25 percent of the ejidatarios rented out their entire parcel, and 13 percent, some part of it. Another study shows that in the state of Hidalgo in 1967, 46 percent of the ejidatarios were renting out their parcels; in the famous Nueva Italia ejido zone (well known because of the frustrated attempts at collectivization there) in 1957-58, 35 percent of the ejidatarios rented their parcels, and ten years later the ratio had risen to 55 percent.[33] In irrigation district 03 at Tula, in the state of Hidalgo, it was reported that in five municipalities a group of forty-four property owners, who owned 1,320 hectares, rented an additional 2,415 hectares from ejidos and private minifundistas. Uncovered there as well were five tenant farmers without any property at all who were renting 600 hectares.[34]

A study dedicated to this problem and conducted in Apatzingán provides an example of the norms followed in rental agreements with ejidatarios:

> 1. The investors never took a single parcel; it was always a number greater than four, with six to ten irrigated hectares each. 2. The decisions about the crop and the method to be employed remained the strict responsibility and under the complete authority of the investors. . . . 3. From the moment in which the contract was signed, the land passed directly under the control of the lessee. 4. "The contracting parties agreed that the share going to the ejidatarios will be set at 10 percent of the total gross value of the harvest, estimating the value of such shares . . . at the sum of 400.00 pesos in cash per hectare, plus the payment of the ejido tax and water fees." 5. The payment of the following shares to the ejidatarios was made: 50 percent at the moment the contract was signed, and the rest three months later, after discounting the costs of improvements made on the parcel by the one who rented it.[35]

It should not be surprising, then, that the legislation would be adapted—tardily—to reality. In effect, the 1971 Agrarian Reform Act permits the rental of ejido parcels.[36]

In 1960 the census recorded 6.5 million hectares in the hands of 21,000 renters. Although the census figures must be below the real number, the reported total proves significant; in order to have an idea of that total, it is interesting to compare it with the total amount of privately owned cultivated land, which was 11.5 million hectares. It must be assumed that the tenant farmers registered by the census only rented private land and that the lessees of ejido land did not declare their status. That being the case, it is possible to calculate the proportion of private land rented: it can be said that 12 percent of the land in private hands in 1960 was rented (excluding unproductive, hilly, and uncultivated land). The importance of renting can also be measured from the average sizes of the unit of production for each type of land tenure (see table 16). As can be seen in the table, the average size of the rented farms was the largest. In 1970 this average declined considerably, since the crisis prompted a contraction of capital investments in agriculture.

Land rental as it appears in contemporary Mexico does not express a

Table 16

Producers and Land Areas, by Type of Land Tenure, 1960 and 1970

Type of Land Tenure	Number of Producers (thousands)		Area (thousands of hectares)		Average (hectares)	
	1960	1970	1960	1970	1960	1970
Owner	1,290	932	96,958	62,243	75.2	66.8
Tenant	21	27	6,450	3,047	306.4	111.7
Ejidatario	1,524	1,848	44,497	69,724	29.2	37.7
Sharecropper	13	25	952	623	75.8	24.4

Source: Censos agrícola, ganadero y ejidal, 1960–70.

precapitalist relation of production, in contrast to what happened with other forms of land tenure. Indeed, it represents the typical form that agrarian capitalism adopts in order to achieve adaptation of the old forms of property to its needs. This means that capitalist rental brings the earlier forms of land tenure up-to-date, changes their essence, and gives them new content. But at the same time, rental of land reveals the precapitalist character of private, ejido, and communal ownership. The payment of a rent to the one who has beneficial use of and monopolizes the land (whether a large landholder, a small peasant, an ejidatario, or a comunero) obliges the agricultural entrepreneur to give up a part of his profits and compels him to generate superprofits in order to reach the average rate.[37]

Capitalism and Land Ownership

Theoretically—and in the last instance—land that is nationalized and in the hands of the state represents the form of ownership that could best express the necessities of capitalist development.

> We understand that economists such as Mill, Cherbulliez, Hilditch, and others have insisted that the State appropriate the ground rent with the aim of substituting it for taxes. It was the frank expression of the hatred that the industrial capitalist feels toward the owner of the soil, who is, in his eyes, useless and superfluous in the scheme of bourgeois production.[38]

But to materialize, this dream of the bourgeoisie would require the elimination of all the social classes that maintain a connection with the land;

it would necessitate, in sum, erasing with one stroke the entire historical base upon which that very bourgeoisie has built the capitalist regime and political alliances that have enabled it to take power. The nationalization of the land and ground rent is one of those measures that are located on the outer limits of capitalist development and that often appear in the programs of popular and socialist movements.[39]

The accumulation and expanded reproduction of capital require the concentration of production from the land in large units. Nevertheless, the latter must occur within the frameworks that Mexican historical development imposes and that are expressed in the particular forms of ownership that predominate in the countryside. The panorama of land tenure nowadays looks like an intricate mixture of large properties, an infinity of private parcels in the hands of minifundista peasants, and a corporatized ejido sector. This situation is the result of a political balance of social forces, arduously constructed since the triumph of the Mexican Revolution. The current problem is that the very economic development that this situation has prompted is modifying the previously attained social balance; thus, the stability of the political apparatus and the structure of power are threatened.[40]

Under these conditions, the Mexican state has two alternatives in order to make way for the concentration of production:

1. the populist solution: collectivization and/or creation of state agricultural enterprises; and
2. the "classic" solution: rental, free circulation of capital.

Of course, the decision about which path to follow is only applicable in the ejido sector. In fact, production on privately owned land follows the second path. To judge from recent tendencies, the "classic" path has been opted for (in a veiled way) in the ejido sector as well, but, simultaneously, the specter of collectivization is being waved before the terrified rural bourgeoisie. Thus, there has been an ingenuous attempt to maintain the sociopolitical equilibrium attained by agrarian reform. However, the factor that destroys that equilibrium cannot be contained by the bourgeoisie: it is the intense process of proletarianization of the peasantry, under conditions of such economic backwardness that the excess population mass is not suitable either for the countryside or for the city. This process is inevitably intensifying, no matter what the "solution" that may be adopted. The so-called collectivization has been a disguised form of organizing state enterprises, totally inefficient and government-subsidized in the majority of cases.

In conclusion, the current land tenure situation is an obstacle that, in one way or another, will have to be salvaged by capitalist development. The "populist solution" ("Blessed are the meek, for they shall inherit the earth"?) could only be put into practice by means of an alliance between the peasant and the governing segment of the bourgeoisie. It would encounter the opposition of very large sectors of the rural bourgeoisie, which would not look favorably upon either the collectivization or the stateization of agriculture, even though that would imply the rise of a new model of capitalist development (state monopoly capitalism).[41] The other alternative implies accelerating the elimination of the peasantry and openly permitting the introduction of capital into the ejido. This solution would break down all possibilities of an effective alliance with the peasantry and could probably only occur under conditions imposed by a despotic government closely aligned with the rural bourgeoisie.

Chapter 5

Social Classes and
Political Power

Clear the way, gentlemen, and let me go back to my old freedom. Let me
go look for my past life so that I may be resurrected from this present death.
I was not born to be a governor or to defend islands and cities from enemies
that would attack them. I know more about plowing and digging and
pruning vines than I do about laws or the protection of islands and king-
doms. St. Peter is well enough off in Rome; by which I mean that each one
should follow the trade to which he was born. In my hand a sickle is better
than a governor's scepter.

—Sancho Panza
*On abandoning the governorship of
the Island of Barataria, from Cervantes,*
Don Quijote de la Mancha

The Social Classes and the Historically
Determined Social System of Production

ALTHOUGH the analysis of class structure has been developed
continuously over the foregoing pages, we must now treat it
explicitly and directly, without sidestepping some important
theoretical problems. It will be of interest to review the few studies of the
social classes in the countryside that have been done in Mexico in order
to situate ourselves more easily in the controversy. Within the group of
researchers concerned with class analysis of the countryside, it is possible
to observe two positions. One defines social classes principally on the basis
of the relations of ownership with the means of production. Rodolfo
Stavenhagen, for example, concludes that "social classes in the countryside
are defined above all in relation to ownership of land, and by the scale
of this ownership."[1] The other position considers the place occupied in a

historically determined social system of production to be the fundamental element of the definition of social class. Of course, following Lenin's now-classic definition, the relation to the means of production, the role played in the social organization of labor, and the form and amount of social wealth appropriated are simultaneously considered as criteria. Ricardo Pozas has recently proposed this approach.[2]

Without a doubt, the second criterion is the most satisfactory, and it is the one that has been used in this study. The very study conducted by authors who do not pose the problem correctly, on a theoretical level, itself proves us right. For example, in the Stavenhagen book mentioned above—in spite of its definition of social class—the existence of four social classes is established by inference from the analysis of the two historically given social structures: the semi-capitalist structure and the capitalist structure. The first puts minifundista small peasants face to face with a commercial bourgeoisie; the second structure puts the large landholder (or foreign plantation company) in opposition to the agricultural laborer.[3]

In contrast, and paradoxically, the cited study that, in theoretical terms, correctly sets forth the analysis of the social system of production in order to locate the social classes does not apply its own propositions in practice. If the concept of a "historically determined social system of production" is understood in a nondialectic way, as is the case, one arrives at erroneous conclusions. In that study the system of production is defined as capitalist *tout court*, and therefore it accepts the existence of only two classes: the bourgeoisie and the proletariat.[4]

Of course, the authors mentioned define various strata, sectors, or levels within each class in order to flesh out the situation. Table 17 presents simplified outlines of the class structures that they propose. As the table shows, Stavenhagen places a special emphasis on the form and scale of ownership. The rural bourgeoisie and the property owners are the two dominant classes, and they are distinguished from one another because the former is not essentially an owner of land (it is linked to the tertiary sector, although it is closely tied to, and sometimes confused with, the other). The minifundista peasants and the proletariat, the two exploited classes, are also distinguished from one another by their respective relations to the means of production. But the distinction between property owners and minifundista peasants, although partly based on the size of the land, apparently takes into account differences in the system of production (capitalist and semi-capitalist).

Indeed, the Pozas analysis rigidly applies the criterion of ownership of the means of production without taking into account differences in the system of production, since it considers only the existence of the capitalist system. Ultimately, the differences between these two evaluations of the class structure derive from the authors' differing understandings of the

Table 17
Two Views of Class Structure

Class	Sectors or Strata
Stavenhagen	
1. Rural bourgeoisie (commercial)	
	Ejidatarios
2. Minifundista peasants	Property owners
	Family
3. Property owners	Average
	Large
4. Agricultural proletariat	
Pozas and de Pozas	
1. Agrarian bourgeoisie	Large bourgeoisie
	Average and petty bourgeoisie
	Strict proletariat (day laborers)
	Semi-proletariat (domestic servants, peons,
2. Agricultural proletariat	minifundistas)
	Subproletariat (unemployed)
	Lumpenproletariat

Source: Rodolfo Stavenhagen, "Aspectos sociales de la estructura agraria en México," in *Neolatifundismo y explotación* (Mexico City: Editorial Nuestro Tiempo, 1968), 43–55; Ricardo Pozas and Isabel H. de Pozas, *Los indios en las clases sociales de México* (Mexico City: Siglo XXI Editores, 1971), 139.

Note: In another, more recent text, "La población campesina," in CDIA, *Estructura agraria y desarrollo agrícola en México*, 2:63–90, Stavenhagen defines five classes: ejidatarios, private minifundistas, mid-level property owners, large landholders, and agricultural day laborers. Here the criterion of mode of production is definitively abandoned in defining classes. Generally speaking, the analysis of social classes in Stavenhagen's texts is not very precise.

historically determined system of production dominant in Mexico, which is actually the key concept.

I define social classes as large groups of persons (1) which form a non-exhaustive asymmetrical system within a given social structure; (2) within which are established relations of exploitation, dependence, and/or subordination; (3) which form relatively impermeable units (with little vertical social mobility); (4) which tend to be distributed along a stratified continuum the two opposite poles of which are represented by oppressed and oppressors; (5) which develop in some moment of their historical existence their own forms of ideology (whether in a nonsystematic, rudimentary way or with complete self-awareness), which express directly or indirectly their common interests; and (6) which are distinguished from one another basically in accordance with

1. the place they occupy in a historically determined social system of production (relations with the means of production and/or distribution, function in the social division of labor, amount of and form of acquiring the social wealth they possess); and
2. the relation they maintain with the system of socioeconomic institutions and organisms of coercion, power, and control, a system that is nothing more than the political expression of the way one or several modes of production are articulated—in a given moment and place.

It is a question of a *system* of classes, not a simple sum or cluster of social groups. This system is asymmetrical, for it contains an unequal distribution of the privileges and discriminations of each group. It is not exhaustive, given that not all the individuals in a society belong to a class; rather, there may be layers of unclassed elements. The boundaries between classes are not rigid: there are intermediate groups that share the traits of two or more different classes, and although generally their existence is transitory and changeable, their presence gives the system the appearance of a continuum.[5]

The social system of production is, for me, the subcapitalist economic formation characterized in previous chapters. It is an agrarian structure within which an articulation of two modes of production has crystallized. However, the bulk of the rural population is not exploited by *two* dominant classes, as Stavenhagen proposes, but by a single one: the agrarian bourgeoisie (agricultural and commercial). Nevertheless, we find, effectively, *two* exploited classes: the peasantry and the agricultural proletariat. This situation is owing to the nonclass character of the simple commodity mode of production, which is articulated with the capitalist mode in a relation of exploitation. In looking at the implications of this fact in some detail, I shall indicate some problems related to the structure of power.

The Peasant Class

For some, peasants are proletarians with a miniscule piece of land; for others, they are petty bourgeois. For me, their specificity lies in the fact that they are exploited as proletarians owing to their petty bourgeois condition. Why?

The peasant is immersed in a particular mechanism of production in which if he were isolated, he himself, like a good petty bourgeois, would be the sole owner of the product of his own labor. In this sense, the concept of self-exploitation proposed by Alexander V. Chayanov proves revealing.[6] But the peasant is not isolated, and his insertion into the bourgeois economy transforms the self-exploitation into exploitation by the dominant class of the one who works the soil. He "auto-exploits" himself for the benefit of others. Unlike the worker, the peasant does not offer the market his labor power, but the fruits of his work on the land. But there is a similarity: both the fruits of the land and wage labor are sold to the market for the price necessary to permit the reproduction of labor power. Thus, one can speak of the *proletarian* character of the exploitation of the peasant, who nevertheless lives in a petty bourgeois (simple commodity) situation.

Indeed, the economic characterization of the peasant gives him his structural base: the simple commodity mode of production.[7] But the articulation of this mode of production with capitalism places the peasant in a double status of petty bourgeois and proletarian, under a double designation in which the peasant is neither totally bourgeois nor completely proletarian. Its articulation with the capitalist system blocks the peasant mass from any alternatives of development as bourgeoisie. On the other hand, the petty bourgeois nature of its mode of production eliminates the revolutionary potential that it could develop as a proletariat. Only alliance with the proletariat, under the political leadership of the latter, enables the peasantry to develop a revolutionary consciousness.

Thus, strictly speaking, the peasantry is made up of the independent producers who basically live from working their smallholdings, that is, the peasants who were characterized in chapter 3 as divided into two strata: the *average* and the *well-to-do*. The term *average peasants* means those producers who generate a sufficient amount to maintain their families at a low level that enables them to subsist but not to save. Beginning at this subsistence level, one continues superimposing layers of peasants with increasingly higher incomes, up to the point of reaching a well-to-do range, which borders on bourgeois status. Furthermore, the great mass of small producers is so miserable that they cannot strictly be classified as peasants; one is dealing with *semi-proletarians* and with *pauperized peasants* (see chapter 3).

The figures in table 18, rounded off, give an idea of the numerical significance of these peasant strata. The difference between the definition presented in table 18 and those of Stavenhagen and Pozas (see table 17) lies fundamentally in the fact that here I am making a complete, precise distinction between agrarian bourgeoisie and peasantry, while Stavenhagen and Pozas place them in the same class.[8] Moreover, those defined by Stavenhagen as "minifundista peasants" are actually, for us, semi-proletarians and pauperized peasants. In sum, we conceive of the existence of a peasant *class* defined by its particular mode of production; in Marx's

Table 18
Distribution of Peasants, by Social Strata, 1950–1970

Stratum	1950		1960		1970	
	No.	%	No.	%	No.	%
Well-to-do peasants	30	1	70	3	300	12
Average peasants	290	12	300	12	200	8
Pauperized peasants and semi-proletariat	2,100	87	2,100	85	2,000	80

Source: Derived from table 9.
Note: Numbers represent thousands of individuals, on the basis of the economically active population over twelve years of age.

terms, one would be dealing with *smallholding peasants*. As has been seen in the foregoing analyses, this conception of the peasantry as a class has great importance in the interpretation of the agrarian structure, political system, and economic evolution of Mexico, for this class is situated as a creation of the Mexican Revolution and as a creature of distorted capitalist development itself. As such, the peasantry is a key for understanding the complex of problems affecting a historic era.

The metaphor of Mexican Bonapartism, based on the peasant masses, has recently been used to describe the country's political structure. The *caudillismo, caciquismo,* and *presidencialismo* have the feel of examples of a variety of what Marx (and, later and insistently, Gramsci) called Caesarism or Bonapartism. It is, in fact, a matter of an excellent, although inadequate, concept for cutting through the problem. Marx's words, referring to the French peasants, seem to have been written for Mexico. The smallholding peasants, he wrote,

> are incapable of asserting their class interests in their own name, whether in Parliament or in a convention. They cannot represent themselves and must be represented. Their representative must appear to them both as their lord and master and a ruling being of unlimited power who protects them from the other classes and sends down rain and sunshine from above. The political influence of the smallholders is therefore finally expressed in the subordination of society to the executive authority.[9]

There is something that attracts one's attention in Marx and Engels's statements on the agrarian problem: as a rule, studies on the importance of the peasantry's political participation are accompanied by observations and allusions to the "relative independence" of the state. The situations in which weak capitalist development is shown in the existence of hybrid, transitional forms in agriculture and in society in general also generate "independent" forms of political power. This is precisely the German situation that Hegel reflected: in Germany, wrote Marx and Engels in 1845, "the land was being cultivated under a system that was neither the small-holding system nor the large crop system and that, despite the persistence of serfdom and the feudal offering of services, never pushed the peasantry toward emancipation, as much because this type of exploitation did not allow an actively revolutionary class to arise as because it did not have at its side the revolutionary bourgeoisie corresponding to a peasant class with those characteristics."[10] Further on they concluded:

> The impotence of each one of the spheres of life (one cannot speak of estates or classes, but, at most, of future estates and classes) did not permit any of them to take over exclusive hegemony. And that resulted as a necessary consequence in the fact that during the era of the absolute monarchy, which here cloaked itself in the most feeble form, a semi-patriarchal form, that special sphere to which it was assigned by the division of labor, the administration of public interests acquired *an abnormal independence,* carried further yet by the modern bureaucracy. *The state, thus, constituted itself as an apparently independent power,* and it has maintained up to today, in Germany, this position that in other countries is purely transitory, a transitional phase.[11]

The state's independence is nothing more than an appearance. But under conditions of transition to capitalism, or when the previous modes of production are not yet disappearing, the dominant classes do not achieve an "exclusive hegemony," and social groups mediating between the "sovereign will" and the society appear. This perspective undoubtedly has its roots in Hegel's philosophy of the state. At the same time, eras of transition reveal the true character of the state with special clarity in the violence that the dominant class exercises over the society. It is precisely in the course of examining the primitive accumulation of capital (i.e., the era of transition to capitalism) that Marx expresses his well-known ideas on the role of violence: "Force is the midwife of every old society which is pregnant with a new one."[12] In the same place, Marx defines the power of the state as "the concentrated and organized force of society,"[13] basis of the methods of primitive accumulation of capital. It is during this transitional period that it is revealed that the state's violence is a tool of the emerging dominant class: the bourgeoisie. However, at the same time, the violence contributes to giving the state that necessary aureole of independence and power over the classes.

In 1895 Engels explained the characteristics of states that arose from nonproletarian revolutions in this way:

> Until that date [1848], all revolutions had been reduced to the overthrow and replacement of one particular class domination by another; but all the previous dom-

inant classes were only small minorities compared with the dominated mass of people. A dominant minority was overthrown, and another minority grasped the helm of the State in its place and molded the state institutions to its interests. This role always belonged to the minority group prepared for domination and called to it by the state of economic development, and precisely for this reason, and only for this reason, the dominated majority either intervened in the revolution in favor of that domination or tranquilly accepted the revolution. But setting aside the concrete content of each one of the cases, the form common to all these revolutions was that of being minority revolutions. Even when the majority cooperated in them, it did so—consciously or unconsciously—in the service of a minority; but this, or simply the passive attitude, the nonresistance on the majority's part, *gave the minority group the appearance of being the representative of all the people.*[14]

To the extent that proletarian struggles—independent and revolutionary— are increasing, the dominant class is losing that mediating "appearance." Nevertheless, there is a popular class that because of its economic situation remains inscribed in that condition of "spectator" or "collaborator" with the dominant minority. It is the peasant class, which even in the full development of the capitalist mode of production has an objective tendency to behave like a precapitalist class, like a nonpolitical class. It is the class in which Hegel posited the role of mediation par excellence, "the peasant class *raised to a higher power,* the nobiliary ownership of the land."[15]

It is important to note here the problem in the specific conditions in France, where a bourgeois revolution had destroyed, as it had not in Germany, that very peasantry "raised to a higher power" (i.e., the nobility) and had prompted the rise of an enormous mass of smallholding peasants. According to Marx,

> Only under the second Bonaparte does *the state seem to have become completely autonomous.* The state machine has established itself so securely as against bourgeois society that it needs as leader only the head of the Society of 10 December, a fortune-hunter from foreign parts, chosen as leader by a drunken soldiery bought with drams and sausages, whom he must ever and again bribe with more sausage. . . . Nevertheless, the authority of the State is not suspended in mid-air. Bonaparte represents a class, indeed the most numerous class in French society, the peasant small-holders.[16]

The most important thing is to point out the mechanisms and the conditions behind this apparent autonomy of the state. For Marx, the fact that Louis Bonaparte was the representative of the most numerous class—the peasants—did not give the state a "peasant character." On the contrary, political power thus reaffirmed its capitalist nature. Let us see how Marx explained this in another text:

> The empire, with the *coup d'etat* for its certificate of birth, universal suffrage for its sanction, and the sword for its scepter, professed to rest on the peasantry, the

large mass of producers not directly involved in the struggle of capital and labour. It professed to save the working class by breaking down Parliamentarism and, with it, the undisguised subserviency of Government to the propertied classes. It professed to save the propertied classes by upholding their economic supremacy over the working class; and, finally, it professed to unite all classes, by reviving for all the chimera of national glory. In reality, it was the only form of government possible at a time when the bourgeoisie had already lost, and the working class had not yet acquired, the faculty of ruling the nation. It was acclaimed throughout the world as the saviour of society. Under its sway, bourgeois society, freed from political cares, attained a development unexpected even by itself. . . . The State power, apparently soaring high above society, was, at the same time itself the greatest scandal of that society and the very hotbed of all its corruptions. Its own rottenness, and the rottenness of the society it had saved, were laid bare by the bayonet of Prussia, herself eagerly bent upon transferring the supreme seat of that *regime* from Paris to Berlin. Imperialism is, at the same time, the most prostitute and the ultimate form of the State power which nascent middle-class society had commenced to elaborate as a means of its own emancipation from feudalism, and which full-grown bourgeois society had finally transformed into *a means for the enslavement of labour by capital.*[17]

Just as Hegel demanded, the empire took the peasantry as a mediating social base:

Let it be clearly understood, however. The Bonaparte dynasty represents not the revolutionary but the conservative peasant, not the peasant who wants to force his way out of his social sphere of existence, the smallholding, but one who rather wishes to consolidate it; it represents not the country people who by their own efforts and in conjunction with the towns hope to overthrow the old order, but on the contrary those who, apathetically imprisoned in this old order, hope to see themselves together with their smallholdings rescued and raised to honour by the ghost of the Empire.[18]

Thus, here it is not the peasant "raised to a higher power" but, instead, his conservative, reactionary, petty bourgeois side that is representing the role of the mediating class. But the conditions are similar: the bourgeois society still maintains in its core old relations of production, which capital has not yet managed to subjugate and destroy. Marx expressed it quite clearly:

The struggle against capital in its developed modern form, at its salient point, the struggle of the industrial wage-labourer against the industrial bourgeois, is in France a partial phenomenon which, after the February days, was the less able to furnish the national content of the revolution, since the struggle against secondary capitalist methods of exploitation, the struggle of the peasant against usury and mortgages, of the petty bourgeois against the wholesaler, banker and the manufacturer, in short against bankruptcy, was still hidden in the general revolt against the finance-aristocracy. . . . The French workers could not advance one step, or disarrange the bourgeois order by a single hair until the course of the revolution had aroused the mass of the nation, peasants and petty bourgeois, standing between the proletariat and the bourgeoisie.[19]

The function of repression and violence is quite important in the construction of a bourgeois state in a society where the capital-labor contradiction is still not totally widespread and where, therefore, the mass of the people are subject to "secondary modes of exploitation" by capital and not to the modern, advanced and fundamental forms of exploitation: wage labor. But the violence is not only an ingredient of the class struggles that are found at the basis of the conflicts for control of the government. For Marx, there is a structural relation between the peasant mass and the army, the principal means of the exercise of violence on the part of the state. Although peasant society has seen how its "cultured portion" (Hegel) was decapitated by the bourgeois revolution, the conservative sectors of the peasant class resurrect the nobility in the army; in this way, the very social base of Bonapartism sharpens the sword of repression for the state:

> The army was the smallholders' point of honour, transforming them into heroes, defending their new possession against external foes, glorifying their newly-won nationality, plundering and revolutionizing the world. The uniform was their gala dress, war was their poetry, the smallholding itself, extended and rounded off in imagination, was their fatherland, and patriotism, the ideal form of the sense of ownership.[20]

To the extent that the smallholding peasants confront their true enemy, capital, and see how their economy is slowly ruined, they cease to form a base for Bonapartist government. In capitalist society, the smallholding economy is an exhausted mode of production moving in reverse. Bonapartism bases its strength on the peasantry's illusion of going back to a situation in which capital did it little harm and was its ally:

> All *idées napoléoniennes are ideas of the undeveloped, fresh and youthful smallholding.* They are senseless for the worn-out smallholding. They are merely the hallucinations of its death struggle, words turned into phrases, spirits turned into ghosts. But the parody of imperialism was needed, to free the mass of the French nation from the burden of tradition and to work out clearly the opposition of the power of the state to society. With the progressive destruction of the smallholding system, the state structure founded upon it collapses too. The political centralization required by modern society can only be built upon the ruins of the military and bureaucratic machinery of government which was forged in opposition to feudalism.[21]

The form of state based on the peasant population has a transitional character. To the extent that the peasants are ruined and are absorbed by capitalist society as proletarians, the Bonapartist government continues to lose its social base and tends to collapse.

The state's autonomy, which presents itself at certain historic junctures, is nothing but an appearance, a deception, an illusion. The exploited classes lack the revolutionary consciousness of their own interests and become the passive agents of mediation between the society and the state. But it is quite important here to distinguish between the social classes that, like the proletariat, have conditions for developing a revolutionary consciousness and those classes that, because of the nature of their insertion into capitalist society, are condemned to disappear without engendering a class consciousness of their own that might become a revolutionary alternative.

It is necessary to distinguish between the appearances of the state's autonomy prompted by the "hallucinations of [the] death struggle" of the peasantry and those caused by the fact that the proletariat is still not aware of the revolutionary possibilities of its class. In this latter instance, it is a matter of the youthful illusion of a class that is still inexperienced and of distortions caused by the predominance of the ideology of the dominant classes. The peasantry's situation is, on the other hand, similar to the Hegelian ideal of civil society: the peasants form a multitude of private interests. "The smallholding, the peasant and his family; next to it another smallholding, another peasant and another family. A number of these make a village, and a number of villages a department. In this way the greater part of the French nation is formed by the simple addition of units of corresponding size, much as many potatoes in a sack make up a sack of potatoes."[22] The objective conditions and the mode of production that are found at the base of peasant society lead to a social environment propitious for a situation in which a mediating force is inserted between the peasant class and the state. The peasants do not constitute a "class on their own behalf"; they exemplify the Hegelian idea of a civil society divided into particular, private interests. It is not by chance, then, that Hegel would see in them (and in land ownership generally) the element from which he was able to infer the class destined to serve as mediator between the state and the society.

This brief examination of Marx's theses about the peasantry has led us to the concept of "civil society." In fact, the Marxist analysis of the French agrarian situation in the mid-nineteenth century seems to follow the Hegelian model, in which the reign of misery and corruption in peasant civil society must be controlled, channeled, and regulated by the universal sovereignty of the state. But there is a noteworthy difference between Marx's model and Hegel's: the former refuses to generalize the civil society–mediation–state scheme to all capitalist societies and uses it exclusively for understanding the relationship between peasant society and the state. For Hegel, civil society is the equivalent of prepolitical society; that is, it is what the English philosophers and economists called *natural society*, in contrast to *civilized society*. In a certain sense, Marx continues the Hegelian tradition; in fact, for Marx, the peasants were "the class that represents barbarism within civilization."[23] Hegel produces an important innovation in political thought: he applies the concept of natural, barbarous, precivilized, and prepolitical society to the sphere of modern economic relations. Thus, Hegel's *civil society* is no longer the prepolitical, but the nonpolitical, as opposed to the *political society* (the state). For Hegel, all economic relations belong to the private world of the civil society; for Marx, peasant society is a specific type of economic relation with a precapitalist character, and therefore, it is inserted into capitalist society in a way comparable to the way Hegel inserts civil society into the state.

The objective economic situation of the smallholding peasantry causes Marx to see in this class a set of economic relations without its own political superstructure. These are economic relations that are worn out but extant in the interior of capitalist society. Their decrepit (precapitalist) nature and their subjugation to the capitalist mode of production hinder them from developing their own political demands. The peasants are, therefore, a living example of nonpolitical civil society: "They cannot represent themselves and must be represented" (Marx). In their relations with the state, then, they generate a specific form of mediation that contributes to giving the political power of another class an appearance of autonomy and legitimacy.

The peasantry is not capable of controlling power, nor of leading an alliance of classes of which, ultimately, it forms a part, nor of representing itself politically; that is so because of the traits of the mode of production in which the small peasant, who is exploited as a proletarian owing to his petty bourgeois condition, is immersed. In this contradiction I find one of the deepest roots of the similarly paradoxical Mexican political structure. The Mexican bourgeoisie takes advantage of this feature of the peasantry in order to control power effectively with a solid popular base. The Mexican Revolution is the history of the struggles and alliances between the bourgeoisie and the peasantry, a history that transpired in the midst of the distressing contradictions between a politically impotent peasantry and a sector of the bourgeoisie that did not easily find a new and different political alternative to that of the Porfirian landholding bourgeoisie that had just been overthrown. The bloc of classes and the reformist accord that Lázaro Cárdenas achieved, twenty years after the "official" termination of the revolution, represented the political solution of the contradictions and the point of departure for the current Mexican system.

The "vacuum of power" and the equilibrium of the sectors in conflict during the revolution, as well as postrevolutionary caudillismo and Cardenista populism, can be explained in terms of Caesarism or Bonapartism, in which a "strong man," a *caudillo* or a president, attains the support of "third forces": the peasants. However, Caesar had his Brutus, and Napoleon his Waterloo; even the tragicomic version of the latter, Louis Bonaparte, faced the beginning of the end in Querétaro. But where does Mexican Caesarism stop?

The class alliance established by Cárdenas, which implied in some way the peasantry's sharing in political power, through intermediaries, was virtually shattered between 1940 and 1946, that is, between the assumption of power by Avila Camacho (who, curiously, was nominated as a presidential candidate by the National Peasant Confederation) and the reforms in Article 27 of the Constitution introduced by Miguel Alemán, in order to guarantee the right of *amparo* (writ of relief) to landholders. What remains unexplained is the continuity up to our day of the Mexican political system forged in the Cárdenas era, that is, what the politicians refer to as the institutionalization of the Mexican Revolution and what, if we wanted to continue using the concept, ought to be called democratic Caesarism.[24] Nevertheless, the concept of Bonapartism or Caesarism, which explains the moments of crisis and the peasantry's political impotence, does not establish anything but the bases of an analysis that remains to be done.

Once a revolution has been completed, every bourgeoisie that has come to power is faced with the problem of how to ensure the maintenance and reproduction of the political system that it has just installed. As organized in Mexico, the economic system ensures the reproduction of the basic elements of the productive forces (the means of production and labor power) under the specific conditions that have been discussed. But it is also necessary to ensure, in Althusser's terms, the reproduction of the relations of production, which, as he correctly points out, cannot be explained only in terms of the economic base; rather, it is necessary to understand the role of the ideological-political superstructure.[25] This problem is expressed by the Mexican bourgeoisie in its very own terms: the need to institutionalize the revolution. The state's role is fundamental, and the entire future of the country is going to depend on the type of power that the bourgeoisie manages to consolidate.

With regard to the agrarian structure, the bourgeois state faces the complicated problem of ensuring the continuity of a structure in the process of transition; that is, in addressing the agrarian sector, the Mexican state reflects precisely the contradictions of a structure whose process of development toward capitalism is indispensable for the bourgeoisie, but a structure that, under the specific conditions of backwardness in which it occurs, can cause the downfall of the entire political system. It is necessary to control that process, even to slow it down, in order to keep a part of the rural population tied to the land. Through agrarian reform, support from the ejido and minifundista sector, and political control of the rural masses, the Mexican state manages to ensure the reproduction of the relations of production in the countryside: it ensures the continuous state of violence, struggle, and plunder typical of the process of permanent primitive accumulation. To that end, it manages with extraordinary ability a double political game: the populism that partially satisfies peasant demands and the defense of the interests of the large agrarian bourgeoisie. Both facets of this political game have deep historic roots; the populism draws its symbols from the Zapatista revolution and obtains its reality from the Cardenista reforms. The agrarian capitalist interests pull back from the liberals' defense of private property and are consolidated in the policies of Miguel Alemán.

This is not, however, simply a matter of two political strands interwoven throughout Mexican agrarian history. They also represent two different political structures brought together under a single political system. One of them is the structure of the direct power of the bourgeoisie; the other we can characterize as a structure of mediation. The first is expressed in the economic power of the agrarian bourgeoisie, which manages and manipulates official and private resources in order to develop itself. The second comprises the "revolutionary" organizations and institutions that "defend" the peasant: the National Peasant Confederation (CNC), the League of Agrarian Communities, part of the activity of the Department of Agrarian Affairs and Colonization, and so forth.

The structure of mediation has its origin in the consolidation of the official party carried out by Calles and in the institutionalization of popular and peasant participation in the state, ensured by Cárdenas. The rural popular masses quite quickly lose this share of power, which becomes a bureaucratized system that captures, to a certain extent, the support (forced or spontaneous) of the poorer classes and manipulates the situation in terms of the needs and interests of the classes in power. The high degree of institutionalization achieved (legally or informally) by this structure of mediation explains in large measure the well-known stability of the Mexican political system.

This system extends its tentacles into the most distant corners of the Mexican countryside, in a deformed version of a supposed democracy. The key to the structure of mediation consists in the fact that it permits and uses peasant popular participation up to a certain point, beyond which the interests from below are rearranged through a curious political alchemy into the interests of the large agrarian bourgeoisie, whose clearest-thinking leaders understand that it is necessary to keep the process of capitalist development within populist channels. Víctor Flores Olea was correct when he said that "in the features of our economic structure, with its uneven, combined growth, and in the features of our political system, we believe that we have found an essential *adaptation*, a *functional* correspondence that would explain the stability within the polarization of our development."[26]

The existence of two structures of domination is observed not only at the institutional level; it is also expressed in a division of the rural bourgeoisie. On one hand, an important sector of the latter advocates the elimination of the ejido and tries at all costs to slow down the timid impulses for agrarian reform, but the other sector defends agrarian reform and declares itself in favor of coexistence between the private and the ejido sectors. The former, not very skillful, tries to push the direct forms of domination; the second understands the need for mediation. The struggle between the two sectors explains to a large degree the features of the agrarian policy of each regime.

In spite of everything, in the long run, the bourgeoisie's own class interests tend to impose themselves on the structure of mediation. This is quite clear these days, when the possibility of land distribution among the peasants is becoming limited, as much because almost all the latifundios that still exist are well-disguised as because the capitalist sector in agriculture, more vigorous every day, is not disposed to permit it. What happens is that the development of capitalism clashes openly with the existing forms of ownership; the minifundio, the ejido, and the communal lands are increasingly a troublesome obstacle to the free circulation, investment, and concentration of capital in agriculture. It is not surprising that, as noted previously, the Federal Agrarian Reform Act promulgated in 1971 hides under various layers of legal artifice an effort to adapt the legislation to the development of capitalism in the countryside. This signifies the beginning of a serious deterioration in the structure of mediation, which has used the ejido sector as a shock-absorbing cushion. To the extent that capitalism develops in the ejido and minifundio sector, with the consequent proletarianization and expulsion of labor, the stability of the political system in the rural zones will be doomed to the same degree. In fact this is already happening.

Another interesting aspect in the power structure derived from the Mexican agrarian situation is its internal dialectic. Mediation and direct power function as two substructures or opposite poles that integrate the unity of the political system. Between the structure of mediation and that of direct power, there is not merely one ongoing struggle; instead, this internal contradiction causes changes in the system to develop in accordance with a dialectical game. In this internal dialectic, crises are resolved when mediation turns into direct power, and the latter into mediation.

In order to better understand this pattern, it will be useful to take the example of caciquismo (bossism) as it operates in many regions of Mexico.[27] Many of the caciques who control vast regions of the Mexican countryside had their beginnings in the agrarian reform process, of which they were the promoters and from which they obtained their power. Even those caciques of whom this is not true attain their power by means of a complex network of coparenthood, friendships, debts, favors, and threats that enable them to control the peasant communities. Every system of bossism implies in its origin a structure of mediation in which the cacique obtains power by means of the support he attains from the community he represents; however, the power the community bestows on him is exercised in accordance with interests alien to it. Nevertheless, with time, this system comes to a halt, the cacique has learned how to turn his power into wealth, and he exercises his control in a despotic, arbitrary manner. From that moment on, he ceases to be useful to the system and finds himself with opposition from the formal system of power: the municipal president, with a part of the official party behind him, the local representatives of the federal government, and so on. A struggle begins in which the official system slowly builds a new structure of mediation, for it needs firm support in the community to eliminate the cacique. Both poles of the internal contradiction of the power structure assist in their own destruction and annihilation. To the extent that economic and political forms that contradict the dynamism of the dominant capitalist system are encouraged, mediation rapidly generates corruption. On the other hand, to the degree that the exercise of direct power breaks down traditional political and economic forms, it causes serious imbalances in a system that is not capable of absorbing, either politically or economically, the forces liberated by the process of modernization. Thus, day by day, the possibilities for the double dialectic game of the power structure are narrowed down, and the end of the present Mexican political system draws near.[28]

The Rural Bourgeoisie

The nucleus of the rural bourgeoisie is made up of the few thousand farmers who control capitalist units of production. But it is not possible for the notion of the rural sector of the bourgeoisie to be restricted in this way; the mere existence of intensive financial and commercial activity tied to agriculture should make us think about expanding the concept of rural bourgeoisie.[29] Moreover, in considering the political functions of the rural bureaucracy and technocracy and the role of (state or private) monopoly capitalism, we should determine to develop a system of stratification of the rural bourgeoisie that will enable us to understand its internal structure.[30]

The research carried out permits me to suggest the existence of four strata or segments of the rural bourgeoisie:

1. Large agrarian bourgeoisie
2. Mid-level agrarian bourgeoisie (well-to-do farmers)
3. Rural commercial bourgeoisie
4. Rural bureaucracy (agro-political bourgeoisie)

The *large agrarian bourgeoisie* is formed by a privileged sector of agrarian capitalist enterprises; this segment of the bourgeoisie is closely tied to agricultural production and to the monopolistic sector of the economy. We can distinguish three strata within this segment: the landholding bourgeoisie, the agro-commercial bourgeoisie, and the agro-industrial bourgeoisie.

The landholding bourgeoisie has "nurtured its capital through various generations dedicated to agriculture"; as such, it bases its power not only on the accumulation of capital but also on land ownership.[31] It must be pointed out that within this stratum there is a sector that is not very efficient and seems to have inherited the traditional vices of latifundismo along with the land (see chapter 3). However, one must observe that the existence of an inefficient sector of capitalist farmers is not only a reminiscence from the past: agrarian reform itself and the very governments arising out of the Mexican Revolution favored a form of "political" accumulation of capital and land, which has quite often swollen the sector of inefficient agrarian bourgeoisie. Further on I shall discuss this type of agro-political bourgeoisie.

The agro-commercial and agro-industrial bourgeoisie, on the other hand, have not generally originated in the agrarian environment: the source of their capital has been business or industry; or rather, it derives directly or indirectly from high finance, as an arm of big monopoly capital. Moreover, these strata of the bourgeoisie tend to base their profits on a combination of commercial or industrial activities with agriculture; their base generally is not formed by land ownership, but by the management of large amounts of capital (one typical example is big merchant lessees of land). The agro-industrial bourgeoisie is not as developed as the agro-commercial; for example, in a study of the two hundred largest private fortunes, only two represent an agricultural-industrial combination, while twenty-three are agro-commercial (agriculture–commerce and services).[32] This latter type of capital is the principal form of penetration of the monopoly sector into agricultural production: large enterprises that control the marketing are simultaneously financing production. Indeed, that is the path the industrial capital must take in order to link itself with agricultural production; it is the case with the agro-industrial enterprises, such as pasteurizing plants, packing plants, cotton gins, sugar mills, food-products plants, and so forth, which establish ties with the agricultural production sector by means of the agro-commercial bourgeoisie. The three strata of the large agrarian bourgeoisie are closely connected; indeed, they are inseparable. The glue that joins them together is financial capital.

In the rural zones, there is a segment of capitalist farmers at the head of units of production that do not constitute large enterprises, although they do in fact report substantial earnings. This group could be categorized as *mid-level agrarian bourgeoisie*. To a great extent, they have appeared recently, which is to say as a parallel product of agrarian reform; the group is made up of former well-to-do peasants who have managed to become bourgeoisie. They are the modern rancheros spawned by the Mexican Revolution. Along with the large agrarian bourgeoisie, these farmers have been the determinative base of support for the rapid growth of Mexican agricultural production since 1940. At the core of this segment, we also find an inefficient, backward sector, which is in danger of disappearing from the rural scene.

The mid-level agrarian bourgeoisie still has not developed production on a large scale nor in a totally entrepreneurial way. The owner's direct labor in the organization of production is quite important here; the organization of some of these farms, or ranchos, recalls somewhat their recent peasant past. Generally, they are represented politically by the regional organizations of so-called *pequeños propietarios* (small property holders), which are very strong pressure groups.

The third segment of the bourgeoisie is the *rural commercial bourgeoisie*. Behind it, we find the least developed forms of merchant capital (not connected with production, parasitic, usurious, and monopolistic). The large commercial fortunes that invest in agriculture I have defined as agro-commercial. The merchant capital referred to here, in contrast, generally has a parasitic relation with agriculture; it feeds more on the misery and ruin of the peasant than on the wealth of the bourgeoisie. In the best of cases, it is a question of simple intermediary trade between industry and agriculture, which is limited to obtaining ordinary commercial earnings. But in many cases extraordinary profits are obtained, derived from illegal loans at high rates of interest, cornering of products, arbitrary price setting, and so forth. However, one must also note that the growth of the internal market, owing as much to the proletarianization of the peasantry as to the demand generated by capitalist enterprises, has stimulated the growth of a lively trade in plastic products, clothing, bottled soft drinks, beers and other alcoholic beverages, fertilizers, prepared feed for cattle or poultry, seeds, and so forth, which is established within an important local segment of the bourgeoisie, located in the small provincial cities.

Lastly, one must mention the *rural bureaucracy*, which could also be called the agro-political bourgeoisie: the local and federal deputies from the rural zones, the presidents of important towns, the caciques, the regional presidents of the official party (the PRI), the high-level functionaries and technicians of the Ministries of Water Resources, the Interior, and Agrarian Reform, some ejido commissioners, the chiefs of the military zones, the agents of the public prosecutor's office, judges, and so on.

There is no clearer or more apparent example than the rural zones for demonstrating the bourgeois character of the upper bureaucracy and technocracy: in a large portion of cases, the high political-administrative posts are occupied by persons who possess capital. (When that is not the case, the position is held by an individual who is obviously controlled.) This is true because in the rural zones a division of labor that relieves the rural bourgeoisie of everyday political tasks is still not fully developed. But an inverse phenomenon is also occurring: by means of holding positions representing the bourgeoisie's interests, individuals originally lacking fortunes have managed to accumulate land and/or wealth sufficient to become—objectively and materially—part of the dominant class.

Of course, I am only referring to high political, administrative, or technical positions; the bulk of employees and professionals cannot be considered as part of the dominant class. The important thing is that the social groups allied with the bourgeoisie that help it in capturing surplus value through various mechanisms (political, administrative, etc.) should also be considered as part of the dominant class.

The dominant class on the rural scene is no longer represented by the latifundista, whose best-known image is that of the big land monopolist and idle man of means surrounded by superfluous luxuries. Nevertheless, in many places there is still a desire to hold on to the idea of the large landholder as the peasant's enemy. In fact, the dominant exploiting class in the Mexican countryside is the rural bourgeoisie, composed of the segments and strata enumerated here. It is true that inefficient and parasitic sectors still exist, especially among the landholding bourgeoisie and the mid-level agrarian bourgeoisie, the commercial bourgeoisie, and the agro-political bourgeoisie. But nowadays these groups see their power as seriously threatened and contested by the landholding-entrepreneurial, agro-commercial, and agro-industrial bourgeoisies, which, supported by technocratic sectors of the agro-political bureaucracy, lead a struggle against archaic forms of political domination. Apparently, the different segments of the rural bourgeoisie tend, these days, toward three conflicting political positions:

1. A traditional current tied to the influence of the caciques, quite corrupt, which receives support from the most inefficient groups of large farmers and from the rural commercial bourgeoisie. I shall label it *old-style populism*.
2. A position tied to the interests of big monopoly capital, to the needs of the agro-commercial and agro-industrial bourgeoisie. This position

is characterized by its interest in the promotion of infrastructure projects and by the support it gives to measures to "modernize" the political structure.

3. A current supported basically by sectors of the mid-level agrarian bourgeoisie, which are attempting to replace the traditional forms of power through renewed systems of mediation that, even as they facilitate the enrichment of this mid-level bourgeoisie, permit extending the era of political equilibrium that has been experienced in the countryside. We shall call it *neo-populism*.

The old-style populism represents the interests of the class segments that benefit directly from the alliance and the articulation between the bourgeoisie and the peasantry. Here we find portions of the rural bourgeoisie embedded in the now-exhausted structure of mediation that was forged during the period of agrarian reform (caciques, moneylenders, acaparadores, decadent farmers, corrupt functionaries, etc.). In comparison, the private monopoly interests of the most modern segment of the rural bourgeoisie are seeking a reorganization of political power that will eliminate the growth of parasitic excrescences at the core of the agrarian economy. The interests of state capitalism have found an ally in some sectors of the mid-level agrarian bourgeoisie, and they fight the old structure of mediation—the old-style populism—for control of the peasant communities. During the years 1970–1973, this tendency sought with little success an alliance with the agro-commercial and agro-industrial segments, a search that has given way to a type of technocratic populism.[33]

The Rural Proletariat

The most visible sign of the penetration of capitalist relations of production into the countryside is the presence of more than 3 million day laborers, who represent more than half of the population economically active in agriculture. If we include employees and family members who have assisted without remuneration, the total population lacking land rose to around 3.5 million persons in 1960. In 1970, the total decreased (to 3.03 million), but it increased in relative terms (from 57.4 percent to 59.3 percent of the total population economically active in agriculture).

The rural proletariat is twice as large as the industrial proletariat, notwithstanding the fact that it lacks political or union organizations to represent it. It is numerically the most important segment of the Mexican working class, but it is the social force that has the least political presence and the weakest capacity to exert pressure. Its very existence as a class continues to be ignored through use of the label "peasants without land," or the euphemism "ejidatarios with rights reserved." In 1967 the CNC, an official organization affiliated with the PRI, was given a serious warning as to the political importance of agricultural day laborers and the urgent need for the "massive organization of these workers into rural unions, affiliated with the CNC."[34] However, the CNC has never managed to follow this advice because the rural proletariat demands two things that the bourgeoisie cannot give it: land and work.

There is no usable land in a condition to be distributed to more than 3 million persons, nor does the dynamism of the entrepreneurial system attain the levels necessary to absorb them completely as salaried labor power. Thus, the demands of the rural proletariat are an attack on the survival of the system. If, for example, the state takes up requests of the type made by the peasants, it will not be capable of satisfying them: agrarian reform can no longer advance very much further along the path of endowment with land. The result is the increasingly numerous land invasions.

If, on the other hand, the proletariat initiates a struggle for increasing wages and for obtaining secure, steady employment, the large entrepreneurs will refuse: what madness to increase rural wages significantly when the labor supply is so much greater than demand! Thus, the struggle of the rural proletariat has turned back toward demands of a peasant character and has been channeled by the peasant movements, properly speaking. The last great example of that is Rubén Jaramillo's battles in Morelos; but when they took on an overtly proletarian ideology and character, the government did not hesitate—on that account—over the use of violence and murdered the peasant leader in 1962. The peasant character of the struggle of the rural day laborers has been maintained up until now, but with a tone that is more violent every day, expressed, for example, in the invasions of land.[35]

These days, rural day laborers are experiencing a transitional phase with respect to the nature of their struggle. Little by little, after each land invasion, each march, each demonstration, and each protest, the authentically proletarian struggle will continue to appear—aiming its blows directly at the bourgeoisie and its political representatives, asking not for a peasant Arcadia or for a Barataria island but, rather, for a new socialist world, asking not for reforms in the system but, instead, to take power, asking not for land in bits and pieces but for all the land.

Chapter 6

And If the Peasants Become Extinct . . .

"But the Emperor has nothing at all on!" said a little child.
—Hans Christian Andersen
"The Emperor's New Clothes"

IN THE preceding chapters I have given a panoramic vision of Mexican agrarian structure and of the interpretation I propose for understand-standing it. Next, it seems indispensable to me to approach the topic from a more concrete, more precise perspective in order to show in the following chapters how it is possible to analyze three issues that to me seem crucial for understanding present-day Mexico: the crisis of the political system, the extinction of the peasantry, and the indigenous culture. In contrast to the preceding chapters, the final three chapters of this book are an application of my methodology to situations of juncture and to concrete cases, with the objective of showing the need to apply a multifaceted analysis that will avoid economism and reductionist interpretations. These three chapters were originally written as independent essays.[1]

The three problems I treat in the final part of the book are closely linked with one another. I consider the way in which the decomposition of the peasantry contributes to the political crisis, to the extent that it erodes the social bases of the system of power. At the same time, the Mexican state finds its strength in the populist and reformist perspectives that are being opened with the processes of refunctionalization and protection of the peasant economy. This specific articulation of economic and political phenomena, which I have called permanent primitive accumulation, has its particular expression in the regions where the peasantry forms part of some ethnic group: very complex ideological phenomena occur there, enabling one to understand how cultural contradictions become forms of political mediation. It will be possible to observe the curious ideological transfigurations of exploitation (racism), mediation (liberal *indigenismo*), decomposition of the peasantry (technocratism), and its refunctionalization (populist demagoguery).

To me, it seems appropriate to approach these topics by beginning with the most obvious critical point of the Mexican political system: the mystery of the presidential succession. From this starting point, I will unravel the confusion bit by bit, in order to show how the agrarian structure reveals several key elements of Mexican politics.

The Political Imagery of the Independence of the State and the Mystery of the Presidential Succession

For a system of exploitation of the majority by the minority to be able to reproduce itself requires the presence in the society of, among other things, certain enigmatic fluids summoned together by the bureaucratic witches' sabbath of the dominant politicians: ideological streams that filter into even the most intimate interstices of daily life, with the aim of transforming, to state it as a Pythagorean metaphor, the mystery of the *number* into the reality of the *drama*. In countries that have attained a modern bourgeois democracy, electoral and parliamentary mathematics seem to create political tragedy. Other countries that, like Mexico, live outside the Pythagorean world of Western political arithmetic have varied, original ways of nurturing the mystery upon which the edifice of politics is erected. In Mexico, the democratic, Greek number of votes, creator of political life, has been replaced by a legend of an almost medieval character. It is that of the *tapado* (hidden candidate), who, like a new *golem*, waits until the right cabalistic combination of the letters of the name of God is put into his mouth in order to take on an independent life of his own, for precisely six years. Like the golem of the old Jewish tradition, the Mexican tapado also destroys his progenitor, but he meets his own end in the Talmudic words "no reelection."

Nobody knows how the president is selected in Mexico. All the speculations of political commentators, journalists, historians, and political hopefuls reach the same banal conclusion: the outgoing president names his successor, driven by an incomprehensible, chance mixture of pressures, sympathies, treacheries, and cronyism. Everyone assumes that there is a more or less small group of select politicians, located at the summit of the apparatus, who share in the "secret" of the succession; but for the last thirty to forty years, all of the "initiated" have remained silent about the hidden mechanisms and have jealously borne their secret to the grave. Every six years, nevertheless, "public opinion" racks its brains and is kept on edge in the face of the mystery of the presidential succession.

No doubt remains, however, that within some period of time, let us say by the middle of the twenty-first century, historians will cast a dispassionate look of boredom over the long series of presidential successions that one hopes will not characterize the entire political history of the final two-thirds of the twentieth century. They will have the same wise attitude as do the worker and the peasant of today, who just will not understand that a boring, bureaucratic candidate selection can miraculously become, for the bourgeois and petty bourgeois intelligentsia, an exciting political mystery. Thus, the first Sunday in July at the end of each six-year term has been, for many Mexicans, a day like any other, one on which the ballot boxes are filled with votes, much as the speeches that the politicians make on the other days of each year of each six-year term are filled with empty words. It is true that sometimes the boring ritual appears to be bathed in blood, but that does not affect the essentially bureaucratic ceremony of the presidential successions. After all, the internal struggle to obtain the presidency of the Republic is no different in form from the obscure battles unleashed among office workers trying to attain command of some humid, mildewed subaltern tax collection office. It does not cease to be disturbing that for decades the occupancy of the highest political position in the nation has been decided in such a low fashion; nevertheless, it is not possible to fail to recognize that this political mechanism forms part of what is perhaps the most highly perfected bourgeois state machinery in Latin America.

It is precisely this advanced, sophisticated character of the Mexican state that enables one to explain how the banality in the form of presidential selection has become the principal mystery that political science in Mexico seeks unavailingly to solve. Only a profoundly capitalist state in a country where the modern bourgeois class has taken power by the revolutionary path can manage to impose, in such a radical, enduring fashion, the complex of historical myths and ideological byways that in Mexico justify and prop up bourgeois hegemony. At the same time, the despotic, enigmatic mechanism for choosing the president was forged in an agrarian country; consequently, the peasantry was a fundamental part of the system. It is probable, moreover, that the peasants are the ones who possess the key to the mystery.

In reality, the mystery of the presidential succession reduces to the following proposition: in Mexico there is a state so autonomous of the class struggles, so Bonapartist, so exceptional, so revolutionary, so national, so far above society and so arbiterlike that it is capable of self-reproduction and self-nurture without the need for intervention from the social forces. The state assumes that it is the determining actor of the society, that it gives life to the social classes and ordains and determines the form of economic development. To whom can it occur, under these conditions, that the state is nothing but a superstructure, whose characteristics inundate its roots in the conditions under which civil society lives? This idea recalls the Marxist tradition of thought. It is worth reproducing a little-known sentence written by Marx a few years before his death: "The apparent supreme independent existence of the State is in itself only an appearance and . . . it is in all its forms an excrescence of the society; just as its very apparition occurs only at a certain stage of social development, it disappears again as soon as society reaches a stage not previously attained."[2]

It is interesting to propose here an alternative plan for a mystery. What conditions will cause the disappearance of the so-called Mexican political system? What type of crisis will finish off the bureaucratic ceremony of the presidential successions? These questions cancel out the postulate of an unhealthily autonomous state, deus ex machina of the social dynamic. These uncertainties brusquely confront us with what, deep down, almost all of us know: that the six-year personality of the one chosen by the PRI to govern the country lacks *historical* significance, that the mystery of the presidential succession is nothing but the sleep-inducing vapor of political ideology destined to hide the *fundamental* historical fact, namely, that the bourgeoisie has hegemony in Mexico, to put it bluntly, which is at times how one has to say things in countries where the imaginary clothes accumulate haphazardly on the naked body of the emperor. Of course, in Mexico's history, the peasants occupy the place of the child who discovers the emperor's nakedness; the difference consists in the fact that here the peasants pay for their discovery with their lives. But before continuing with our story, let us take a look at what the emperor's clothes are hiding.

The Triple Invisible Domination of the Oligarchy, the New Rich, and the Technocracy

First. No one will have failed to recognize the presence of a repressive, authoritarian, and despotic political tendency in Mexico; many, moreover, have suffered from it in person. Does it owe its existence only to the bad humor that is awakened in some politicians in the face of the upsurge of outbreaks of opposition? or to the presence of pressure groups with fascist tendencies? On the contrary, I believe that it is possible to locate the roots of this tendency—certainly the most powerful but not totally hegemonic—in the concessions that one part of the political bureaucracy is accustomed to making to the segment of the bourgeoisie that enjoys the double peculiarity of having an old tradition and of forming a structural part of the financial oligarchy. One is dealing with a bourgeoisie that was born in the past century, that has its own history, its Porfirian original sin, and that has, therefore, known different types of states. It is for this reason, among others, that it does not identify itself fully with the "revolutionary" state forged by Carranza, Obregón, Calles, and Cárdenas and that it maintains a certain autonomy with respect to the government. It is precisely this relative independence that enables it to exercise a decisive weight in the political apparatus without having attained, however, complete political hegemony.

This bourgeois sector has crystallized into a political sector sufficiently well identified that it operates in a unified way: the regional bourgeoisies of Monterrey, Guadalajara, Puebla, and Saltillo are its most obvious expression, and the Employers' Confederation of the Mexican Republic (COPARMEX), its sharpest (noneconomic) political tool. One is dealing with a bourgeois segment that has been oriented by preference to the promotion of large enterprises for the manufacture of intermediate and capital goods in close association with foreign capital; it also includes the large commercial bourgeoisie, the brewers, part of the agrarian bourgeoisie, and the large livestock ranchers. Accordingly, it does not look favorably on "excessive" state intervention in the economy and is opposed to a fiscal policy that will empower state monopoly mechanisms and impose taxes on the high-income brackets. The "solution" for this sector sets out to channel state action toward increasing exports (of raw materials, petroleum, maquiladora products, manufactured products of large transnational enterprises that have a sure market). Moreover, the state should, in the view of this bourgeoisie, take charge of the large infrastructure projects (dams, communications) in order to open the way for private capital. From the viewpoint of a modern, refined politician, this position seems to represent a barbarous appetite of the bourgeoisie for accumulating capital by the most rapid routes, with the help of the imperialist system; it seems to reflect a brutal, undisguised interest in profit on the part of the bourgeoisie, desiring the dividends for itself and leaving the dirty work to the state, lacking a certain modern sensibility that might contain and channel the development of capitalism in Mexico in a global way, with the fewest possible conflicts.

The vocation for hegemony that this bourgeois segment undoubtedly has is crudely embodied in the image of the ultrareactionary, antidemocratic bourgeois. Its efforts toward achieving hegemony are more apparent and more menacing every day: it has managed to create its own union system (the Federación de Sindicatos Independientes, or Federation of Independent Unions), which in Monterrey, for example, brings together more than 70 percent of the industrial proletariat; one of the most important broadcasting media—television—is almost totally in its hands, as are several large-circulation newspapers. Its skillful effort at infiltration and control in the Ministry of the Treasury, one of its most important channels for exerting pressure, appears to have advanced quite far. (It is well known that the gift of a packet of stock certificates to high-level functionaries achieves something more than simply buying them off: it turns the bureaucracy into bourgeoisie.) Its proximity to two extraordinarily sensitive sectors of the Mexican economy, exports and tourism, situates it in a favorable position to influence strongly, and sometimes decisively, the course of the state's economic policies. Similarly, this sector has taken an important step in the political realm: the creation of the Enterprise Coordinating Council, which was begun under the presidency of a wise theoretician and politician from among the bourgeoisie, the brewer Sánchez Navarro.

The political segments of a class do not always coincide with the economic strata into which it is divided; that is the case with the bourgeois segment referred to here. This is probably the cause of the crude, brutal, and incomplete nature of the political positions this segment asserts; these positions do not set forth a refined plan or model of the *general* interests of the entire bourgeoisie. In fact, this is a segment of the monopoly oligarchy, but absent from it is a key economic group whose presence here would flesh out the profiles of an entire economic stratum and would permit the financial oligarchy as a whole to present itself with greater political unity. The absent economic group referred to is that of the big bankers, who manage the real nervous system of the monopoly economy, who for years have supported a position very close to that of the state, and who maintain very intimate ties to executive power and to the public sector of the economy. This peculiar isolation and the singular placement of the big bankers (at whose head figures Legorreta's Banamex group) form a bulwark against the hegemony of the monopoly oligarchy. This clique was enormously strengthened in 1982 when all private banks were nationalized.

Second. Is there any reason why the portion of the bourgeoisie that has continued to rise thanks to the support of the "revolutionary" state should not feel deeply "revolutionary"? In the already solidly established existence of this segment of the bourgeoisie, the political current that permits itself some populist whims, that believes itself enormously nationalistic, that has often been linked with the mediating mechanisms of the political apparatus, and that supports various forms of state interventionism in the economy finds a secure base and a certain safety. In the crystallization of this political segment, historic elements and economic characteristics intersect as well. This is a group of "new rich" that grew up in the shade of state protectionism, of the policy of import substitution, of tax exemptions accorded by the government, and of the indirect subsidies that they receive (e.g., special rates for electricity consumption). In spite of the fact that this is the bourgeois sector most closely tied to central power, it is the least independent and presents the blurriest political profile: it comfortably lets itself be represented by the political bureaucracy, which at the same time contributes to swelling the ranks of this segment permanently by encouraging forms of accumulation of capital among high-level functionaries. While this political segment is not dominant on its own, a part of the political bureaucracy exercises hegemony in its name and for its benefit. This new bourgeoisie also has its own geographic seat: the Federal District and the state of Mexico (the industrial zone of Mexico City and its periphery).

From the viewpoint of the state and its political bureaucracy, this segment of the bourgeoisie has proven to be the most "manipulable," the one that adapts with greatest ease to the economic development models proposed by the state. However, this segment has encouraged various reformist currents opposed to despotic, repressive forms and seeking new alternatives for *apertura* (opening) for the political situation. Less unified and less coherent than its counterpart, the northern bourgeoisie, it has been, paradoxically, along with the bankers, closest to the decision-making power. Its reformist positions manifest themselves especially on agrarian subjects, where they promote reforms to eliminate the obstacles that the concentration of private ownership of land presents to the concentration and circulation of capital; measures such as the collective (and efficient) ejidos, the Water Act limiting land ownership to twenty hectares, and the Mexican Food System are viewed positively or at least are not hindered by this segment. In the interior of this group, some weak political outbursts demanding a certain democratization of the system have occurred. This has been the case with the entrepreneurs who timidly hint at their wish that a less repressive, more parliamentary system might function in Mexico.

These days this segment already shelters a significant portion of the large bourgeoisie that is oriented toward the production of direct consumer goods (as an effect of the process of substitution of imports of such goods), but it also contains layers of mid-level entrepreneurs who are persistently looking for all kinds of protective measures from the state to enhance their wealth. For many years, CANACINTRA (the Cámara Nacional de la Industria de la Transformación) managed to channel the interests of this segment of the protected, "revolutionary" bourgeoisie. However, CANACINTRA never succeeded in being entirely an organ for expression of their interests and was always more a form of governmental control.

Third. The enormous, confused political bureaucracy that directly controls the state apparatus contains within it a great diversity of political groups and sectors. But to the extent that modern financial capitalism has continued to grow stronger, a modern technocracy that represents and constitutes an even newer segment of the bourgeoisie has developed: the sector linked to state capitalism. The sector's interests are still quite submerged in and colored by the old forms of paternalistic backwardness that have, to a large extent, characterized the state's economic policy. Nevertheless, these days, the interests tied to the large infrastructure projects, oil, electricity, steel, urban construction, ejido production, marketing, state financing, and so forth, form a conglomerate of economic activities with a marked character of their own. Planning, organization, and efficiency are the concepts that guide the high state technocracy in its struggle to control the key mechanisms of economic development.

Nowadays, political hegemony in the interior of the Mexican state is found in the hands of a triple alliance of this state technocracy, the big bankers, and the new "revolutionary" bourgeoisie. This power bloc, which is surrounded and protected by an infinite number of groups and sectors of very diverse nature, represents the totality of interests of the bourgeoisie. This bloc would not enjoy relative stability if a political accord had not been reached with the bourgeois sector having the most oligarchic leanings, by virtue of which the hegemonic bloc holds the reins of power directly but permits that sector to interfere constantly and significantly in the decision-making processes.

The Decomposition of the Peasantry and the Political Crisis

During the six-year term of Luis Echeverría (1970–76), the triple alliance appeared in the guise of a tentative, disconcerting *apertura democrática* (democratic opening). Use of this term has represented an attempt to indicate how the governing elements have decided to open the windows so that the people might admire from afar the spectacle of a democracy promised but not yet in place, and so that perfumed breezes might enter, making people forget, among other things, the massacre of Tlateloco in 1968. But the sweetness of the "democratic opening" only showed that the country was going deeper into a profound political crisis.

In fact, the politics of apertura had as a basis a slight reaccommodation of the dominant bloc: a greater rapprochement between some of the interests that I have called the new bourgeoisie and the political model of the state technocracy, for the purpose of a somewhat battered, frustrated attempt to control the oligarchy's ambitions. The most important political objective of this effort was precisely that of halting the slow destruction of the traditional mediating mechanisms that had afforded the country great stability over a long period. This degeneration of the state's legitimacy has been at once the cause and the effect of the cracks and crevices that have continued to appear in the hegemonic bloc. The erosion of the structures for mediation and legitimization of bourgeois power not only indicates the decrepitude of certain institutions (the CNC, the Confederación Nacional de Obreros Públicos [CNOP], the Ministry of Agrarian Reform, etc.) but also implies—to the extent that it concerns agriculture—the dramatic process of annihilation of a social class that until ten or fifteen years ago was the most numerous one and the repository of the most cherished myths of the Mexican Revolution: the peasantry.

The Mexican peasantry as we know it today is in a certain sense an invention of the bourgeoisie, which created it in its own image and likeness. After drowning the revolutionary peasantry in blood, the bourgeois sector that consolidated its power as a result of the Mexican Revolution began a process of indispensable reforms in order to open a clear channel for capitalist relations of production. In this way, as a fruit of the fear, the shrewdness, and the socializing petty bourgeois dreams of the dominant classes—but also as a fruit of the popular struggle—the modern Mexican peasantry was born. In succeeding phases of history, the Mexican peasant continued acquiring his present-day character: Obregón and Calles imagined him as a North American *farmer;* Cárdenas consolidated him as a minifundista trapped in the capitalist market, with some collectivist touches, but yoked to the state apparatus. Many years later, the "agrarianism" of López Mateos spread the image of a semi-proletariat endowed with a sliver of arid or mountainous land. Each government makes its own particular contribution to the process of modeling the Mexican peasant. Thus, as a result of intrigues and alliances that in their day expressed the correlation of political forces, in which the great peasant struggles were subordinated, there arose bit by bit the heterogeneous mass called ejidatarios, minifundistas, comuneros, and so on. The Mexican peasants are not the reminiscence of a dark past but the by-product of the growth of capitalism (although "underdeveloped"—if I may be permitted the paradox!).

The Mexican peasantry was situated by capitalist logic as the intermediate pole of attraction between two basically antagonistic classes: the proletariat and the bourgeoisie. Its role had to be political as well as economic: a balancing factor in the class conflicts and an element in fixing in place the labor power that the country's economy could not employ in industry or services. Here is the paradox of Mexico's underdevelopment: in order to grow, capital has required in Mexico a historic type of production, the peasant smallholding economy, that is called upon to disappear in modern society. Like all paradoxes, this is a matter of a contradiction of reality itself; the contradiction consists in the fact that capitalist relations of production need and, simultaneously, destroy the smallholding peasantry. But this contradiction is expressed differently at each political juncture. For example, during the Cárdenas era the need to create a peasant economy prevailed, even at the cost of sacrificing some interests of the rural bourgeoisie.

Today the situation is different, and this contradiction is colored by the presence of new elements: the advanced decomposition and proletarianization of the peasantry and the significant, decisive presence of (both private and state) monopoly capital in agriculture. These new conditions, combined with the agricultural crisis, have signaled the need to reorganize the reformed (ejido) sector of agriculture. The possibilities for reorganization waiver between two extreme alternatives:

1. permitting the free circulation and concentration of capital in the ejido sector, that is, the open encouragement of an agrarian bourgeoisie on ejido lands and the consequent expulsion and pauperization of thousands of ejidatarios (the path of private monopoly); and
2. directing the concentration of capital in a controlled fashion, financed by the state, in the form of collective ejidos, cooperatives, and/or decentralized state enterprises (the path of state monopoly).

The evidence enables us to assume that during recent years there have been several skirmishes between different factions of the dominant class in order that one alternative or the other might prevail. On one hand, the new Agrarian Reform Act approved during the Echeverría administration allowed the leasing of ejido land in a veiled way, and no serious official effort to restrain the concentration of land that the renting of ejido parcels implies was observed. On the other hand, the Echeverría government made a certain commitment to the organization of collective ejidos and cooperatives, a commitment that, while it went a little beyond traditional demagoguery, did not succeed in fostering a significant, efficient collective agriculture sector. Nor did the government use the new Water Act, which could legally impede land concentration in the new irrigation districts. One could say that a critical equilibrium was created between the two extreme alternatives. It is evident that the dilemma was not resolved during Echeverría's term, and a virulent agricultural lockout in Sinaloa and Sonora put the incoming president on notice that the rural bourgeoisie was not disposed to back down. The concrete result of this lockout was quite significant: the government found itself obliged to make room for, and to permit representation of, agricultural entrepreneurs on a tripartite commission of the highest rank that was supposed to decide agrarian matters of the greatest importance. The absence of any representatives of agricultural laborers on this tripartite commission is certainly quite significant. In fact, it was the López Portillo government (1976–82) that, in implementing the Federal Agricultural Development Act, opted for the first alternative, slightly tempered, however, by the reformist features of the Mexican Food System.

Whatever shape the process of concentration and accumulation of capital in agriculture assumes, there is no doubt that the era in which the peasant smallholding economy could have a key role in the political and economic equilibrium of the Mexican agrarian structure is coming to its end. For the dominant classes, the problem consists in getting rid of the smallholding peasantry without causing political chaos and, at the same time, finding an alternative path of capitalist development. For the exploited classes, the problem consists in directing the process of dissolution of the peasantry, not toward an attempt to recover its primitive status, but toward the consolidation of proletarian forms of struggle directed at combating the most modern capitalist forms of exploitation. The process will be long and difficult, for on either side of the line of fire there are still traces of the populist romanticism that does not wish to see the old peasantry disappear.

What is the nature of the crisis Mexican agriculture has been experiencing? According to some hopeful populist theoreticians, it is a structural crisis of the capitalist, or neo-latifundista, path that has been making way for the revitalization of the small peasant economy. In reality, the confluence of two different types of crisis has significantly confused the picture. On one hand, the great world crisis that began openly in 1974 (of which the previous world agricultural crisis was a harbinger) made itself felt in Mexico, especially in the enormous contraction of exports of agricultural products and production of industrial inputs; thus, it affected principally capitalist agricultural enterprises. On the other hand, however, the crisis of the peasant economy, the high costs of which resisted market prices less and less, has advanced inexorably from the early 1960s on. The simultaneity of the two crises during the years 1974–75 was truly catastrophic for Mexican agriculture. Inflation has had a terribly disorganizing effect for the small peasant economy: on one hand, this type of economy does not respond automatically and positively (by increasing production) to price increases for agricultural products; on the other hand, the increase in the cost of living simultaneously, and contradictorily, causes impulses to raise production and to seek more sources of wage labor outside the family agricultural unit.

It must be observed that not only have the two crises been devastating for the small peasant but they have profoundly affected the most backward, most inefficient sector of the rural bourgeoisie, which supports itself thanks to ground rent and to superexploitation of labor. This sector has the combined economic vices of the peasant (inefficiency) and the bourgeois (greed) but does not bring together the qualities of effort in labor of the former or the efficiency of the latter. Thus, Mexican agriculture has been passing through a stage of purification. In spite of the fact that, generally speaking, the agrarian bourgeoisie has had difficulties, which it has largely transferred to the peasant and the agricultural worker, during the next period of recuperation from the cyclical crisis the modern sector of the class dominant in the countryside will find itself strengthened and with the path ahead clearer. Clearer and purified from the *economic* point of view, for the monopoly alternative will appear with greater purity; however, it will not be the same from the *political* perspective. From the economic point of view, the crisis is the intersection of a crisis of over-production (linked to the world situation) with a crisis of the inefficient traditional economy; the simplest solution would seem to be the monopoly way out (under private and state direction). But this solution bristles with political problems, for it inevitably implies the elimination of a large part of the smallholding peasantry. Nevertheless, there does not seem to be another alternative, unless one contemplates global change of the system. For these reasons, the López Portillo government tried to provide a double solution to the double crisis: populist reformism with the Mexican Food System and apertura for capital by means of the Agricultural Development Act, which legalizes the rental of ejido land.

I want to get beyond one possible criticism of what is stated here, for previously there has been no shortage of PRI theoreticians seeking to interpret my thesis in a particularly clever way: they imagine that the Marxist interpretation suggests that the capitalist organization of agriculture is promoted with the goal that proletarianization will bring with it a new mode of production, the socialist mode (and they accuse us of coinciding with the bourgeoisie in this interest in promoting capitalism). Even the most dogmatic, most schematic Marxist would contemplate a thesis of this nature with repugnance. To begin with, Marxists do not "propose" forms of, or plans for, capitalist development; furthermore, in Mexico, no one has called on them to propose anything of the kind. (One should not confuse Marxists with certain intellectuals from the PRI's IEPES [Instituto de Estudios Políticos, Económicos y Sociales] who delude themselves into thinking that someone is going to pay attention to what they suggest.)

Marxists, starting from a praxis, verify and analyze the process of capitalist accumulation, and when they propose reforms, they do so with a social and political effort oriented toward *overthrowing* the capitalist system. Every Marxist knows that there are no formulas for putting the revolutionary moment in place; our critics seek to put in our mouths the absurd idea that the more capitalism there is, the more social contradictions and, therefore, revolutionary possibilities there will be. The violence of the ruin of the peasantry horrifies our critics, and, in a borrowing from romanticism, they do not know how to "propose" anything beyond protective measures, which in the end protect the exploiter more than the exploited. Marxists, on the other hand, are aware of the rebirth of the peasant in the figure of the worker, join in that process, and endeavor to

138

examine its political consequences with the aim of enriching revolutionary practice.

The six years of "apertura" under Echeverría demonstrate the ineffectualness of an autonomous "populist" alternative with a neo-Cardenista slant, which, in the name of the "revolutionary" bourgeoisie in alliance with the technocracy, would be able to implement a model that would favor the development of capitalism in the countryside and simultaneously prevent the proletarianization and pauperization of the peasantry. On the contrary, application of the Echeverrista model showed the following:

1. The collectivization of the ejido rapidly reaches a crossroads: it creates either a corrupt, paternalistic system (as in the sisal-producing ejidos in Yucatán) or efficient enterprises that accelerate the proletarianization of the peasant and migration to the cities (as in Sinaloa).
2. The capitalist enterprises with ejido participation, whether cooperatives or not, create a polarization and a confrontation between a minority of peasants undergoing "kulakization" and a majority of agricultural day laborers.
3. Broad sectors of the agrarian bourgeoisie are violently opposed to ejido collectivization and have not allowed it to displace them from the irrigation districts in which they rent ejido land on a large scale.
4. The plan for new reforms in the countryside has not been useful in reconstructing the battered structure of mediation and legitimization (the CNC, the PRI, the Ministry of Agrarian Reform, etc.). Indeed, the independent, almost spontaneous peasant struggle has become more acute (land invasions, guerrilla warfare), important concessions have been made to the bourgeoisie (the tripartite commission), and the "agrarianist" bureaucracy has lost the power to bring pressure to bear within the state and has had to resort to absorbing corrupt populist groups (Serrano's CAM, Garzón's Confederación Campesina Independiente [CCI]) in order to recover its lost image a bit (the Ocampo Pact).

It is worthwhile to single out some aspects of the last two points enumerated. First, the discontent of the agrarian bourgeoisie (expressed in the lockout as well as in the murdering of peasants) was a part of the unhappiness of the oligarchic segment of the bourgeoisie. Although it grudgingly tolerated Echeverría's *aperturismo* during the presidential succession process in 1975–76 (it was too busy safeguarding its own economic interests from the effects of the crisis), it struck back at the government for its democratic caprices: it directly precipitated an internal crisis in the only truly important officially authorized (rightist) opposition party. Thus, the National Action Party (PAN) did not manage to select a presidential candidate, and the PRI-government candidate had no remedy but to run a ridiculous electoral campaign without legal opponents. This situation, anomalous for a state that claims to be democratic, meant a serious blow to the factions that were supporting the relative independence of the technocracy and political bureaucracy. In fact, because the future president and his team had come to power in such unfavorable, illegitimate circumstances, they found the proverbially ample possibilities of maneuvering with executive power straitened.

Second, the upper political bureaucracy also lost independence, owing to the fact that it no longer finds itself comfortably installed at the peak of a pyramid of mediations that has caciquismo as a base. The modernization of agrarian capitalism and the ruin of the characteristic social base of caciquismo—the peasant communities—brought about the need to replace the caciques, who had, moreover, largely ceased to perform their traditional mediating functions adequately and had degenerated into local and regional despots. But the formal administration—municipal and state—does not always find itself in a situation to take over and to ensure the status quo without unsettled moments. Thus, the political faction that quixotically fought against the injustices of the bosses lost its Sancho Panza in the course of the struggle; that is, it lost a good part of the peasantry that served as its squire and as a shock-absorbing cushion. In this way, it set up the agrarian bases of a political crisis.

In sum, and for the purposes of the argument outlined in this essay, we can locate three series of factors that can, in the short run, modify the peculiarities of the political process in Mexico:

1. The changes in the social composition of the rural masses as a result of the polarization and de-peasantization inherent in the expansion and concentration of capital in agriculture.
2. The rise of a new order of social and political conflicts in the countryside, in which an enormous mass of day laborers and a growing agricultural proletariat are beginning to figure as principal protagonists. These problems, united with the economic crisis and the tensions that migrations to the cities generate, have contributed to weakening important sectors of the powerful classes and to increasing their distrust with respect to governmental political mechanisms used to overcome conflicts (collective ejidos, the Water Act, cooperatives, the new Agrarian Reform Act, the unification and centralization of rural credit, the Mexican Food System, the Agriculture Development Act, the blocking of union organization, the Ocampo Pact, denunciations of caciquismo, demagoguery with regard to nationalization of irrigation districts, etc.).
3. The gradual disappearance of the peasantry as the social base of the PRI-government, the crisis of the structures of mediation (e.g., caciquismo), the failure or limited character of the reforms in the agrarian

structure, and the strong pressures from the agrarian bourgeoisie, which
have undermined the relative autonomy of the political bureaucracy,
which was itself attained thanks to the agrarian policy of the governments of the Mexican Revolution.

In Mexico, the process of de-peasantization affects the whole of the
society: the so-called demographic explosion, the squandering of labor
power, the growth of the so-called marginal sectors, the violence against
the private ownership of land, *bracerismo* (the temporary migration of
laborers to the United States), runaway migration to the cities, unemployment, low wages, and so forth, are phenomena that seem to be closely
linked to the gradual disappearance of the peasantry. The Mexican political system is not well prepared to resist the avalanche of conflicts and
problems that continue to appear one after another during the process of
accumulation of capital in the countryside.

The political crisis came to a head because divisions and serious differences appeared among segments of the hegemonic bloc. The oligarchy
mistrusted the technocracy to the extent that the latter lost autonomy
and legitimacy and demonstrated that it was not very adept at absorbing,
organizing, and mediating for the proletarianized masses in the countryside. The new bourgeoisie, which had less and less every day, was dispersed
across a broad spectrum of political factions, losing a certain coherence
that gave it the assurance of being indulged and protected by the state,
and also losing confidence in the reformist plans that it had timidly
supported. The result was that its alliance with the state technocracy
appeared weakened to the same degree that its traditionally limited political and economic unity had been eliminated. As a consequence, the
failure of the technocratic populism encouraged by a certain rapprochement between technocrats and new bourgeoisie—which was one of the
marks of the beginning of Echeverría's term—caused demoralization or
disorientation in the ranks of the bureaucracy to increase and ignited
considerable ill will among the small and middle-level urban bourgeoisie.

I make no attempt here to state that the fundamental cause of the
symptoms of political crisis resides in the breakdown of the small peasant
economy and the consequent proletarianization of the rural masses. I am
simply trying to underscore the great influence that these factors exercise
over the change in the rules of the political game. In order to emphasize
the importance of the rural factors of the crisis, it is interesting to cite
two further aspects of the problem. First, it is enough to state that the
hub of the sociopolitical dynamic has moved from the countryside to the
city; however, those governing have not yet totally accustomed and adapted themselves to the idea that it is no longer so easy to respond to, for
example, the rural vote in order to demonstrate the system's legitimacy

in the face of the growing open or veiled opposition of important sectors of workers or middle strata in the cities.

Second, and this is quite important, it is possible to observe the enormous influence that the recent agrarian conflicts have had on the structure of the army. From 1960 to 1975, a period in which the peasant struggle intensified considerably (Rubén Jaramillo, guerrilla warfare in Guerrero and other regions, organization of the CCI [today CIOAC, Central Independiente de Obreros Agrícolas y Campesinos], invasions of land, work stoppages in sugar-producing regions, etc.), the army fulfilled a repressive function essential to maintaining the status quo in the countryside. As a result, especially in the 1960s, the army was modernized technically and logistically; it trained elite corps for so-called counterinsurgency or irregular warfare and for controlling "civil disturbances" and acquired large quantities of modern armaments from Belgium, Israel, and the United States to replace its antiquated weapons. (Symptomatically, the large purchases of armaments and ammunition occurred in 1961 and 1968.) The Echeverría administration inherited an already relatively modern army that, aware of its political importance, acquired in its confrontations with popular struggles, puts pressure on the government with the goal of finding a place of greater prestige and importance within the state. The results have been obvious: notable improvement in the living conditions of officers and soldiers, renewal of commands, and, especially, a significant leap in the organization and level of military education. In 1972 a plan for Military Educational Reform was begun; among other things, it led to the creation of an important military university. On the technical side, there has been a total renovation of the air force, which until 1974 was practically nonexistent. (That year, about fifty airplanes and twenty helicopters were purchased—unprecedented figures.)

The important political services made available to the dominant classes by the army, especially in the rural zones, not only have modernized and politicized it but have caused the rise of new tensions within the armed institution, which are revealed in a certain reluctance by a more cultivated segment of the officer corps to carry out bloody and repressive tasks and in a great polarization between, on the one hand, the elite corps—well-armed and well-paid—and, on the other hand, a sizable sector of soldiers who live poorly in inhospitable areas, condemned to a nomadic existence. But at the same time, behind the so-called civic action programs, which are obviously of North American inspiration, one discovers the attempt of a pro-imperialist segment of the officer corps to hide, behind the cartoon figure of the good soldier who plants tree seedlings, distributes food, and restores schools, the executioner of discontented peasants.[3]

The Mexican political system has been, in a certain sense, a three-legged table. It was supported upon a three-class base: the bourgeoisie officially called middle class, the workers, and the peasants. The key to "institutional" and "revolutionary" continuity of a state situated—apparently—atop a class struggle rests to a high degree, although not exclusively, on the peasant base of the system, today weakened and wobbly. It is increasingly clear that the table is going to remain supported by two legs, and even so, it teeters visibly, for the working class has begun a movement toward labor union independence, and dangerous cracks are appearing in the bourgeoisie. It is true that a military boot could temporarily offset the instabilities; but the myth of the State of the Mexican Revolution would be ruined forever, and with it the bureaucracy that it has served. A democratic alternative would also be able to attain a certain reestablishment of the balance, and above all, it would open the way to new options. But although these two paths are in sight, what is most probable is that the Mexican government will stubbornly insist on living off the lost (or daily more illusory) mediations of an institutional power that seeks the solution in all of us but turns over the helm only to a few. It will also be a path toward its ruin, slower and less painful than a military coup, less costly for some sectors of the bourgeoisie than the democratic outcome, but, on the other hand, more dramatic inasmuch as it can hurl the society toward those dangerous states of ennui that are the breeding ground for despotism. In any event, the Mexican state will suffer seriously from the process of the extinction of the peasantry: an impossible, ongoing annihilation.

Chapter 7

... An Impossible, Ongoing Annihilation

It vanished quite slowly, beginning with the end of the tail, and ending
with the grin, which remained some time after the rest of it had gone.
—**Lewis Carroll**
Alice in Wonderland

The Collapse of Technocratic Populism

DURING Luis Echeverría's presidency, a political alternative that
would provide a way out of the agrarian crisis in Mexico was
developed. This alternative, which I have called *technocratic populism* and which arose under the sign of state capitalism, collapsed pre-
cipitously in 1976. It is worth examining this process in detail for the
purpose of drawing some lessons from it.

In opposition to the corrupt, despotic power of the old caciques, supported by the most inefficient, parasitic sectors of the rural bourgeoisie,
there was an effort to form an incipient alliance between the interests of
big monopoly, agro-industrial and agro-commercial capital and the interests of the mid-level agrarian bourgeoisie. For this alternative to have been
politically viable would have required the political bureaucracy to arouse
a certain peasant popular base, which ought to have been attracted by two
major steps: ejido collectivization and land distribution. Here, the inchoate
alliance began to founder, for the first measure directly affected the large
lessees of ejido lands (and inspired ideological repugnance in a sizable
portion of the bourgeoisie as well), and the second directly assaulted the
landowning agrarian bourgeoisie. These measures were up against, not a
weak, obsolete rural bourgeoisie, but a modern, powerful sector of agricultural entrepreneurs, which had developed in the heat of agrarian reform

itself. So great was the failure of the technocratic populist plan that the new government, headed by José López Portillo, put its principal directors, the two ex-ministers of agrarian reform, into positions from which they would not attempt any more new political adventures: Augusto Gómez Villanueva lived in a golden exile in the Mexican embassy in Rome, and Félix Barra went to prison for fraud!

Let us take a look, then, at the political events that led to the elimination of the populist sector from agrarian policy. Toward the end of 1975, with a year to go before the end of Echeverría's presidential term, it was already clear to everyone that the policy of ejido collectivization had failed decisively. In great haste the government turned to the expedient of land distribution in order to recapture lost popular strength. In October 1975, peasants invaded private lands in the Valle del Yaqui; in November, the government distributed some land, but it was of very poor quality. At the end of November, the large farmers received a harsh blow: the expropriation of a latifundio (2,507 hectares) was announced; its owner was no less than Alicia Calles de Almada, daughter of ex-president Plutarco Elías Calles (who was, moreover, the founding father of the new, "revolutionary" bourgeoisie of northwest Mexico). A few days later, 4,387 hectares of good-quality irrigation land in the Valle del Yaqui were expropriated and distributed to 433 peasants from San Ignacio.

The northern agrarian bourgeoisie, the country's most modern and most powerful, responded to these measures quite energetically: it decreed an agricultural lockout for December 1. Although the lockout occurred in wheat-growing zones where the harvest had practically finished, it had a big political impact because it took place at a moment when agricultural production was declining conspicuously, causing Mexico to begin importing large quantities of wheat and corn for the first time. Moreover, the farmers from the north (principally from Sonora and Sinaloa) left the PRI government-controlled National Small-Property Confederation and established the National Agriculture Union. The process of expropriation of latifundios and land distribution was halted.

But matters did not stop there: apparently, the populist group decided to play one last card a few weeks before the presidential term ended. On October 7, 1976, the minister of agrarian reform, Félix Barra, stated, "Before President Echeverría's government ends, all the latifundios of Sonora and Sinaloa will be distributed." Immediately, land invasions began, encouraged by the National Peasant Confederation (the PRI's CNC) and apparently blessed by the government. The Ministry of Agrarian Reform declared that in those two states there were eighty thousand hectares of irrigation land and fifty thousand hectares of summer pasture on properties subject to expropriation. The peasants applying for land, consequently, denounced the most important latifundistas, who were, it should be said in passing, some of the most typical products of the institutionalization of the Mexican Revolution. Many were descendants of revolutionary politicians and military men—the families of Calles, Obregón, Borquez, Ramos, Bours, Esquer, Topete, Vargas, Parada, Zazueta Ruiz, Clouthier, Creel, and so forth.

The first defensive act of the capitalist farmers consisted in resorting to the agrarian amparo (writ of relief) (in Sinaloa, 550 complaints for relief were filed, and in Sonora, 600) with the goal of blocking the expropriation process until December 1, the date on which the Echeverría government was to end. During the first week of November, negotiations between the farmers and the government took place: the former offered twenty thousand hectares, but the government insisted on expropriating eighty thousand hectares of sham parcels. The situation was quite tense, with thousands of peasants beginning to surround and even invade the lands to be expropriated, under the vigilance of the police and army, who had been mobilized but who limited themselves to observing. It was a race against time: the owners, for their part, had succeeded in delaying the constitutional hearing on the amparo lawsuit they had interposed against the agrarian action.

Nevertheless, on November 18, eight thousand Sonora peasants began to take possession of thirty-seven thousand hectares of irrigated land and sixty-one thousand hectares of summer pasture in the Yaqui and Mayo valleys. The furious capitalist farmers directly accused Félix Barra and Augusto Gómez Villanueva of violating the amparo law. In the face of this situation, negotiations precipitated between the government and the CAADES (Confederation of Farmers' Associations of the State of Sinaloa) were concluded in Sinaloa: the confederation agreed to turn over ten thousand hectares of irrigated land and three thousand of summer pasture, in place of the thirty-nine thousand hectares originally requested. In Sonora, the farmers, supported by the merchants, maintained a protest strike until 11:00 A.M. on December 1, the moment at which the new president and his cabinet took office.

The new government openly declared that its principal goal was to organize production. In December, in a settlement meeting with the governor of Sinaloa and the minister of agrarian reform, the president himself succeeded in getting the peasants "to agree to" leave the invaded properties and "to wait for the legal process." At the same time, a legal battle was developing, for the expropriated Sonora farmers formally accused former president Echeverría of contempt for the amparo law. In Sonora "the leader" of the League of Agrarian Communities (of the PRI's CNC) recognized that the land distribution had been hasty. The official tone had totally changed, and the reaccommodation of political forces began. Let us look at a typical example: on the occasion of the celebration of the anniversary of the agrarian act of January 19, 1915, the governor of Vera Cruz censured the "pharisees of agrarian policy." Four days later, the supreme leader of the CNC "resigned" from his office in order to take a position at the head of the National Foundation for Ejido Development, a state enterprise in the process of liquidation. In February, the new CNC leader declared that demagoguery would give way to work. In May, López Portillo had a working meeting in Ciudad Obregón with the "small" property owners affected and declared that there were "doubts" about 17,600 hectares out of the 37,000 distributed. Negotiations began immediately between the Sonora agricultural landowners and the Ministry of Agrarian Reform for the payment of indemnification for the 17,600 hectares of irrigated land expropriated.

Peasant Economy and Capitalism

In order to understand the collapse of the technocratic-populist alternative, we must look at the specific forms that insertion of the peasant economy into the capitalist context assumed. During the late 1960s and early 1970s, the process that I have called permanent primitive accumulation of capital manifested itself as a slight diminution in the polarization of land distribution, accompanied by an increase in the inequality of income distribution.

During the sixties, two parallel phenomena occurred with respect to land distribution. First, the 1960 and 1970 censuses reveal that during that decade the ejido land area increased from 44.5 million hectares to almost 70 million. Four thousand new ejidos were created, and the population employed on ejido lands increased by more than 1.5 million persons. Second, the number of small units of production on private land (fewer than five hectares) decreased during the same period by more than 40 percent; the number of units of more than five hectares also declined, but in a much smaller proportion (13 percent). The total population employed in the private sector declined by more than 1.5 million persons. The enormous decrease in the number of units of private production reflects, in part, a change in classification by the 1970 census: no longer was the parcel of land taken as a unit; instead, the unit was the owner who exploited one or more parcels with the same resources. Nevertheless, the decline in the figure for personnel employed (confirmed by the population census) reveals that the number of small units of production did indeed decline (see tables 19–21).

The simple data in tables 19–21 reveal clearly the dialectic link between the ruin and proletarianization of the peasantry and the expansion of state protectionism that sought to compensate for the imbalances and conflicts inherent in this process. But it is necessary to look at the situation in detail in order to discover its specific characteristics, which, in spite

Table 19

Land Distribution, 1960 and 1970

Type of Land Tenure	Number of Parcels		Total Area (ha.)		Cultivated Area (ha.)	
	1960	1970	1960	1970	1960	1970
> 5 ha.	447.0	388.0	123,259	69,263	12,219	9,675
< 5 ha.	899.0	522.0	1,328	881	1,269	710
Ejidos	18.7	22.7	44,497	69,724	10,329	12,753

Source: *Censos agrícola, ganadero y ejidal,* 1960–70.

Table 20

Personnel Employed in Agriculture, 1960 and 1970

Type of Land Tenure	Total		Producer and Family Members	
	1960	1970	1960	1970
> 5 ha.	1,213	1,535	995	723
< 5 ha.	2,104	1,191	2,104	868
Ejidos	3,545	5,111	2,870	3,711

Source: *Censos agrícola, ganadero y ejidal,* 1960–70.

Table 21

Average Area per Producer and Family, 1960–1970

Type of Land Tenure	Total Area		Area Cultivated	
	1960	1970	1960	1970
> 5 ha.	123.9	95.8	12.3	13.4
< 5 ha.	0.6	1.0	0.6	0.8
Ejidos	15.5	18.8	3.6	3.4
Total	28.2	26.4	4.0	4.4

Source: *Censos agrícola, ganadero y ejidal,* 1960–70. Data are given in thousands of farms, hectares, and persons.

of formal similarities, were quite different from those that prevailed in the golden age of land distribution, during Lázaro Cárdenas's presidency in the thirties. While in the Cárdenas era the smallholding increased in importance in a way parallel to the distribution of ejido land, in the sixties the opposite occurred. While land distribution in the thirties paralleled significant growth in agricultural production, three decades later we observe a critical decline in agricultural production. While under the Cárdenas administration agrarian reform generated a peasant base of legitimizing support for the state apparatus, in the sixties the sharpest confrontations were those between the peasant movement and the government.

What was taking place within the ejido sector was highly complex. One must point out that this sector was extraordinarily heterogeneous, and its unity derived essentially from its peculiar legal and political situation. On the one hand, the ejido sheltered and protected extremely backward, unproductive, pauperized and/or proletarianized sectors of the peasantry; on the other hand, powerful tendencies toward the monopoly concentration of capital began to develop within it (e.g., in the production of tobacco, sugarcane, cotton, and coffee). Various indicators show the increase in the spread of capitalist forms of production in agriculture; the best indices for demonstrating this tendency are those that refer to the weight of investments in wage labor and chemical fertilizers (see table 22).

Although in the total value of agricultural production, ejidos increased in importance, the yield of the labor employed declined, owing to the increase in the massive presence of ejidatarios with very small plots of the worst quality, fruit of distributions that did not touch the good lands of the latifundios. Thus, the average area cultivated per producer (plus family members employed in production) dropped in the ejidos from 3.6 hectares in 1960 to 3.4 hectares in 1970, although the average total area increased (from 15.5 hectares to 18.8). Table 23 shows the changes that occurred in the distribution of the value produced and the population employed.

Table 22
Percentage of Total Expenditure on Wages and Chemical Fertilizers, 1960 and 1970

Type of Land Tenure	Wages		Chemical Fertilizers	
	1960	1970	1960	1970
> 5 ha.	28.9	34.2	6.1	8.8
Ejidos	18.0	37.6	5.5	12.6

Source: Censos agrícola, ganadero y ejidal, 1960–70.

Table 23
Land Distribution, 1960 and 1970

	Percentage of Total Value of Agricultural Production		Percentage of Total Population Employed in Agricultural Jobs	
Type of Land Tenure	1960	1970	1960	1970
> 5 ha.	53.5	44.7	28.2	19.6
< 5 ha.	5.7	4.0	26.8	15.2
Ejidos	40.8	51.3	45.1	65.2

Source: *Censos agrícola, ganadero y ejidal*, 1960–70.

The data in table 23 require some explanations and commentary. First, the increase in the organic composition of capital in the capitalist sector caused the decrease in the population employed on properties of more than five hectares. Second, the same factor, but combined with the absorption of several hundreds of thousands of new ejidatarios, caused the weight of ejido production to increase enormously without any decline—indeed, just the opposite—in the population employed in this sector. Third, the great weight of the value of ejido agricultural production should not encourage errors of overestimation: if the value of livestock production, of animal and forest products, is added for 1970, we have the following percentages: more than five hectares, 51.2 percent; fewer than five hectares, 11.8 percent; and ejidos, 37 percent. Finally, the economic crisis and the processes of concentration of capital caused the decline of production on plots of fewer than five hectares and, above all, caused an abrupt decline in the number of small property owners.

The Double Crisis of Mexican Agriculture

What we see in the evolution of census statistics is only a hint of the problem, for this information is incomplete and is disaggregated in such a way that it is quite difficult to make an accurate interpretation.[1] However, as a starting point, we may outline the following phenomena: (1) the sector of small private property (fewer than 5 hectares) was by 1970 in a stagnant situation; (2) the rapid development of the sector of properties of more than 5 hectares had come to a halt by 1970; and (3) the ejido showed strange and contradictory behavior: by 1970, production still demonstrated a tendency toward growth, but profit rates were falling.

Behind this situation was a contradictory relation between the expansion of the capitalist sector and the small peasant economy. Since the 1950s, capitalist development had begun to erode in a serious way the small agricultural economy, which was one of the central features of social stability in the countryside. In fact, toward the end of the fifties, agricultural growth rates declined abruptly, to an average of 2.5 percent per year. Given that the poor peasantry was responsible for a large part of production, it is evident that any critical situation in their economy had immediate repercussions in the national agricultural economy. The problem was that the efficient, developed capitalist sector did not produce enough products to feed the Mexican people. Moreover, it had shifted its production toward commercial crops for export, for use as industrial raw material, and for nonbasic, or "luxury," food. The fact is that capitalist agriculture was not capable of sustaining the economic system without relying on food imports.

For these reasons, redistribution of ejido land was reinitiated during the sixties: it was necessary to protect the peasant sector from crumbling, in the hope of a greater growth in the capitalist sector. Also for this reason, there was a contradictory behavior in the ejido sector: it expanded but did not avoid the crisis of small ejidatarios. Nevertheless, the government's agrarian policy did not succeed in eliminating the danger. The situation erupted in the seventies: to the ruin of the peasant economy was added a typical economic crisis, with overproduction phenomena and collapsing prices in the capitalist sector. The only way out was to import food, at the expense of increasing foreign indebtedness on the part of the state. The 1978–81 oil boom was merely a short interruption in this tendency.

Let us briefly scrutinize the commoditization process in agricultural production. From 1940 to 1970 the proportion of output sold by production units rose from 53.6 percent to 87.0 percent. If this jump seems quite impressive, it is all the more so if we consider that its thrust really took place during the first decade of the period. In fact, the percentage of production sold in the market increased from 53.6 percent in 1940 to 82.1 percent in 1950. By 1960 this proportion had actually decreased, although insignificantly, to 82.0 percent. Thus, the crucial fact is this: after the Cardenista agrarian reform, most of the agricultural production was taken to the market. The administrations of both Avila Camacho and Alemán were clearly committed to the modernization of Mexican agriculture.

As table 24 indicates, there are certain differences in the rate of output sold in the market, depending on the land tenure system. In general, production units with more than 5 hectares always sold a greater proportion of their output, closely followed by ejido units. Private operations with

Table 24
Percentage of Production Sold, by Type of Land Tenure, 1940–1970

Type of Land Tenure	1940	1950	1960	1970
> 5 ha.	55.7	89.4	87.0	88.2
< 5 ha.	40.0	78.7	67.0	81.0
Ejidos	54.2	72.4	77.0	86.2
Total	53.6	82.1	82.0	87.0

Sources: Derived from *Censos agrícola, ganadero y ejidal,* 1940–70.

fewer than 5 hectares of land, the vast majority of them peasant units, behaved more erratically. In 1950 they sold a greater proportion of their output than ejidos (78.7 percent compared with 72.4 percent), but in 1960 the percentage went down to 67.0, only to increase again in 1970 to 81.0 percent. Two interesting points to keep in mind are (1) that most of the agricultural output went into the market, regardless of the social relations of production that gave rise to it; and (2) that following the Cardenista land redistribution, from the outset the state directed ejido production toward the market. This full-fledged commoditization process placed the peasant economy in a quite vulnerable situation, with dramatic results in the late sixties and early seventies.

The 1970s began with decreases in production in most of the important crops. Corn production, which had stagnated in the mid-sixties, collapsed in 1972 and did not increase again until the early eighties. The pattern for beans was similar. On the other hand, commercial crops such as cotton, sesame, sugarcane, and tomatoes also joined the crisis in the early seventies. Except for the tomato crop, there was no meaningful recovery during the eighties, in contrast with the cases of corn and beans. Cotton, sesame, and sugarcane have entered a long-lasting critical phase.

Let us take a closer look at the behavior of cash and subsistence crops. We will look first at trends in production, prices, and land area for several crops. Next, we will examine historical trends in national consumption and production of one crop from each type. Chart 1 shows the trends in wheat production and prices from 1940 to 1983. It clearly shows the date when the Green Revolution was introduced, particularly in the northwestern irrigation districts. Introduction of Green Revolution technologies boosted production to the extent of making Mexico self-sufficient in wheat for a decade and a half. Between 1947 and 1955, increased wheat production was due to increases in land area cultivated. This rush to wheat production was induced by the government in the early forties, when it set wheat

Chart 1

Wheat: Production, Mean Prices, and Land Surface, 1940-1983

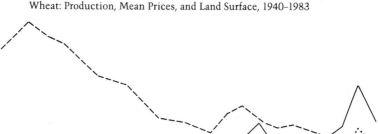
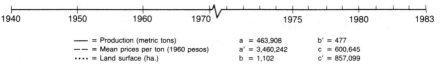

—— = Production (metric tons)	a = 463,908	b' = 477
— — = Mean prices per ton (1960 pesos)	a' = 3,460,242	c = 600,645
•••• = Land surface (ha.)	b = 1,102	c' = 857,099

Sources: DGEA, *Agenda agrícola* (Mexico City: Secretaría de Agricultura y Recursos Hidráulicos, 1983); idem, "Consumos aparentes de productos agrícolas, 1925-1982," *Ecotecnia Agrícola* 7, no. 9 (1983).

prices above those on the international market. After 1955, augmented production was due to Green Revolution technologies. The area of land dedicated to wheat production continued to expand until 1970, but it increased at a slower rate than production. The trend toward a decline in wheat prices appeared in 1955, along with increased productivity, and continued through 1975. Thus, during the same period, wheat production rose at a slightly higher rate than that at which prices fell. From the producers' point of view, however, this trend was endurable insofar as declining prices were offset by increased productivity. But the point of saturation was reached in 1970, when wheat production began to decline, and domestic consumption had to be complemented with imports. From 1970 on, wheat prices continued to fall, with a short break in 1974-1975. At the same time, wheat imports had an important presence during this period (see chart 2).

Although wheat is typically a cash crop, the behavior of its production and prices does not exhibit clear capitalist responses to market fluctuations. During the seventies and early eighties, we do observe a close rela-

Chart 2

Wheat: National Consumption as a Percentage of Production, 1940–1982

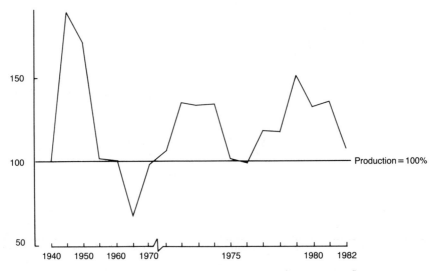

Source: DGEA, "Consumos aparentes de productos agrícolas, 1925–1982."

tion between production and prices. However, production does not always decline after periods of falling prices, and this was not a time of increased productivity, either: production increases occurred because of the dedication of additional land to the crop. Perhaps part of the explanation of this inconsistency lies in the fact that a large number of ejidos were engaged in wheat production, and their decisions as to what to produce were often determined by the official credit institution. In turn, the Ejidal Bank made many of its decisions upon a political basis rather than an economic one.

Two cash crops for which we do observe a more clearly positive correlation between production and prices, in a typically capitalistic fashion, are cotton and sesame. Chart 3 shows production and price trends for these crops, and we can visually determine that correlation. In the case of cotton, there is a noticeable discrepancy for the 1960–70 period. An important explanation for this lag is that cotton is a very labor-intensive crop. From 1970 on, however, the correlation between price and production is much higher and positive. In fact, despite the discrepancy pointed out above, if we allow one year for reacting to prices, we obtain a correlation coefficient of +0.6 for the whole period 1940–83. The case of sesame reveals a similar situation.

The behavior of corn production has been different from that of wheat. From 1940 to 1972, Mexico was virtually self-sufficient (see chart 4). Dur-

Chart 3

Cotton and Sesame: Production and Mean Prices, 1940–1983

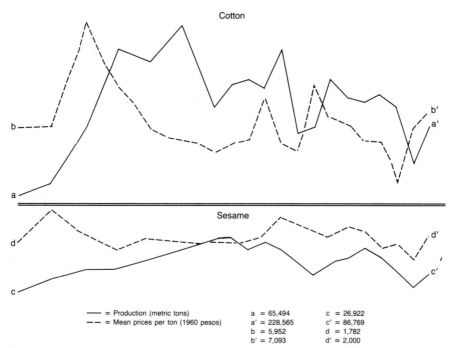

Cotton

Sesame

—— = Production (metric tons)	a = 65,494	c = 26,922
– – = Mean prices per ton (1960 pesos)	a' = 228,565	c' = 86,769
	b = 5,952	d = 1,782
	b' = 7,093	d' = 2,000

Sources: DGEA, *Agenda agrícola* (Mexico City: Secretaría de Agricultura y Recursos Hidráulicos, 1983); idem, "Consumos aparentes de productos agrícolas, 1925–1982," *Ecotecnia Agrícola* 7, no. 9 (1983).

ing much of this time the government held corn prices down with "guaranteed prices," which were supposed to represent a subsidy to corn producers. In fact, real corn prices decreased for most of the period considered. The only years in which there were real price increases were 1963 and 1975, when the "guaranteed prices" were upwardly revised by the Mexican government, already in the midst of the crisis. What is most striking regarding corn production and prices is that their trends show a negative correlation coefficient of –0.4, when we allow one year for reaction to price changes. I believe that this negative correlation occurs because of the peasant logic under which most corn production takes place (see chart 5).

The predominantly subsistence character of corn production does not mean that all the corn produced is consumed by the peasant family. Part of it is sold in order to purchase other use values indispensable for reproduction. Moreover, corn is usually produced as insurance against starva-

Chart 4

Corn: National Consumption as a Percentage of Production, 1940–1982

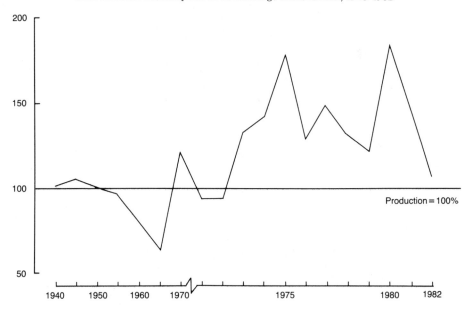

Source: DGEA, "Consumos aparentes de productos agrícolas, 1925–1982."

tion. Thus, when corn prices rise, a smaller quantity of it is required to achieve the balance between work and consumption. Conversely, when corn prices fall, production must increase in order to meet the consumption requirements of the peasant unit. This behavior also indicates the very limited flexibility many peasant units have in adapting to market conditions. Given the scarcity of their capital and the generally low quality of their land, they cannot shift production to other crops easily enough. Since access to land is usually restricted, peasants can only rely on increasing the use of the single resource over which they have control: domestic labor power.

Chart 6 shows a very similar behavior in production and prices for beans, also typically a subsistence crop in Mexican culture. We may note an exception in significant bean production increases for 1980–81, which are positively correlated with price increases. The most likely reason for this is the application of the Mexican Food System (SAM) development strategy. The SAM was implemented in 1980 by the López Portillo administration as a strategy aimed at attaining self-sufficiency in basic grain production. Although official declarations stated that self-sufficiency

Chart 5

Corn: Production, Mean Prices, and Land Surface, 1940–1983

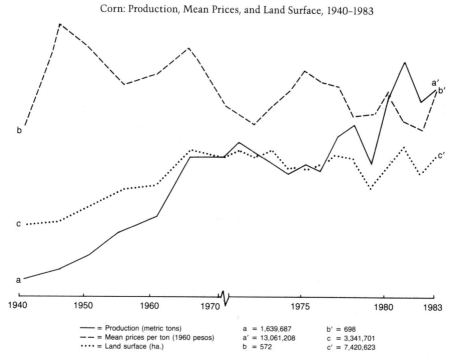

—— = Production (metric tons)	a = 1,639,687	b′ = 698
— — = Mean prices per ton (1960 pesos)	a′ = 13,061,208	c = 3,341,701
•••• = Land surface (ha.)	b = 572	c′ = 7,420,623

Sources: DGEA, *Agenda agrícola* (Mexico City: Secretaría de Agricultura y Recursos Hidráulicos, 1983); idem, "Consumos aparentes de productos agrícolas, 1925–1982," *Ecotecnia Agrícola* 7, no. 9 (1983).

would be achieved by strengthening the peasant economy in rainfall agricultural zones, much of the production increase actually took place in irrigation districts. This indicates that government incentives were so appealing that quite a few members of the agrarian bourgeoisie opted to seize the opportunity to profit with basic grains. In fact, production rose in 1980 not only for beans but for corn as well (see charts 5 and 6).

The preceding discussion of price and production tendencies has pointed up the manifestation of the double crises in these spheres. Generally, production and prices have been falling, with short interruptions of only a few years' duration. The production increases brought about by the SAM were extremely expensive for the federal government, and in 1982 there were disastrous results, owing in part to below-normal rainfall levels. As soon as Miguel de la Madrid took office in December of that year, the SAM strategy was abandoned. Although the concept of self-sufficiency and

Chart 6

Beans: Production and Mean Prices, 1940–1983

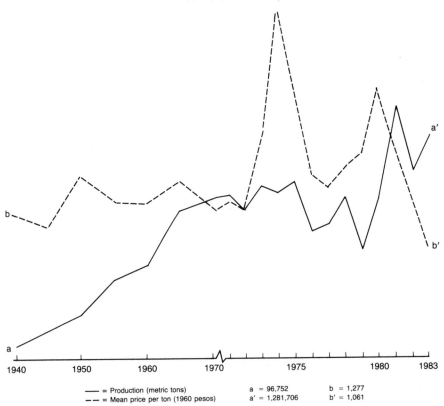

—— = Production (metric tons)
– – = Mean price per ton (1960 pesos)

a = 96,752   b = 1,277
a' = 1,281,706   b' = 1,061

Sources: DGEA, *Agenda agrícola* (Mexico City: Secretaría de Agricultura y Recursos Hidráulicos, 1983); idem, "Consumos aparentes de productos agrícolas, 1925–1982," *Ecotecnia Agrícola* 7, no. 9 (1983).

the preoccupation with it remained, no significant amount of resources was devoted to encouraging production of basic grains under the De la Madrid administration.

Despite the widespread redistributions of land in the sixties, the erosion of the peasant economy continued at a very considerable pace. This was partly because the lands distributed during the Díaz Ordaz administration were of a very poor quality for agriculture. In fact, the total area redistributed in his administration was a little over 25 million hectares, a larger area than was distributed under Cardenismo. Nevertheless, only 2.4 million hectares, or 9.6 percent, of this land were arable. In contrast, Cárdenas distributed close to 20 million hectares, of which almost 5 million, or 25 percent, were arable. Thus, the Díaz Ordaz agrarian reform reduced the proportion of arable land in ejidos from 23.2 percent in 1960 to 18.3 percent in 1970.

Hence, the redistribution in the sixties could not halt the tendency toward the ruin of the peasant economy. The manifestation of such ruin was already clear by 1970, when a large proportion of agricultural producers were no longer able to sustain a simple reproduction level by relying only on their agricultural units of production. The processes of de-peasantization and semi-proletarianization were already fully under way.

What we find at the beginning of the seventies is the simultaneous explosion of two crises: the acceleration of the small peasant's ruin, and the drop in prices, which brings down production in the capitalist sector (after a typical period of overproduction). This explains the intensity of the crises. Moreover, the double crisis was both a preview and one of the causes of the national economic crisis that hit bottom in 1976, during the Echeverría administration, which was forced to devalue the Mexican peso significantly.

Populist Romanticism

Is it possible to hope for a resurgence of the small peasant economy as an alternative to the crisis of the capitalist system? What is happening in the small private properties sector, along with the political defeat of the group that promoted a populist-style alternative within the state, seems to indicate a negative answer to the question. But the growth of the ejido sector is inserted into a much more complicated process, for, in effect, there is no "peasant alternative" in Mexico today. However, no other alternative is viable if it does not leave a place for the small peasant economy.

It is precisely because of this situation that the controversy over the characteristics of the agrarian structure is intensifying in Mexico today. From any viewpoint, it is apparent that during the seventies and eighties the Mexican countryside experienced an intense crisis that flowed beyond the boundaries of a narrowly rural context and shook the entire society. Nowadays, all sectors recognize the exhaustion of the old forms of struggle or reform and are proposing new paths: the government proclaims the end of the land distribution phase, the agrarian bourgeoisie puts a halt to its tolerance of the state's *campesinista* caprices, the guerrilla movement accepts, implicitly or explicitly, its defeat, and the independent mass movement announces the end of the traditional populist features of its political line. The government attempts to promote forms of state monopoly concentration and organization, the bourgeoisie cries out for a policy that will favor the productivity of the capitalist sector in agriculture, and the forces of the left determinedly seek the independent organization of the pauperized masses in the countryside, particularly the rural workers.

From the viewpoint of the independent socialist organizations, settling accounts with the agrarianist past is of crucial importance. The Marxist interpretation of the agrarian problem has an extraordinary relevance in Mexico, for it signifies, at the level of the ideological struggle, the precise definition of the boundary between the theoretical-political space of the bourgeoisie and petty bourgeoisie and the space that is specifically socialist. In sum, the enormous weight of the populist agrarianism that the Mexican Revolution of 1910 and the Cardenista reforms have bequeathed us must be set off clearly from the proletarian positions and must cease overwhelming the independent popular movement that is beginning to grow in Mexico. There is a need for a socialist vision not only of the characteristics of the bourgeois class and its forms of domination but also of the other classes and nonproletarian popular sectors (principally the peasantry) that often become especially solid bases for legitimization of bourgeois power. This is what I am attempting in some fashion to initiate in a polemic way in this book. The controversy that the book is advancing has flowered, and I would like to add to it here by using the opportunity afforded me by a text by the North American researcher Robert Wasserstrom for that purpose.[2]

In the name of a poorly understood and worse considered populism, Wasserstrom accuses me of nothing less than failing to accept that "within the peasant communities there are distinct social classes" and denying the existence of class struggle in the countryside. My critic's confusion is total: from the affirmation of the existence of a nonclassist simple commodity mode of production, one cannot by any means derive the idea that there is no class struggle in the Mexican countryside nor that, in the very heart of the peasantry, a profound, advanced process of class differentiation does not exist. Nevertheless, he insists on arbitrarily ascribing to me a "dualist" interpretation of Mexico similar to the interpretations of Ricardo Pozas, Gonzalo Aguirre Beltrán, and Rodolfo Stavenhagen (authors who, moreover, hold positions fundamentally different from one another's) because I have defined and distinguished *two* modes of production in the countryside (the simple commodity mode and the capitalist). Beyond trying to demonstrate that his criticism is groundless, I would like to explore the reasons that have prompted such extensive animadversions on the definition of the peasantry by its insertion into a simple commodity mode of production ("a common petty bourgeois type" of economy, as Lenin said). I dare to assume that the principal cause lies in the fact that such a concept implies setting the peasantry apart *as a social class distinct from the proletariat.* All the accusations of dualism, of not seeing the revolutionary potential of the peasantry, of pointing out its petty bourgeois traits, which limit its capacity to function as an independent force, and so forth, derive, in my judgment, from the rejection of a socialist interpretation of the peasantry, which reflects the perspectives of another, different social class (the proletariat).

Thus, the background of the controversy has an eminently political character: I am accused of advocating an interpretation that is alien, external, to the peasantry, which is *relatively* true. But now let us see just what is the "inwardness" in the name of which he criticizes me. To understand the peasant, Wasserstrom tells us,

> is neither to treat him as a reactionary nor to desire his proletarianization through the superior strength of capitalism. It is to live with him, to speak his language, to bring him our theoretical reflections so that he might teach us and criticize us. Only in this way will we achieve our principal goal: to radicalize the social sciences, decentralize scientific research, and—it must be said—demystify the role of the researcher, guru of an academic, unfeeling Marxism.[3]

A typical outburst of populist romanticism! In reality, what is our critic complaining about? That Marxism brings, necessarily, a vision of the world different from that which emanates from the peasantry and that only by understanding the *difference* in class interests that separates the peasantry from the proletariat will it be possible to realize the alliance of classes that Lenin, like Mao Tse-Tung, not only proposed but put into practice. But today this "alliance" manifests itself in a new and different way: as a formidable process of expansion of the revolutionary subject in which class differences are no longer based on agreements about subordination.

The horror that use of the concept *simple commodity mode of production* inspires in some critics illustrates my argument: to define the mode of production in which the peasantry lives implies defining its specific character, its transitory historical character (that is, asking about its internal contradictions, its mechanisms of exploitation, the ways in which class contradictions are expressed within it, etc.). It is important to point out that the interesting arguments carried on by Marxists with respect to the concept *mode of production* during recent years have left, notwithstanding the richness of the controversy, a vicious sequel: defining a mode of production in a given society would seem to imply putting up an insurmountable, overwhelming structural barrier that abstractly separates different segments of the society. In fact, the influence of structuralism on Marxism has meant that many researchers effectively apply this concept in a mechanical fashion. To my way of thinking, the definition of a mode of production implies the concrete historical determination of the manner in which relations of production and productive forces are organized. It is not, then, an analytic-descriptive concept but a historical-explanatory one. Thus, the concrete understanding of the small peasant economy contributes to explaining that dual tendency toward its reproduction and its destruction.

What is the difference between those who, like Wasserstrom, "defend the peasantry" and those who "treat it as reactionary"? On this point, our North American researcher is quite clear: in opposition to the "Mexican tradition of *grandes théories,* another type of research in the countryside was developed, research carried out above all by foreigners." Who? Manning Nash, Frank Cancian, Erik Wolf. . . . In sum, Wasserstrom recommends that we pay homage to the empiricism of North American anthropology, which apparently gives us the model for revolutionary interpretation of the Mexican countryside. Should we also perhaps agree that studies like those undertaken by the Harvard Chiapas Project—through which our critic made contact with Mexican reality—represent a guide for revolutionary action? Let us recall, simply, that that project was denounced some years ago as a sort of imperialist "Camelot Plan."[4] The supposed "principal goal" of these researchers averse to the *grandes théories* (read: Marxism) is, according to Wasserstrom, "to radicalize the social sciences, decentralize scientific research, and demystify the role of the researcher." I doubt very much that these three demands have arisen out of the peasant communities in which the North American anthropologists have been immersed, not exactly like "fish in water," in the Maoist fashion that our critic lays claim to, but more like some dubious foreign body. In contrast, the principal goal of the so-called insensitive Marxist gurus is the revolutionary transformation of capitalist society; perhaps they commit the sin of living in the world of grand theories, but those very theories are the ones that illustrate the great revolutionary processes. Taking the risk of sinning on the side of utopianism is always more worthwhile than falling into the petty bourgeois ambit of petty demands for a radicalization, decentralization, and demystification of research—empty words that can serve any cause.

Populist-inspired theses, with authentic revolutionary vocation, have also developed within currents of Marxist thought. The magazine *Cuadernos Agrarios* most openly brings together Marxist formulations of the populist theses. A controversy has developed in this magazine with respect to my statements on the peasant economy; my critics try to show that transfers of value do not exist within agriculture, from which they infer that there is no relation of exploitation (of unequal exchange) between agrarian social classes located in different modes of production. I will refer here to Armando Bartra's essay on ground rent.[5] His entire critical argument with respect to transfers within agriculture rests on a false assumption: its point of departure is the notion that the leveling of the profit rate refers solely and exclusively to the distribution of excess value among the different branches of production and cannot in any way be transferred to the distribution of profit among individual capitals that operate in a single sphere. The error consists in believing that a sphere of production is defined exclusively by the identity of the use values that it produces, when in reality the determining factor is, for the problem that concerns us, identity in the organic composition of capital, even if there is no identity of use values. Marx was quite explicit in this regard: "It is only within the same sphere of production, where the organic composition of capital is therefore given, or between different spheres of production with the same organic composition of capital, that the mass of profit stands in exact proportion to the mass of capital employed."[6]

Thus, all the discussion to the effect that there are no transfers within agriculture is left up in the air if one ceases to consider the agrarian sector of a relatively backward country as a homogeneous sphere of production, from the standpoint of the organic composition of capital. It is obvious that within a sphere of production with similar organic composition of capital, there are no transfers between enterprises. But it does not follow from this that there are no transfers within agriculture, for in Mexico at least, the latter cannot be identified as one homogeneous branch of production, in the sense that Marx uses the concept in order to explain the formation of the average rate of profit. Indeed, reality shows that the agriculture of the so-called underdeveloped countries is quite far from representing a homogeneous set of elements and that, at the very least, diverse forms of production and even different modes of production exist. This situation prevents starting from the assumption that agriculture in these countries functions as one sphere (or branch) of production in the leveling of the average rate of profit.

The problem is complex, but Armando Bartra wanted to simplify his criticism by arbitrarily imposing on me the idea that the superprofits of the entrepreneurial agricultural sector derive directly from the peasant sector, from which he would infer that *all* struggle for land is a populist fiction. He even manages to mangle a quotation on unequal exchange, eliminating my reference to the industrial sector, in order to "prove" that my interpretation falls into the phony critical scheme that he has constructed. My analyses of the transfer problem lead me to a conclusion different from the one he assigns to me: it is the bourgeoisie *as a whole* that benefits from peasant surplus labor. Much less did I ever think that such transfers derived *directly* from the peasant sector. The mass of peasant surplus labor is thrust upon the society through market mechanisms and is redistributed among the different branches of production, including agriculture itself, in accordance with a complex set of factors that rests, ultimately, on the different organic compositions of capital.

It is apparent that there are other aspects that irritate my critic and that they are not made explicit. When he is scandalized by a statement (which he takes out of context) to the effect that peasants have inherited and fulfilled certain of the functions of the landholder, it is evident that what my critic does not like is the term *landholder*, which reminds him of the peasant's petty bourgeois side. Nowhere do I state that the peasant fulfills the role of the landholder because he obtains a rent beyond the profit, by selling his production. That is an absurdity. The peasantry, to the extent that it is landowning, monopolizes a portion of the land: that is its function as landholder, a ragged landholder, for it obliges the capitalist to generate a superprofit (rent) if he wants to invest in those lands; this phenomenon is quite common in all the irrigation districts in Mexico.

These misunderstandings lead me to state outright what seems to me to be the underlying problem. The populist interpretation refuses to accept the petty bourgeois nature of peasant production, a nature that proves apparent when one confirms the simple commodity character of peasant production and the peasantry's links of ownership with the land. It seems that Armando Bartra would like to shut his eyes to this evidence and to emphasize exclusively the peasant's revolutionary character. The fundamental duality of the modern peasant escapes him.

Good evidence of this duality is provided by Armando Bartra himself in his study of Chontalpa.[7] It is obvious that there the peasant wavers between the interests of the Plan (a state monopoly enterprise with peasant participation) in terms of profitability and efficacy, and the need for organized struggle on the part of workers who will not be compromised by the profitability of the enterprise. That is, even in the specific conditions that indicate an insertion of the peasant as a (disguised) wage laborer into the context of a spuriously collective enterprise, the nexus of the peasants' ownership with the land and with the unit of production leads to a conflict in the face of the objective proletarianization to which he is subjected. What political conclusion can be drawn from this? Armando Bartra contends that the *principal* force state capitalism faces here "is not the political potential of the new class that is being shaped but the old, deeply rooted potential for peasant rebellion, which refuses to disappear." Of the "new class" he says: "In the first place, proletarianization appears as political decomposition and ideological deterioration that shape a phase of reflux and passivity." In turn, the peasants "can be a point for the definitive struggle to create a new social order in which the peasant condition will no longer be condemned to disappear, transformed into proletarian slavery." We are dealing, in sum, with the old populist thesis: set in opposition to the most refined, modern forms of capitalist exploitation (state monopoly concentration) is the alternative of the peasant struggle. I do not doubt the great revolutionary potential of the peasantry. But that potential is expressed in *precise, concrete historic conditions, not in a general, abstract way.* The social classes are not in and of themselves bearers of a pre-established historical destiny: it is the specificity of the structures and mechanisms of exploitation, of the accumulation of experiences in the struggle, that turns them into revolutionary forces. The specific situation of Mexico shows us that the peasantry, led in the majority of cases by the dominant classes, has already left a deep impression of its revolution-ary potential, just as its petty bourgeois side has already exhausted its revolutionary potential. Now it is the proletarian side's turn to stand out. This facet of the peasant, stifled and kept quiet by populism for so long, today finds itself surrounded by conditions favorable to its political de-velopment. These conditions have been established by the dead-end street in which the peasant economy finds itself—as a massive, national solu-tion—and by the aggressive development of the modern forms of capital-ism in agriculture.

The Dynamism of the System

Michael Redclift and David Goodman point out, quite correctly, the dif-ficulties in understanding that (a) the development of the capitalist agri-cultural economy causes a tendency toward the ruin of the peasantry, but (b) the capitalist sector cannot exist without a noncapitalist environment.[8] This means that Mexican agrarian structure is tangled up in a permanent contradiction.

We have various alternatives for interpreting this situation. Redclift and Goodman seem to suggest that the capitalist sector is not a dynamic force and even question whether it is specifically capitalist in nature. On the other hand, if we assume the existence of dynamism in the capitalist sector, it will be necessary to prove why, in spite of everything, the peasant economy continues to reproduce itself. In my judgment, the discussion should center on determining the characteristics of the linkage between the two types of economy.

If the development of the large-scale commercial economy had as a basis only mechanisms for superexploitation of wage labor, and if this super-exploitation required as a condition a peasant economy that would con-tribute to regulating the price of labor power (keeping it at low, "infrasub-sistence" levels), in this case the capitalist economy would apparently find the way blocked. In my judgment, however, the articulation of the peasant economy should be analyzed as a relation with the entire capitalist sector, not only with the large agricultural enterprises. In this way we can locate two great series of contradictions: (a) those that arise from the expansion of capitalist relations of production, which tend toward the ruin of the peasantry and generate a process of proletarianization and/or pauperization; and (b) those that arise from the entire capitalist sector's difficulties in absorbing productively the masses in the process of being proletarianized and/or pauperized at the same rate as the peasantry is ruined and that generate a *process* of refunctionalization of the peasant economy.

The two processes, in a feedback effect, cause a peculiar dissociation of the agrarian sector from the capitalist economy. Thus, in effect, as Redclift and Goodman point out, the unemployed and underemployed peasant rural mass operates as an industrial army of reserve, and as superexploitation wages are established, it permits a segment of the large enterprises, to put it that way, to develop in nonentrepreneurial forms (as renters) with low organic composition of capital. But parallel to this is another segment of capitalist agriculture that operates under entrepreneurial criteria, which constantly increases its organic composition of capital and organizes itself in modern monopolistic agro-industrial and agro-commercial groups.

We could ask why, given the ample facilities for superexploitation, modern enterprises, inserted into mechanisms of expanded reproduction of capital, are being developed. Could we assume that in fact the capitalist path is blocked and that dynamism can only be channeled through the small peasant enterprise? But reality shows us that there are elements of dynamism (expansion, reproduction, growth) in the capitalist sector. We can find the answer to this problem in the inevitable crises of the capitalist system: inflation and the decline of agricultural prices affect in an especially acute way all the most backward enterprises, many of which find themselves obligated to modernize or to perish. This enables us to understand that the capitalist agrarian sector, if it is developing in a modern entrepreneurial form, does not require a peasant environment: but the entirety of the capitalist economy does indeed require a refunctionalization of small noncapitalist units, for it is not in any shape to absorb the population expelled from agriculture. The dimensions of the pauperized rural mass greatly exceed its functions as an industrial army of reserve. It must be noted that some of the measures for protecting the peasant economy (see, e.g., guaranteed prices) reinforce the entire backward sector (whether peasants or latifundistas). It is a matter of a vicious circle, but only relatively so: it can be characterized as permanent primitive accumulation of capital, a process that simultaneously contains capitalist exploitation under primitive forms, destruction of the peasant economy, expanded modern accumulation of capital, and refunctionalization of the noncapitalist economy.

It is necessary to underscore that it is not entirely a vicious circle (its "permanent" character is relative), since the forms of expanded accumulation of capital and of refunctionalization of the peasant economy slowly rise to higher levels of organization, division of labor, productivity, and so forth. Thus, forms of monopolistic concentration of capital and cooperative or collective organizations (often brought together among themselves in state development plans) are appearing. These are phenomena that are being inserted into the spiral of permanent primitive accumulation, that do not manage to break it, but that do modify some of its tendencies.

Chapter 8

The Indigenous Peasant and Indigenist Ideology

T HIS chapter attempts to explore why the so-called native problem continues to be important even though the "indigenous culture" in Mexico has disappeared, its basic aspects eliminated through the workings of the modern, "civilized" forces of capitalism.[1] Today, the ancient institutions of the indigenous people, their traditional economy, their customs, and their religion exist only precariously, totally submerged, distorted, and subjugated by the structures of the dominant society. Nevertheless, behind the term *Indian* one discovers a network of exploitation that seems to recreate the old colonial domination of the Indian in new forms. The objective is, then, to observe how capitalist society has managed to absorb the complex of socioethnic conflicts inherited from the colonial past. The goal of the analysis will not be, at any point, to find "survivals" from the Indian past that may still exist as small islands in an ocean of capitalist, industrialist civilization; that task we leave to traditional anthropology. Our job must be to try to understand the concrete and the specific of an underdeveloped society that has been injured in the past by an interethnic conflict and still has open wounds; that is, the old Indo-colonial situation, which has been eliminated from the economic structure, appears under a new guise at the level of the ideological practices of Mexican society. The question is, How is the Indian exploited today, when the Indian as such has not fully existed for a long time?

The laboratory in which we will attempt to answer this question is the Valle del Mezquital. For decades this region of Mexico has represented the most notorious example of misery and exploitation; the name Valle del Mezquital has been synonymous with Valley of Death. In 1938 the well-known anthropologist Alfonso Fábila spoke of the Indians of the Valle del Mezquital in this way:

The Otomí race, the largest ethnic group after the mestizos, could not be in a more precarious or more lamentable condition. No matter which side it is viewed from, unless it is considered by a non-Western criterion, their state reveals total defeat. This situation is not a new one, but has come down to them from the most ancient times. Always subject to a centuries-long servitude. First under the Toltecs and Aztecs, then under the Spanish conquerors and the creoles, and today under the latter and the mestizos, who have retained all the economic resources that would enable them to live in a rational way. Thus, they have continued to retreat day by day further and further up toward the slopes and peaks of the mountain ranges, whose barren soils deny them a living, and therefore they lead a miserable existence there, no matter which aspect it is judged from, even that of their individual liberty, because they have been surrounded and suffer all sorts of *insults*.[2]

The same author said of the Otomí that they were, "among the most ancient ethnic groups, the one that has from the most remote times been subjected to the servitude of other groups, and for that reason and for many other causes, those who have studied them hold the opinion that they are an inferior race or that they are descended from the Chinese people, although Francisco Pimentel, relying on study of their language, has disproven the latter assertion."[3] More than thirty years later, the writer Fernando Benítez stated:

If I were asked which Indian group has made the most vivid impression on me, I would unhesitatingly respond, "The Otomí," for the ingratitude of their environment and their condition as slaves, rather than making them hard and egoistic, have permitted them to maintain and to refine what is not precisely a feeling of communal solidarity typical of the Indians, but the exceptional one that every man is a god and merits the respect and devotion due the gods. A man who attributes this transcendent quality to human beings, a starving man with this ontological sense who has succeeded in transcending slaughters and pain through that concept of human dignity is worthy of our resolute aid in freeing him from his caciques, from the rapacious exploiters who embody the ancestral figure of the Old Coyote, the god of Discord, a sort of Otomí Cain who has tried to destroy them by setting brother against brother.[4]

A great deal has been written on the Valle del Mezquital. The scientists' cold analyses have been followed by ardent denunciations from humanist spirits or the empty demagogic statements of the politicians. Journalists and writers have shed tears on discovering the situation of the Valle del Mezquital Indians. Behind all the words one discovers a stark reality: a people that has lost its culture is living crushed under the march of a capitalist society that imposes its conditions on dominated peoples. In the myths of the fusion of three cultures (indigenous, Spanish, and mestizo), this same capitalist society has resurrected a cultural reality that it had itself murdered. However, the Indian reality reappears in bourgeois ideology in an inverted, distorted way, as a new tool of domination.

In the Valle del Mezquital I wanted to observe this ideological phenomenon empirically. First, I will attempt to show some aspects of the image that the regional dominant classes have of the indigenous people. I will link the exposition to certain aspects of the economic and political order that I have investigated.[5]

The Dominant Classes on the Native Problem

The Discriminatory Attitude:
"They have always been shiftless and apathetic"

Among the numerous interviews with people belonging to the rural bourgeoisie, it is striking to note the high frequency of cases that present a frankly, openly discriminatory attitude with a racist bias toward the indigenous people. The interviews with these people brought the conversation around to answering two basic questions: Why are the Otomí so poor? and, What do you think of the Otomí? Let us look at some examples.

One of the richest farmers in the region, a true millionaire who permits himself the luxuries of safaris to Africa, owning an airplane, being a patient of a Mexico City psychoanalyst, and having a car equipped with a radio-telephone, answered as follows:

> "Well, you've read some history, haven't you? The Otomí have *always been shiftless and apathetic* as long as anyone has known anything about them. . . . They are difficult people, obstinate *by race.* I have lived with them a great deal in remote places. . . . You have already seen in history how the Otomí exchanged their families, their daughters, their women; they have no idea of what they are doing: *They're a difficult race, but that doesn't mean that they can't be integrated into our society."*
>
> "By what means?"
>
> "Well, through education, the young people and the children could be integrated, but the old people, you're just not going to make them change now. I am interested in, for example, your group's doing an experiment with the Otomí people, to get to know them in depth: start a cooperative among them, *so that you see that they have very little desire to change.* If you want to do the experiment, I'll help you."

I declined the rich agricultural entrepreneur's proposal to do "experiments" with the native people in order to prove their inferiority. What is surprising about these statements is that they did not come from a buyer, a usurer, or a merchant middleman of a traditional type, but from one of the region's most modern capitalist entrepreneurs.

Another very wealthy farmer, the son of a regional cacique and the leader of an association of large and mid-sized landowners, made similar statements:

"Well, I think that the Otomí are poor because they have no aspirations for anything; they are people who are content just to go along, who have no ambitions of any kind."

"Do you believe that there is some solution?"

"Well, for the people today, I think not; for the future generations, I believe that with schools. . . ."

Another person, a merchant and distributor for a large beer company, expressed himself in a similarly forceful but simplistic way:

"Well, I believe that they are half-*burros*, they lack training."k

"Why?"

"They've been isolated from civilization."

An ex-deputy, formerly a cacique and today a powerful farmer, introduced new cultural factors in order to explain the inferiority of the indigenous people; but he got tangled up in the explanation:

"Well, in the first place, they lack culture. I mean that the Otomí are people forgotten by nature. . . . The Indian is a totally isolated type, he—like the peasant— brings with him a complex from the times of the conquest: they were the persecuted people. . . . But the one who frees himself, that one is dangerous: I mean that he can distinguish himself like any other person, and if he manages to enter into a cultural environment without improving himself, he is a harmful individual. If he succeeds in improving himself, he becomes one of the protectors of his own kind."

This person, who was, as he admitted, of remote Indian origin, argued irreconcilable contradictions that led him to frankly racist, discriminatory positions. On the other hand, a mid-level merchant who aspired to attain a political position in his municipality denied the obvious. He answered the question, Why are the Otomí so poor? as follows:

"They're relatively poor; compared with others, they're not really poor. That they have not developed culturally is quite a different matter; but that they're poor, no. You'll see, for example, if you go out to the barrios and to the little towns, that they are completely humble people, very poorly dressed, but they have a few head of cattle, they have a sliver of land, they have a place where they plant alfalfa or some vegetables; so, it isn't exactly that they are very poor, but that they still aren't very well developed."

This "culturalist" orientation in discriminatory attitudes is often accompanied by an explanation that tries to see the causes of the inferiority of the indigenous people in climatic or ecological conditions, and so forth. For example, a rich livestock owner who a few years ago was an important official in the local administration and who also was former president of the regional livestock owners association said:

"The hundreds of years that they have lived on this sterile land have led to their having no ambitions; the majority of the people are lazy for that very reason: the heat, the dust, the lack of water, prevent the body from taking on its active rhythm. Then, these people are satisfied with going down to the market on Mondays; they bring their *ayates* (textiles), their *lechuguillas* (agave), their *shite* (by-product of the lechuguilla fiber), which they get between Friday and Sunday because Monday is the day they use for going to market. They come and get drunk; Tuesday they use to rest up from the hangover, Wednesday, well, the same, they don't do anything. I believe that these are the most essential points as to why these people have remained in this state."

"What could be done in order to change this situation?"

"To my way of thinking, teach them to work, not as in the times of the Inquisition, with blows, with kicks, no. It's necessary to train these people, to find a convincing means for leading these people."

The principal problem that a large part of the dominant class notes is the apathy, laziness, or lack of culture of the indigenous population. In the eyes of the exploiters, these "defects" are fundamental, for they limit the possibilities of immersing the Otomí in more modern relations of exploitation. The solution is to find "a convincing means for leading these people." This "convincing means," as we shall see, has already been found: the indigenist policy. One of the most famous founders and promoters of indigenism in Mexico, Manuel Gamio, was asking the same question at the beginning of the century—posing it in his own way—that we were asking the exploiters in the Valle del Mezquital:

Why does the Indian not know how to think, to lead, to make his revolutions triumph, forming as he does the majority of the population, with his physical energies possibly superior, and possessing intellectual abilities comparable to those of any race in the world? This is owing to his mode of being, to the developmental state of our indigenous civilization, to the intellectual stage in which its individuals have come to a halt.[6]

Inspired by Franz Boas, Manuel Gamio's thinking reflected, as did that of our Mezquital bourgeoisie, the imperative need to "solve" the native problem by integrating into "civilized" life a population that was not considered capable. Of course, subsequent development of indigenist policy did not retain colonial-style racist aspects, but it did retain the need for integration as its basic premise. At the same time, the country's economic development was itself "solving" the problem: the native peoples were engulfed by capitalist development in such a way that their specific economic features (e.g., communal structure) were totally eliminated or redefined. The bourgeois sector whose ideology with respect to the Indian we have presented no longer has any direct interests in maintaining relations of a "colonial" sort with the Otomí. Its position is overtly racist, like that of someone who wants to "eliminate" a bothersome situation, and it as-

172

sumes an attitude toward the Indians like that of a person dealing with a parasite. The Indians are of little importance to this modern bourgeoisie: it does not earn a living off them as such, nor does it require their ignorance of Spanish, their relative isolation in communities, or their misery in order to succeed in business.

The Technocratic Attitude:
"To teach them to replace inadequate cultural patterns"

Another set of attitudes with respect to the Indian comes from officials, professionals, and technicians, who generally look for the causes of Otomí misery in the geographic environment, in de-capitalization, and in other "objective" factors. They do not adopt openly discriminatory positions as do the rural bourgeoisie. The head of an important irrigation zone in the Mezquital, an engineer and government official, explained to us:

> "The Otomí are in an ecological zone that is unfavorable to them. This zone has no wealth; that is, it has no natural resources that enable them to develop themselves. They do not have fertile soil, nor are there pasture lands for raising good cattle. . . . There is no irrigated agriculture, nothing but dry farming; and that is unstable, because there is no guarantee of harvesting anything, and even less so when the land is arid. I believe that wealth will have to be brought in from elsewhere, the resources would necessarily have to come from outside, they would have to industrialize . .f. I believe that is the only possibility because the ecological conditions are quite unfavorable."

This tendency not to see the problem in the region's social relations and to blame the "environment" or external causes is quite symptomatic of a way of avoiding the core of the issue. Another example is that of a high official from a state development organization, a person of Otomí origin, who seems to find the root of the problem in industrial society.

> "There is a series of reasons that explain Otomí poverty. They have devoted themselves exclusively to cottage industries like the making of ayates, which was the main occupation that the population had. It was very remunerative, especially in the colonial era, because there were many mining centers that used the rope, the sacks, and so on. . . . But plastic and many other things have come to replace these products, and the same problems that sisal has had in Yucatán are occurring. Thus, the prices of ixtle and lechuguilla remain the same as the prices thirty or forty years ago . . . so that those who cut lechuguilla live in a situation of greater poverty, much greater poverty; they are five or ten times poorer than forty or fifty years ago. This is due, I repeat, to the displacement of textiles by other products."

Out of these ideas develops a paternalistic policy that attempts, fruitlessly, to defend the "noble savage" from the evils of modern industry or to protect him from the hostility of the geographical environment.

173

A rich merchant who corners tomato production also offered an opinion on the problem:

> "The Otomí are so poor because they are located in a poor region or because they lack the education to be able to seek satisfaction in an adequate way. But they are being helped, a lot has been achieved; the people from around here, we're able to see that, over time, there have been many positive things accomplished. Slowly, which is the way it has to be. Given their lack of education, the evolution is slow."

But the geographical determinism easily turns into a value judgment on the "shiftless" nature of the Indian. A former municipal president said:

> "In the region there are places that are quite barren; they lack water even though they have land. There are many who have an ejido, a hectare or two: they plant one year, it doesn't yield them anything; they plant another, it doesn't yield them anything; they get fed up, and they leave it. It's that we don't get much rain here . . . this region is quite barren."
>
> "But there are rich farmers in the region. Why are the Otomí in particular so poor?"
>
> "Some . . . don't work."
>
> "They don't work?"
>
> "For lack of encouragement, they don't work."
>
> "Why?"
>
> "Well, the people are like that, they don't work. For example, if I were poor, I'd go to work in a factory in Mexico City or I'd go work on a ranch. I'd take on some overtime, and I'd improve my family with better food. I'd improve myself, and also— if possible—the boss for whom I worked."
>
> "The boss would benefit?"
>
> "Of course! He would benefit, and I would, too, because then I would earn the best salary. . . . But if I don't work much, only work two or three days, and pass the time drinking in the saloon, while my children are starving to death. . . ."
>
> "What do you think would be the solution to this problem?"
>
> "Well, it would be difficult for me, well . . . How to make an Otomí do it? No, there are things they don't know. You can't work with machinery for tomatoes in the same way that you scrape a maguey plant. . . . It's up to them to make an effort."

A rich farmer from the irrigated zone complained of the Otomí's lack of interest in work:

> "They ask these people from around here to work, and they don't want to, they don't like to go to work. I believe that's why they're poor, for I don't see any other reason. . . . Of course, the land is very barren, they lack resources, communications, electrification, water. . . ."
>
> "And why do you believe that they don't want to work?"
>
> "Well, it's just a person's habit, that he doesn't like to work."
>
> "And why do you believe that they have this habit?"
>
> "Well, who knows? . . . I just wouldn't know what to tell you."

For the technocrat group, the solutions to the native problem are linked to the introduction of irrigation, new techniques, industries, drinking water, and so forth. "Civilized" society is responsible for bringing the progress that the Indians have been incapable of achieving. It is a widely held opinion that the Indian's ills are rooted, not in social relations, but in "objective" factors. Introducing new conditions will be enough to change the situation. Manuel Gamio, the indigenist thinker quoted previously, expressed the need to introduce new situations in the following way:

> For the advancement of the total population as well as for the formation of an integral nationality, it is urgent not only to obtain the economic betterment of the groups that we are discussing but also that they be taught to replace the defective cultural elements that currently make their existence so poor and difficult with others that will be more satisfying and that will broaden and diversify their basic aspirations and needs.[7]

The Demagogic Attitude:
"So that the native will be integrated into national society, ideally on a basis of equality."

The use and manipulation of the "native problem" are, in the Mezquital as in other zones of the country, tools for greasing the political machinery of domination. From this perspective, the Indian's situation is a base of support to facilitate political control and to ensure that class relations do not reach the point of an acute conflict. The manipulation of the Indian problem for these purposes takes two forms:

1. The use of ethnic identity as a means for controlling the population. This usage is almost always found behind the so-called *cacigazgos* (cacique system).
2. The assertion of political power on the basis that the native problem has been "solved" by the government. It is common to find this idea among local politicians who have attained positions (e.g., as deputies) by "election."

We found one example of the former situation behind the power of an Otomí cacique who had controlled the distribution of irrigation water in the Ixmiquilpan region for decades. After considerable conflict and struggle, the cacique had no choice but to retire personally from the water control office; however, he left his acolytes there. One of them, a close relative of the cacique, is a very rich, young, dynamic agricultural entrepreneur. We spoke with him:

> "With respect to the post I hold on the Water Board, well, I believe that Don Martiniano [the cacique] had very good intentions. . . . But as he was alone and could not get people to help him, well, I thought that one of my responsibilities was to work with him on whatever I could. . . . Then I came here to try to speed up the

175

administration a little, *aware that the Otomí are very touchy*. . . . I tried to have them better served, and since I arrived, I've tried to give them all the attention possible, with the advantage that, because I know how to speak Otomí, just when they can't make themselves understood, I speak to them in their language and ask them, 'What's the problem?' and I get things resolved for them quickly. I try to help them as much as possible. . . . When they have a lot of unpaid water bills, the only thing I can do is to go to Don Martiniano and say to him, *'Hombre!* Wouldn't it be possible for you to forgive these people part of their debts. They have very little money. . . . ' "

These words hide the complicated system of favors and debts that sustain the cacique's iron control over the Indians. Neither the big entrepreneurs that we quoted at the beginning nor the technocrats look favorably on this system of bossism, because for the former, the caciques themselves, who are almost always Otomí, are contemptible, and for the latter, this system complicates the possibilities of introducing new technology and services. Nevertheless, for both the former and the latter, the cacique is "necessary" to control the situation.

On the other hand, a conversation with a deputy to the local congress, a young lawyer of Indian ancestry, enables us to look into another form of demagoguery. Faced with a question as to the existence of discrimination against the Otomí, he tried to camouflage the obvious:

"Discrimination? No, here there isn't any, there definitely isn't any. Because we understand that they are people who have been somewhat marginalized but who have a right to something better. There's no discrimination here, absolutely none, there's no problem like that here. The mestizo treats the Indian well; besides, the Indian won't put up with that anymore . . . he often experiences some mistreatment by some bad official. Also the government is trying to get all types of abuses against them denounced."

In any event, this deputy has absorbed the demagoguery quite poorly. It was particularly surprising to learn that he holds the chair in Greek and Latin etymology in the undergraduate college of a provincial town. Nevertheless, he scornfully referred to his mother tongue, Otomí, as a "dialect."

The situation that this local politician paints for us is the one that the official indigenist administration wants to attain. From the viewpoint of official indigenism, government policy should facilitate "the move from a caste situation to one of class so that the Indian may be integrated into the national society, ideally on a basis of equality."[8] Of course, a new class status does not imply, not even ideally, a situation of equality. We have already observed how the most modern entrepreneurs view the Indians, not as a class, but as an *inferior caste.* What one actually observes is that the process of integration and acculturation of the Indian does not bring with it the elimination of the racist ideological "distortions," but, on the contrary, raises them to a new plane. Why, in spite of the technocrats' work to "develop" the Indians and to bring them civilization, does the bulk of the rural bourgeoisie continue to look on them as inferior races? Undoubtedly it must be because today's society continues to require the existence of the phenomenon of discrimination.

The Liberal Attitude:
"They are industrious people.
Government intervention is all that's needed."

One (small) group of the local bourgeoisie has an attitude totally different from the predominant one. This is a liberal position that often resembles populism but also seeks paternalistic solutions. At times these ideas mask Christian attitudes about the Indians, which exalt the spirituality of the Otomí. For example, a rich merchant who was president of the Lions Club in the region years ago said,

> "The Otomí are poor in the material, but in the spiritual they are very rich. It is a race for which the government ought to do everything in its capacity to end this material poverty, because they are workers, they are very industrious people. Government intervention is all that's needed . . . that way, their poverty would end."
>
> "And why do you believe they are so poor?"
>
> "Well, just because they don't have anything. They have land that doesn't produce anything but lizards . . . and, nevertheless, as I was saying, they are people who have a quality of their own. You go to the home of any of those Indians, and he spends on a single celebration money that he doesn't have, or they get it somehow. . . . But they are happy, and they give you everything."

Another wealthy merchant, but one linked to indigenist political action, offered a somewhat similar opinion:

> "The Otomí are poor because their lands are very poor. If we look into history a little, we will see that their families sought refuge here, they pushed them here, and then they left them in peace because there was nothing left to take from them. The Aztecs, the Toltecs, were, as I understand it, the ones who hounded them. That is how the Otomí became used to seeing poverty as a shield, so that they would not harm him.
>
> "The Otomí are a very hard-working people, quite industrious. They learn easily what they are taught. A people that manages to survive in the midst of so much poverty and so many hardships is undeniably superior to us, for we would not withstand it.
>
> "Besides they are multiplying, they keep on multiplying. . . . The Otomí are a people who might possibly have experienced a trauma, and they thought that their poverty was a shield so that others would not keep on harming them. And it has been difficult to break down that resistance: I believe that it is already over-

come. . . . We ran up against the initial problem that the Indian did not want anyone to help him, did not want to be redeemed. Later, once he began to see the benefits that he was receiving, the problem was that we no longer could, we didn't know how to deal with so many requests to attend to their problems, because we couldn't solve them all."

In this case, the native's "virtue" is not his spirituality but his capacity for suffering. This conception inevitably leads to the call for paternalistic government activity. But the problems were so numerous that indigenist action rapidly got bogged down: it had to be limited to "alleviating" some of the Indians' material sufferings.

Of great interest was the interview with the municipal president (a merchant by profession) of one of the towns most densely populated with Indians. "Why are the Otomí so poor?" we asked him.

"Because the mestizos exploit them a lot [*laughter*]; it's a phenomenon that happens everywhere."

"They exploit them a lot?"

"Yes, *we have exploited* them a great deal. The Indians have minimal purchasing power, but they are many, and, however little they buy, however little they consume. . . . There is even a saying among the merchants here: 'If you're going to start a business, it had better be for something the Otomí consume . . . because there are so many of them that it will get the business moving.' Well, now, why are they so poor? Well, I don't really know. Because they're stupid? No, definitely not. Because they're lazy? No, not that, either. Because they have been in the Valle del Mezquital for many years? Probably. And I believe that because *they do not think like we do:* because if you're relatively poor, you're not likely to spend ten pesos on a drink, but they will.

"Everybody says that it is because of the zone in which they're stuck: poor soil, meager possibilities for production, and so on, but the idea is for the Otomí to stay with the land that is going to be irrigated; but unfortunately, because of some circumstances I don't know about, it always ends up in the hands of mestizos . . . because that's who can buy it. . . .

"I believe that it is a defect on the part of Maurilio Muñóz [an indigenist official], because he is an anthropologist, to try to preserve the Otomí culture. They don't want them to assimilate. I don't know why they're going to want them like that [*laughter*]. They said: 'How do you know that the Otomí culture isn't better than the one you claim to have?' *But it isn't a question of seeing which is better, but of seeing which is going to win,* as in everything. And unfortunately, ours is winning. So it makes no sense for them to preserve them as Otomí. . . . Absolutely, my culture is worse, I don't doubt it. But now it's the one that dominates; well, once and for all, let them come here."

This curious mixture of "pragmatic cynicism" and liberalism enables one to justify the greediest forms of exploitation. A more advanced, more progressive opinion came from an Otomí schoolteacher, a political leader:

"They say that the Otomí are drunks, degenerates, or lazy, but for me that is not true. In fact, the people are tired of so much exploitation, so much deceit, so many speeches. . . . They only pay attention to [the Otomí] at election time so that they can get their votes, but afterwards they forget about them, and they continue to live in the same old situation, without any progress. But the Otomí himself is not really lazy; what he needs is guidance at work and a fighting spirit to improve his economic condition. . . . But as long as there's no irrigation, I don't believe that there will be any success in improving the people's economic situation."

The liberal attitude of one segment of the regional dominant class is also reflected in indigenist policy. This liberal attitude is the other face of the attitude that I have labeled "demagogic." While the latter affirms the possibility of integrating the native on "a basis of equality" into an unequal society, the liberal viewpoint converts this possibility into a necessity of state. Indigenist policy is thus revealed as a state concern. This has been recognized by Gonzalo Aguirre Beltrán, one of the most brilliant exponents of Mexican indigenism: "Indigenism, basing itself on the mestizo status of the majority of the country's population and on the arrogation of the indigenous past, rationalizes the right that it believes it has to impose a single way out on the Indian: Mexican nationality."[9]

Indigenist Ideology in the National Context

To this point I have allowed only the regional bourgeoisie to speak and have counterbalanced their ideas with some references to official indigenist theory. In using this approach, I wished to make one of the most significant conclusions from our research understood: official indigenist policy is not independent from the interests of the dominant classes in Mexico; on the contrary, these interests find their most polished expression in that policy. As has been seen, and as is obvious, the research did not find one single attitude or position toward the Indians, but a varied range that extends from the most racist ideas to progressive liberal ones. Nevertheless, all of these have one common denominator: they are expressions of the politically powerful and economically dominant sector of Mexican society. Here, we shall term all these expressions ideology, whether advanced by theoreticians of indigenism or by the bourgeoisie itself directly. This leads us to wonder whether there is some specific form of economic exploitation, characteristic of the relation between the bourgeoisie and the natives, that might constitute the basis of this indigenist ideology, which is a national phenomenon and goes beyond the limits of the indigenous regions.

Is There an Indian Economy?

The presence of specific forms of economic exploitation of the Indian would imply the existence of an economic situation for the Indians different from that of the worker or the peasant. In fact, all the positions within the indigenist ideology begin from the following postulate: the Indian constitutes a social category distinct from the rest of the population (whether because of his "racial inferiority," the "climate," his "culture," the "forms of domination," etc.). This does not mean that any viewpoint that considers the Indian as a distinct category is part of what we are calling "indigenist ideology," which is defined by its bourgeois character.

Several recently completed studies clearly demonstrate that the indigenous people (provisionally defined by the language that they speak) are totally integrated into the country's global economic structure.[10] Thus, any theory that asserts the need to integrate the Indian into the nation is only justifying a process of integration ("acculturation") that has already occurred, a *fait accompli*. That is, it is trying to justify the way in which the Indian is integrated into Mexican society.

Moreover, in analyzing the particular features of the economic situation of native language–speaking groups, one observes that the same types of exploitation mechanisms predominate among them as among the rest of the population. One discovers that the Indian is being exploited as a peasant and as a worker (almost always as a peasant). The traditional economic forms of pre-Hispanic or Indo-colonial origin, such as collective labor, commercial ownership, forms of redistribution of wealth (of potlatch-type "leveling"), subsistence consumption, and communal organization are economic mechanisms that no longer fulfill their original functions and are, moreover, characteristics not just of the indigenous population but of the entire peasantry.

Collective labor, in the few places where it continues, is quite detached from the community's productive base. The systems of mutual aid have remained relegated to such work as building schools, homes, roads, and so forth, almost always under state control, thus saving considerable investment in wages for labor. Communal property as a legal form peculiar to the indigenous community has lost its rationale. In fact, it does not differ from ejido ownership. In the few instances in which the communal property is farmland, it is divided into parcels and distributed among the peasants. In the majority of cases, it is rough or forest land and operates just as the communal section of ejido land does. In fact, agrarian reform in Mexico did not stimulate the process of "return" of the old communal land to the peasants; instead, it encouraged in its place the system of "endowment" of ejido land.

The traditional festivals have practically ceased to function to prevent accumulation of wealth within the community and have become an important apparatus for consumption of industrially produced goods that serves to extend the domestic capitalist market. (Many of the traditional celebrations have been rescued from oblivion by the beer-brewing companies, for example.)

Subsistence consumption is an important trait of the entire peasant economy and by no means peculiar to the Indian communities. As I have shown elsewhere, subsistence consumption does not constitute a mode of production, but a form of distribution.[11] Its old productive base, the natural economy, has been replaced by a simple commodity economy.

Finally, it is no longer possible to think of the community as an economic unit. Studies conducted in the Valle del Mezquital and in other areas enable one to affirm that the economic organization of the community is not self-sufficient, indeed far from it.[12] The results of this research demonstrate that a very high percentage of the community's expenditures derive from earnings obtained outside—from jobs as day laborers, industrial workers, domestic laborers, migrant workers in the southern United States, and so forth. This means that the community's existence is not explained by the community itself.

In conclusion, it is not possible to think that an indigenous economy, differentiated from the national economy, exists as a segment of the whole society. In sum, there is no "indigenous mode of production" distinct from the simple commodity or capitalist economies. This is not to say that in the interstices of market relations there is no infiltration by parasitic merchants, moneylenders, and acaparadores, who take advantage of the Indian's ignorance of Spanish, much as they take advantage of any poor peasant's lack of education, to appropriate part of the wealth produced by the indigenous peasants. However, these intermediaries are nothing but vultures who eat the leftovers from the grand feast at which the great domestic and international bourgeoisie wolfed down the Indo-colonial world. The paradox of indigenist ideology is that it seeks to put all the blame on these intermediary scavengers, long after most of the cake has already been eaten. Indigenist ideology is a search for a sacrificial lamb to expiate the guilt of the modern bourgeoisie. We shall return to this topic further on.

Forms of Political Domination and Economic Change

If there is no special economic basis distinct from the commodity-capitalist system to account for the widespread phenomenon of indigenist ideology, is it possible to find an explanation for it in the apparatus of political domination? That is, if there is no form of economic exploitation peculiar to bourgeois-Indian relations, perhaps there is a particular political link that gives rise to indigenist ideology.

In examining the remnants of traditional forms of political power of pre-Hispanic origin, we generally come to a common phenomenon that characterizes the political integration of the indigenous communities in the national state. This common phenomenon is the use and manipulation of the local forms of organization by the dominant classes. This phenomenon appears in two basic forms: (a) in the so-called cacique system; and (b) in an articulation of official national administrative mechanisms with the patterns of native organization. These two modalities are not, of course, mutually exclusive; in most cases they merge, but in different regions one observes a predominance of one form or the other. In each case, the political organization of native origin is limited to hybrid forms that have ceased to have a determinative effect.

There is an important difference between these two aspects of the political structure in indigenous areas. Generally, the cacique system tends to keep the Indians within a framework of "traditional" social relations, "isolated" from national society. That is, political communication is monopolized by the caciques, who thereby ensure despotic control over the communities. In fact, this system does not by any means imply the isolation of the indigenous community; rather, it implies that the ties that link it to the country are firmly controlled by key personalities, who ensure political stability through a combination of favors and repression.

Under the second system, control of the community is more administrative than personal. This modality tends to lead to the disappearance of the traditional mechanisms of power, given that it does not need them. This form of symbiosis between official and native power generally exists in those regions where the economic apparatus of exploitation is more capable of maintaining domination on its own. While the cacique system is necessary to protect and reproduce the relations between the (indigenous) simple commodity economy and the capitalist system, in situations where these relations imply the existence of numerous forms of parasitism (e.g., acaparadores, merchant capital, profiteering), the official administrative apparatus, including some traditional features, in turn proves capable of "keeping order" in situations where modern, capitalist exploitation relations clearly prevail. In the latter case, where the predominant economic factors crystallize in agricultural capital and wage labor, the function of intermediaries is not indispensable and, indeed, is only just barely possible. (In any event, the cacique system assumes very individual forms.) The cacique is necessary as long as the working population remains strongly tied to the land and the community.

From the perspective of ideological phenomena, it can be observed that

Table 25

Ideological Tendencies in Caciquismo and Political-Administrative Domination

Cacique System	Administrative Domination
Parasitic ⟶ Racism Merchants	Technocratism ⟵ Officials, technicians, and politicians
Caciques ⟶ Demagoguery	Liberalism ⟵ Industrial bourgeoisie, state policy
Articulation of simple commodity and capitalist economies	Greater development of capitalism

the economic and political situations that foster the cacique system are accompanied, in turn, by the appearance of two contradictory but complementary processes. First, the cacique himself generally relies (as does his group) on the ideological statements that I have described as "demagogic" attitudes in order to ensure communication with and control of the native community. Second, the merchant-usurers who live off intermediary parasitic activities (and who are generally mestizos and sometimes referred to as "ladinos," or "caxlanes") develop a deeply racist ideology that justifies the drastic forms of exploitation of the community.

In turn, the "technocratic" attitude and the "liberal" attitude are the two faces of the ideology that belongs to political administrative domination. These two ideological expressions are the "advanced form" assumed by "racism" and "demagoguery." When the parasitic merchant sector that exercises economic control is replaced by officials, professional politicians, and technicians, racism is transformed into technocratism. At the same time, when the technicians' political power permits the removal of the cacique, traditional demagoguery tends to be replaced by a liberal attitude that represents the interests of the industrial bourgeoisie, which is not present in the native zones but lets its influence be felt through the state. Table 25 presents a schematic view of these trends.

The passage from demagoguery to liberalism and from racism to technocratism is only an initial phase of the ideological process, which corresponds to the reformist transition from a semi-capitalist situation to a totally capitalist one. However, capitalist development in the native zones leads to the appearance of new social actors in those zones: a local agro-industrial and agro-commercial bourgeoisie flourishes, reassuming, as we have seen, racist attitudes. Simultaneously, the local governing political groups rely on more repressive methods for political control. All of this leads to a second phase in the ideological process: technocratism becomes demagogic, and liberalism is transformed into racism. The following outline presents the entire process:

$$\text{Racism} \xrightarrow{\text{Phase 1}} \text{Technocratism} \xrightarrow{\text{Phase II}} \text{Demagoguery}$$

$$\text{Demagoguery} \xrightarrow{\text{Phase 1}} \text{Liberalism} \xrightarrow{\text{Phase II}} \text{Racism}$$

Thus, as if by magic in a process that appears to be a kind of social alchemy, racism has given birth to demagoguery, and demagoguery to racism. Things have apparently come full circle back to the original situation. But the new demagoguery and the new racism have a very different content and explanation. Here is the key to the "native problem" as it appears today, after what we have defined as "phases" of the economic-political-ideological process have wiped out the Indian's social existence by "integrating him" into the capitalist world.

The Janus Aspect of Indigenist Ideology

Next it is necessary to speak separately about the two ideological processes (racism-technocratism-demagoguery and demagoguery-liberalism-racism) in order to attempt to find the real dimension of interethnic relations in the context of sociopolitical development. But one must keep in mind that we are dealing with two indivisible processes, like the two faces of the god Janus: one looking toward the past, the other toward the future, but seeing with the same vision, that of bourgeois thought.

The Discrimination That the System Needs: Demagoguery-Liberalism-Racism

It would be simplistic to imagine that the breakup of the typically peasant structures linked to the capitalist economy, through a more or less accelerated "modernization," would end reliance on mechanisms of discrimination. In the end, this "modernization" did not mean the end of the exploitation; instead, it resulted in its "rationalization" in overtly capitalist terms. On bursting into a system that links noncapitalist economic and political forms with the capitalist market, modern capitalism needs, in principle, to destroy any social, political, or economic situation that implies traditional forms of monopoly of such factors (ethnic castes, caciques, archaic latifundismo). The "reformist" (or, sometimes, "revolutionary") task of modern capitalism is to eliminate these existing situations.

With respect to the phenomenon that concerns us, modern capital confronts the ideology of the cacique, who is, paradoxically, the nondiscriminatory focal point of an exploitation relationship. The cacique is "popular"; his position is based on indigenous traditions and has arisen from within the community. Capitalist interests, on the other hand, "come from outside" and tend to destroy the community. Nevertheless, in their struggle with the cacique, they necessarily adopt a "more advanced" (liberal) ideology that not only upholds the Indian's rights but also offers full state support in solving his problems. Of course, in many cases, in order to establish the state's power in the Indian zones, liberal interests have had to ally themselves with the caciques, whom they have not managed to destroy. Thus, in many Indian areas, liberalism has been bound up with the cacique system, having taken as a base only a single political structure. These were the two tendencies that collided and then became intertwined during the first phase of capitalism's penetration into the indigenous community, during the postrevolutionary period and, especially, beginning with the latter half of the 1930s (the Cárdenas presidency). Indigenist liberalism touched off tough battles with the old racism of the rich Ladinos (and mestizos); but the liberal indigenist spirit, almost always lacking a regional social basis of support, has often had no other choice than to ally itself with the demagogic pragmatism of the caciques and to imitate their conduct. Indigenist liberalism was always an arm of the state; it refused to mobilize the Indian masses themselves and had no young regional bourgeoisie on which to rely for support. Accordingly, liberal indigenism advanced by means of officials, administrators, and teachers. But it represented political and economic interests that had not yet developed in the indigenous areas: those of a rising national bourgeoisie.

But this was the first phase in which liberalism was born. After the liberal indigenist ideology came the bourgeoisie itself, which began to develop locally, in the native zones. Surprisingly, however, this new regional bourgeoisie was not the bearer of a liberal ideology, but had a discriminatory, racist attitude.

If we examine the problem in detail, we discover that for this new racist ideology, the concept *Indian* is not the one the old Ladino usurers had, that economic throwback. For the mestizo merchant, the Indian is the real, concrete person who lives in the communities, speaks a native language, and above all, buys expensive goods from him and sells him cheap products; for this two-bit merchant, the Indian is a poor peasant.

For the new bourgeoisie, on the other hand, the Indian is the ideal image of the day laborer, the peon, the proletarian; to the new bourgeoisie, whether he speaks a vernacular tongue or has special customs is of little importance. For the new bourgeoisie, it is enough for a man to be a ragged fellow who needs to sell his labor power for him to fall into the category *Indian*. The concept *Indian* (or *native*) provides the modern bourgeoisie the perfect justification for the exploitation to which it subjects its wage laborers. The reasoning is the following: modern society has provided the Indians the means to integrate themselves into the national economy on "equal" terms; those who do not succeed in overcoming their situation continue to be Indians, are inferior, have not been capable of "assimilating themselves."

Thus develops the myth of the unassimilated native who is not sufficiently intelligent or quick to rise in the national society. This myth tries to cover up the real fact of exploitation with the screen of a purported nonassimilation. It is said that the Indian is poor and exploited because he is an inferior being. As for the others, they are not exploited. In this fashion, the Indian's situation permits covering up of the widespread exploitation typical of capitalist relations of production. For this reason, the new bourgeoisie is interested in keeping the category *Indian* or *native* alive, whether or not it is an ethnic reality. The truth is that this class is the exterminator of the Indian as an ethnic and cultural category. It has caused the Indian's death, but it needs his corpse as an ideological shield.[13] Racist indigenism is an ideology that nourishes the discrimination necessary to the capitalist system. Capitalist development in the native zones has meant only the death of the old racism and its resurrection in a new guise.

The Policy of the State:
Racism-Technocratism-Demagoguery

We have seen how the annihilation of the cacique system (and its "demagogic despotism"), through the path of bourgeois liberalism, tends to lead to the rebirth of racism. Let us next look at how the path of bourgeois technocratism leads to the rebirth of demagoguery out of the ashes of the old racism. This is the other face of Janus.

I have already explained how the sector of middlemen, merchants, acaparadores, and moneylenders tends to disappear owing to the parallel penetration of modern capital and the national bureaucratic-administrative apparatus for political control. The gradual dominance of the latter is guided not only by liberal inspiration but also by a technocratic attitude and technocratic activity. In fact, this attitude is nothing but the "dehumanized" version of liberalism. The technocrat is responsible for smoothing the way for modern capitalism, for "replacing the [Indian's] faulty cultural features" in order to introduce the new technology, the new education, and the new ideology that will enable him to overcome the challenge of the environment. By favoring the introduction of irrigation, technology, communications, and, generally speaking, infrastructure projects, the activity of the technocrat, who believes that the causes of Indian misery are to be found in the environment, is in fact fertilizing the soil in order that capital might grow and bear fruit.

The state is aware of this process and realizes that the technocratic policy of its own agencies contributes to eroding the very existence of the Indian as an ethnic reality. In fact, official indigenism openly pursues the goal of integrating the Indian into the national reality. Yet, simultaneously, it undertakes the task of rescuing the indigenous culture. Here begins the second phase of the process: the transformation of technocratism into populist and culturalist demagoguery.

Official indigenism proposes an integration process that is supposedly going to enrich the Mexican nationality. The Indian is not going to be simply integrated into (i.e., engulfed by) Mexican class-based society. In the indigenist imagination it is said that the Indian is going to contribute the most positive aspects of his culture to enrich the Mexican nationality, in a symbiosis of the European and the autochthonous that will yield a third culture: the mestizo. Accordingly, Mexican society derives from three cultures in the process of integration, with the Indian—now seen as a cultural entity—playing an important role. This oversimplification of the process of creating the Mexican nationality (which is the fruit of the interaction among not just three cultures but many)[14] has as one goal, among others, the perpetuation, at the ideological level, of the Indian's image. In fact, it demagogically complements the need that the bourgeoisie has for the idea of the Indian as the ideal sacrificial lamb for the guilt of the dominant class.

Thus, after contributing to the social disappearance of the indigenous people, technocratic indigenist ideology resurrects the Indian at the level of cultural reality. The demagoguery consists in proclaiming that indigenous culture enters the society through the front door, as guest of honor, while the real Indian is made to go around to the service entrance, in order to be assimilated as a proletarian deprived of his culture. Accordingly, the government institutions responsible for implementing the indigenist policy have become administrators of a culture plundered of its social and material base, of a culture "cleansed" of the wretchedness that accompanied its bearers, of a culture that can enter the living rooms of the bourgeoisie and appear on television. The state's indigenist policy has contributed to the murder of the indigenous people. Just like bourgeois interests, the state also needs the Indian's cultural corpse in order to nourish the myth of national unity. Much as the three cultures are merged on an egalitarian basis, the social classes—the poor and the rich—find themselves made brothers within Mexican society. The official indigenist institutions are nothing but permanent agencies for the Indian's funeral ceremony, perpetual wakes over the corpse of the indigenous people. It could be said that interethnic relations are essentially an ideological representation of real class struggles. This does not mean that interethnic relations do not exist, but that they function as an ideological apparatus of domination, that they are like a fulcrum of ideological support for the powerful levers of class exploitation.

I have outlined the most significant trends in the interaction of six attitudes within indigenist ideology (i.e., the old racism, the old demagoguery, liberalism, technocratism, the new racism, and the new demagoguery). The analysis has necessarily been schematic and has only attempted to initiate discussion of the problem from a new perspective. These six attitudes merge and are intertwined with economic, social, and political processes in an extraordinarily complex fashion, resulting in a reality very rich in surprises for the researcher. The central idea that can be drawn from our studies of interethnic relations is that those relations have become a part of the extraeconomic mechanisms of an ideological nature that permit the reproduction of capitalist relations of production in Mexico. Interethnic relations do not simply reflect the particular features of social contradictions in the rural zones; instead, they are principally an ideological system that enables these contradictions to persist. They are an ideal image in the mind of the dominant classes that functions as an aid in the exploitation of the dominated classes.

Notes

Preface

1. *Estructura agraria y clases sociales en México* (Mexico City: Ediciones Era, 1974); *El poder despótico burgués: las raíces campesinas de las estructuras políticas de mediación* (Barcelona: Península, 1977); *Campesinado y poder político en México* (Mexico City: Ediciones Era, 1982); and, with Gerardo Otero, "Agrarian Crisis and Social Differentiation in Mexico," *Journal of Peasant Studies* 14, no. 3 (1987).

2. Ernest Feder, "Campesinistas y descampesinistas: tres enfoques divergentes (no incompatibles) sobre la destrucción del campesinado," *Comercio Exterior* 27 (1977): 12. See also Richard L. Harris's version of the argument: "Marxism and the Agrarian Question in Latin America," *Latin American Perspectives* 19 (Fall 1978).

3. Manuel Coello, "¿Recampesinización en la descampesinización?" *Revista Mexicana de Sociología* 43:1 (1981). Luisa Paré, *El proletariado agrícola en México* (Mexico City: Siglo XXI Editores, 1977).

4. Examining the history of the struggle of the French peasants against agrarianism is quite beneficial here. Cf. Phillippe Gratton, *Les paysans français contre l'agrarisme* (Paris: Maspero, 1972).

5. *Ley de Fomento Agropecuario* (Mexico City: Ediciones de la Cámara de Diputados, 1981). Cf. articles 35 and 42. In addition, this act provides another mechanism for the legal rental of ejido and communal parcels (and private ones as well): the Ministry of Agriculture and Water Resources will identify idle lands appropriate for production and will, in the name of the nation, take charge of renting them (see articles 71–89). Furthermore, the act encourages the concentration of small private property, considered to be in the "public interest," by offering tax exemptions for transfers of property "that have as a goal the regrouping of *minifundios* [small landholdings]" (article 69).

6. *Sistema Alimentario Mexicano: primer planteamiento de metas de consumo y estrategia de producción de alimentos básicos para 1980–82* (Mexico City: Oficina de Asesores del C. Presidente de la República, 1980), emphasis added.

7. Comisión Económica para América Latina [CEPAL], *Economía campesina y agricultura empresarial: tipología de productores del agro mexicano* (Mexico City: Siglo XXI Editores, 1982) (study prepared by Alexander Schejtman).

8. The CEPAL study cited indicates that even on the transitional level (which

is located between the peasantry and the entrepreneurs), it would seem "more probable that the forces that tend to position it on the lower stratum are greater than those that would push it toward the level of midlevel entrepreneur" (ibid., 111). See also the critical study by M. R. Redclift, "El Estado frente al campo," *Nexos* 47 (1981). "Cassio Luiselli, the principal architect of the SAM," says Redclift, "has made it clear that the Mexican government's intention is to occupy a *space* in the Mexican countryside. The 'space' that Luiselli has in mind is not that of the peasant economy but that of a rising class within the peasant sector. The measures of the Mexican Food System will have the effect of converting a minority of peasant producers into fully developed small commodity producers, at the same time that they reduce the productive role of the poorest peasants, by denying them access to the land, except as wage laborers paid by the Mexican State."

1. Agriculture and Capitalism

1. The first part of this chapter, as well as other sections of the book, contains portions of an early version of an essay entitled "Peasantry and Political Power in Mexico," prepared for an address to the Tenth Latin American Sociology Congress, Santiago, Chile, 1972.

2. These specific studies comprise: research carried out in 1966-67 on the coast of Michoacán and Guerrero (Mexico), a study in the Venezuelan Andes (1968-69), and research in the Valle del Mezquital (Mexico) completed during 1972 and 1973.

3. Karl Marx, *El capital*, trans. Wenceslao Roces, 3 vols. (Mexico City: Fondo de Cultura Económica, 1959), 3:817. [The English translation used in the text appears in Karl Marx, *Capital: Volume Three*, trans. David Fernbach (New York: Vintage, 1981), 1024. Hereinafter, citations to the third volume of *Capital* will be to the Fernbach translation and will be followed by the volume and page in Roces's Spanish version, in square brackets, as follows: "[FCE 3:(page)]"—Trans.].

4. V. I. Lenin, *El desarrollo del capitalismo en Rusia* (Moscow: Ediciones en Lenguas Extranjeras, 1950), 12ff.

5. See esp. Lenin's comments on Karl Kautsky's book *Die Agrarfrage* in V. I. Lenin, *Obras completas*, 2d ed. (Buenos Aires: Editorial Cartago, 1969), 4:65-192, hereinafter *Obras*; and idem, "El problema agrario y los críticos de Marx," in *Obras*, 5:101-270.

6. Marx, *Capital: Volume Three*, 1018 [FCE 3:811].

7. Ibid., 970 [FCE 3:769].

8. The most exaggeratedly mechanical version of this position, inspired by Louis Althusser, is found in E. Fioravanti, *El concepto de modo de producción* (Barcelona: Península, 1972).

9. Karl Marx, *Elementos fundamentales para la crítica de la economía política (borrador) (1857–1858)*, 2 vols. (Mexico City: Siglo XXI Editores, 1971), 1:21.

10. Ibid., 27–28 (emphasis added). [The English translation appearing in the text is drawn from Eugene Kamenka, ed., *The Portable Karl Marx* (New York: Viking, 1983), 392—Trans.]

11. The respective writings are found in the first volume of *Capital* and in the text entitled *El capital, libro I, capítulo 6 (inédito)* (Buenos Aires: Siglo XXI Editores, 1974). [An English translation of the so-called chapter 6 of *Capital* appears as "Results of the Immediate Process of Production" in Karl Marx, *Capital: Volume One*, trans. Ernest Mandel (New York: Vintage, 1977), 1021. Hereinafter references to the first volume of *Capital* will be to the Mandel translation and will be followed by the volume and page in Roces's Spanish version, in square brackets, as follows: "[FCE 1:(page)]"—Trans.]

12. Marx, *Capital: Volume One*, 1021 [FCE 1:56] (emphasis in the original).

13. Ibid. (emphasis in the original).

14. Ibid., 1026 [FCE 1:61] (emphasis in the original).

15. The discussion has no meaning in a natural economy, where the effect of exchange value is not a useful category for analysis.

16. Karl Marx, *Theories of Surplus-Value*, 2 vols. (Moscow: Progress Publishers, 1968), 1:344 (emphasis in the original).

17. Ibid.

18. Ibid.

19. Marx, *Capital: Volume Three*, 942 [FCE 3:746].

20. Ibid.

21. Marx, *Capital: Volume One*, 275 [FCE 1:124].

22. Ibid., 129–30 [FCE 1:7].

23. Ibid., 137 [FCE 1:13].

24. Ibid.

25. Ibid., 275 [FCE 1:124].

26. This conclusion demolishes the assumptions about a marginal, unproductive peasant population, whose labor would not be "necessary" to society and for whose labor power there would be no "demand."

27. Marx, *Capital: Volume One*, 196 [FCE 1:63].

28. Ibid., 269 n. 24 [FCE 1:120 n. 38].

29. Marx, *Capital: Volume Three*, 117 [FCE 3:45].

30. Ibid.

31. Arghiri Emmanuel, *El intercambio desigual* (Mexico City: Siglo XXI Editores, 1972).

32. Christian Palloix et al., eds., *Imperialismo y comercio internacional* (Buenos Aires: Ediciones Pasado y Presente, 1971), 124.

33. Marx illustrated the confrontation between capitalists and landholders in England by referring to the problem of the Corn Laws.

34. Marx, *Capital: Volume One*, 226 [FCE 1:118].

35. Variants of this illustrative anecdote have appeared in a number of sources. The version presented here derives from Emmanuel, *El intercambio desigual*, 145.

36. Marx, *Capital: Volume Three*, 134 [FCE 3:59].

37. In fact, it is the industrial bourgeoisie, local or international, that benefits most, but it is not the only sector that benefits, nor does this "additional profit" mean very much to it in terms of the volume of its income.

38. Cf. the excellent study by Karl Kautsky, *La cuestión agraria* (Paris: Ruedo Ibérico, 1970), esp. chap. 6, "Grande y pequeña explotación agrícola" (101–38).

39. Sergio Reyes Osorio, "Aspectos de la problemática agraria nacional," *Revista del México Agrario* 1, no. 5 (1968): 71–95.

40. Lenin, *El desarrollo del capitalismo en Rusia*, 7.

41. Centro de Investigaciones Agrarias (CDIA), *Estructura agrario y desarrollo agrícola en México*, 3 vols. (Mexico City, 1970), 1:332ff. Eckstein did research in this study directed by Reyes Osorio.

42. Ibid.

43. Pablo González Casanova, *La democracia en México* (Mexico City: Ediciones Era, 1975).

44. In CDIA, *Estructura agrario y desarrollo agrícola en México*.

45. José Nun, *Superpoblación relativa, ejército industrial de reserva y masa marginal* (Mexico City: ABIIS, 1972).

46. Ibid.

47. See the interesting and suggestive article by F. H. Cardoso, "Comentario sobre los conceptos de sobrepoblación relativa y marginalidad," *Revista Latinoamericana de Ciencias Sociales*, June–December 1971, 57–72. There it is pointed out that Nun did not frame his concept of marginality within the theory of accumulation.

48. Samir Amín, *L'accumulatión a l'échelle mondiale* (Paris: Anthropos, 1970), 11.

49. Christian Palloix, "La question de l'échange inégal," *L'Homme et la Societé* 18 (1970): 27.

2. The Mexican Path

1. Marco Antonio Durán, "Los problemas agrarios mexicanos," *Revista del México Agrario* 1, no. 3 (1968): 60–61.

2. Ibid. (emphasis added).

3. Adolfo Gilly, *La revolución interrumpida* (Mexico City: Ediciones "El Caballito," 1971); Michel Gutelman, *Capitalismo y reforma agraria en México* (Mexico City: Ediciones Era, 1974).

4. E.g., Jesús Puente Leyva, "Acumulación de capital y crecimiento en el sector agropecuario en México, 1930–67," in *Bienestar campesino y desarrollo*

económico, ed. Ifigenia M. de Navarrete (Mexico City: Fondo de Cultura Económica, 1971); and esp. CDIA, *Estructura agraria y desarrollo agrícola en México*.

5. Rosa Luxemburg, *La acumulación de capital* (Mexico City: Editorial Grijalbo, 1967), 322–23.

6. V. I. Lenin, "Los nuevos cambios económicos de la vida campesina," in *Obras*, 1:46–47.

7. Salomón Eckstein, *El marco macroeconómico del problema agrario mexicano* (Mexico City: CDIA, 1968).

8. CDIA, *Estructura y desarrollo agrícola en México*, 1:282–87.

9. Puente Leyva, "Acumulación de capital y crecimiento en el sector agropecuario," 68.

10. "Negative rent" is not a peculiar concept but simply the result of the calculations in specific (noncapitalist) conditions. There is no theoretical pretense in its use; it is an indicator of losses.

11. Kautsky's analysis is found in chapter 5 of his book *La cuestión agraria*. Marx's most systematic, concise treatment is found in *Theories of Surplus-Value*, 2 vols. (Moscow: Progress Publishers, 1968), 2:293ff.

12. CDIA, *Estructura y desarrollo agrícola en México*, table 3-25 (p. 507).

13. The cited CDIA study adds it proportionally to the plots of fewer than five hectares and to the ejidos but not to the larger parcels. The study gives no valid reason for doing so, but this manages to inflate the output of the ejidos and minifundios.

3. The Modes of Production

1. Witold Kula, *Théorie économique du système féodal* (Paris: Mouton, 1970), 25–26.

2. Lenin, "Los nuevos cambios económicos de la vida campesina," in *Obras*, 1:49 (emphasis added).

3. Lenin, *El desarrollo del capitalismo en Rusia*, 157–58.

4. Lenin, "El capitalismo en la agricultura," in *Obras*, 4:126.

5. Lenin, *El desarrollo del capitalismo en Rusia*, 7.

6. Marx, *Capital: Volume Three*, 941 [FCE 3:745].

7. Ibid., 942 [FCE 3:746].

8. This study was carried out in collaboration with Jorge Casas and María Elena Pérez during the second half of 1972.

9. CDIA, *Estructura agraria y desarrollo agrícola en México*, 1.

10. The CDIA designates the following types of farms in accordance with the classifications from the CDIA study (1960 prices): *infrasubsistence*, production less than 1,000 pesos; *subfamily*, production from 1,000 to 5,000 pesos; *family*, production from 5,000 to 25,000 pesos; *average multifamily*, production

from 25,000 to 100,000 pesos; and *large multifamily*, production greater than 100,000 pesos (see ibid., 1:282–86).

11. Ibid., 1:286ff.

12. The use of fertilizers is one of the best indices for measuring the degree of efficiency of the units of production. For example, between 1950 and 1967, agricultural production doubled in Mexico, notwithstanding the fact that the area irrigated increased by only 54 percent. But the use of fertilizers took an astonishing leap: in 1950 fewer than 12,000 tons were used, in 1960 around 470,000 tons were used, and 1968 usage reached almost 500,000 tons (see Puente Leyva, "Acumulación de capital y crecimiento en el sector agropecuario." Cf. Leopoldo Solís, *La realidad económica mexicana: retrovisión y perspectivas* (Mexico City: Siglo XXI Editores, 1970), 74.

13. Marx, *Capital: Volume Three*, 885 [FCE 3:697].

14. Ibid.

15. In relation to this point, Henri Lefebvre makes the following observation:

In fact, the "directionist" setting of prices has made the mechanism of agricultural price determination increasingly bureaucratic. Under the pretext of democracy, the protection of the small agriculture of the small peasant worker, owner, tenant farmer, or sharecropper tries in fact to protect the earnings of capitalist agriculture. In effect, the very development of agricultural production threatened it. The growth of general productivity and of production, the transformation of many fields into grazing lands, bring with them the abandonment of poor lands, left fallow although they are arable. These abandonments threaten to lower the differential ground rent. It is maintained by price setting, destined in principle to ensure a "living minimum" to the small peasants who work land that is poor or poorly situated.

See Henri Lefebvre, "La teoría marxista-leninista en la renta de la tierra," in *Estudios sociológicos sobre la reforma agraria* (Mexico City: Universidad Nacional Autónoma de México, 1964).

16. Marx, *Capital: Volume Three*, 941 [FCE 3:745].

17. Ibid., 942 [FCE 3:746].

18. Lenin, *El desarrollo del capitalismo en Rusia*, 169–70.

19. The information that follows here is derived from A. Calderón Martínez, "El mercado internacional de productos agrícolas," *Revista del México Agrario* 3, no. 1 (1969–70).

20. Marx, *Capital: Volume Three*, 745 [FCE 3:569].

21. Ibid.

22. Ibid., 729 [FCE 3:556].

23. Often cited, for example, is the case of the moneylender who uses bank financing with the aim of lending the capital thus obtained to poor peasants at high rates of interest.

24. Marx, *Capital: Volume Three*, 730 [FCE 3:556].

25. Roger Bartra, *Breve diccionario de sociología marxista* (Mexico City:

Editorial Grijalbo, 1973), 105–6. See the interesting discussion by Sergio de la Peña, "El modo de producción capitalista y la transición al socialismo," *Historia y Sociedad* 1 (1974). See also a critique of the use of the concept in Roger Bartra, "Sobre la articulación de modos de producción en América Latina," ibid., 5 (1975).

26. See in this regard the interesting study by Pierre-Philippe Rey, *Les alliances de classes* (Paris: Maspero, 1973).

27. *Structure* means the complex of internal, stable relations that articulate the different elements of a specific whole; these internal relations determine the function of each element and contribute to explaining the process of change of the whole. The essential characteristic of these relations is that they confer *coherence* upon the whole, give it the quality of unity (see Bartra, *Breve diccionario de sociología marxista*).

28. Puente Leyva, "Acumulación de capital y crecimiento en el sector agropecuario." Cf. Solís, *La realidad económica mexicana*.

29. The state financing institutions are: the Banco Agrario de Yucatán, the Banco Agrario de Michoacán, S.A., the Banco Agrario del Noroeste, S.A., the Banco Agropecuario del Noroeste, S.A., the Banco Agropecuario de Occidente, S.A., the Banco Agropecuario del Sureste, the Banco Nacional Agropecuario, the Banco Nacional de Crédito Agrícola, the Banco Nacional de Crédito Ejidal, the Banco Nacional de Fomento Cooperativo, the Banco Regional de Crédito Agrícola en Matamoros, and the Fondo Nacional de Fomento Ejidal.

30. The agro-industrial enterprises include: Beneficios Mexicanos del Café, S. de R.L. y C.V.; Guanos y Fertilizantes de Mexico, S.A.; Henequén del Pacífico, S.A. de C.V.; Ingenio del Mante; Ingenio Independencia, S.A.; Ingenio Rosales, S.A.; Ingenio San Francisco el Naranjal, S.A.; Maderas Industrializadas de Quintana Roo, S.A.; Maíz Industrializado, S.A.; Refrigeradora del Noroeste, S.A.; and Sociedad Cooperativa de Ejidatarios, Obreros y Empleados del Ingenio Emiliano Zapata, S.C. de P.E. de R.S. The agro-commercial enterprises include: Almacenes Nacionales de Depósito (ANDSA); Compañía Nacional de Subsistencias Populares (CONASUPO); La Forestal, S.C.L.; and Productora Nacional de Semillas.

31. An example of a monopolistic group would be that of the large food products and milling concerns: Ortiz, Olazábal, Gómez, Hernández Pons (Herdez), Pando (linked to the Bancomer financial group), Longoria, etc.

32. In using the term *subcapitalist*, one does not wish to indicate a stage "prior" to capitalism or any noncapitalist stage; it is a term that designates underdevelopment (or a situation of dependency) in a way that alludes more directly to its *capitalist* content. Daniel Cazés has used the term in the same way in his book *Los revolucionarios* (Mexico City: Editorial Grijalbo, 1973).

33. Calderón Martínez, "El mercado internacional de productos agrícolas," 20–21.

4. The Forms of Land Ownership

1. For a more extensive interpretation of the forms of pre-Hispanic property, see Roger Bartra, "Tributo y tenencia de la tierra en la sociedad azteca," in *El modo de producción asiático*, 2d ed. (Mexico City: Ediciones Era, 1974). I have drawn from that text the summary presented here.

2. Silvio Zavala and José Miranda, "Instituciones indígenas en la colonia," in *Métodos y resultados de la política indigenista en México*, vol. 6 (Mexico City: Instituto Nacional del Indígena, 1954), 29–112.

3. Nathan L. Whetten, "México rural," *Problemas Agrícolas e Industriales de México* 5, no. 2 (1953): 75.

4. Eyler N. Simpson, "El ejido: única salida para México," *Problemas Agrícolas e Industriales de México* 4, no. 4 (1953): 18–19.

5. Enrique Semo, *Historia del capitalismo en México: los orígenes, 1521–1763* (Mexico City: Ediciones Era, 1973).

6. Ibid., 260.

7. José Miranda, "La propiedad communal de la tierra y la cohesión social de los pueblos indígenas mexicanos," *Cuadernos Americanos* 149, no. 6, 176.

8. Moisés González Navarro, "Instituciones indígenas en México independiente," in *Métodos y resultados de las política indigenista en México*, vol. 6 (Mexico City: Instituto Nacional del Indígena, 1954), 121–33.

9. Ibid., 126.

10. Simpson, "El ejido," 25.

11. Andrés Molina Enríquez, "Los grandes problemas nacionales," *Problemas Agrícolas e Industriales de México*, supplement to vol. 5, no. 1 (1953); Whetten, "México rural," 78–79; González Navarro, "Instituciones indígenas en México independiente," 130.

12. CDIA, *Estructura agraria y desarrollo agrícola en México*, 2:281.

13. Marx, *Capital: Volume One*, 1021 [FCE 1:609].

14. Ibid., 885 [FCE 1:616–17].

15. I mention only a few: François Chevalier, "La formación de los grandes latifundios en México" in *Problemas Agrícolas e Industriales de México*; Silvio Zavala, *La encomienda indiana* (Madrid: Centro de Estudios Históricos, 1935). There are several studies by the latter author, but particularly interesting is *De encomiendas y propiedad territorial en algunas regiones de la América Española* (Mexico City, 1940).

16. Semo, *Historia del capitalismo en México*, 258 (emphasis added).

17. Marx, *Capital: Volume One*, 271 [FCE 1:121]. A very vivid description of the conditions of the rural laborer can be found in John Kenneth Turner, *México bárbaro* (Mexico City: Cordemex, 1965).

18. Marx, *Capital: Volume One*, 271–72 n. 3 [FCE 1:122n].

19. Miguel Othón de Mendizábal, "El orígen histórico de nuestras clases

medias," *Ensayos sobre las clases sociales en México* (Mexico City: Editorial Nuestro Tiempo, 1970), 14.

20. Molina Enríquez, "Los grandes problemas nacionales," 55.

21. Carlos Tello, *La tenencia de la tierra en México* (Mexico City: Instituto de Investigaciones Sociales [UNAM], 1968).

22. Chevalier, "La formación de los grandes latifundios en México," 178.

23. Whetten, "México rural," 118.

24. Molina Enríquez, "Los grandes problemas nacionales," 37.

25. Whetten, "México rural," 118–26.

26. Ramón Fernández y Fernández, *Notas sobre las reforma agraria mexicana* (Chapingo: Editorial Escuela Nacional de Agricultura, n.d.), 17–18. See also idem, *Cooperación agrícola y organización económica del ejido* (Mexico City: SepSetentas, 1973), 121ff.

27. Chevalier, "La formación de los grandes latifundios en México," 225.

28. Ibid., 236.

29. See "Genesis of the Capitalist Farmer," in Marx, *Capital: Volume One,* 905 [FCE 1:631–33].

30. Molina Enríquez, "Los grandes problemas nacionales," 64 (emphasis added).

31. *Estadísticas sociales del porfiriato, 1877–1910* (Mexico City: Secretaría de Economía, 1956), 41.

32. Unpublished results of Enrique Semo's research in the archives of several haciendas.

33. CDIA, *Estructura agraria y desarrollo agrícola en México,* 2:214–19.

34. Iván Restrepo and José Sánchez Cortés, "Minifundismo y neolatifundismo en un distrito de riego," *Revista del México Agrario* 4, no. 2 (1971): 7–36.

35. Iván Restrepo and José Sánchez Cortés, "El arrendamiento de tierras ejidales: el caso de Apatzingán," *Revista del México Agrario* 3, no. 1 (1969– 70): 49. See also A. René Barbosa and Sergio Maturana, *El arrendamiento de tierras ejidales: un estudio en Michoacán* (Mexico City: CDIA, 1972).

36. In the Código Agrario, the renting of the ejido was permitted only in cases involving minors, widowhood, physical incapacity, and so on. The new law, in its Article 55, continues to prohibit renting in general, with the exceptions that mark Article 76, which permits sharecropping, renting, and the use of wage labor in the same situations as the prior Código Agrario did but adds one more: when it is a matter of "crops or work that the ejidatario cannot carry out opportunely even though he dedicates all his time and effort." The vagueness of "opportunely" and "time and effort" permits them to be translated as "capital"; thus, the ejidatario who does not have the necessary *capital* will be able to rent out his parcel. In this way, the ejido legally opens its doors to capitalism.

37. Of course, the case of small peasant renters is not included here; the latter represent a more advanced variant of sharecropping, and they reflect social

relations typical of a seignorial system or simple commodity economy. In this case, there is no relation between the capitalist and the owner of the land.

38. Karl Marx, *Miseria de la filosofía* (Moscow: Ediciones en Lenguas Extranjeras, n.d.), 157.

39. The expropriation of ownership of the soil and the appropriation of ground rent on the part of the state are the first of the ten measures that, in accordance with the Manifesto of the Communist Party, the proletariat in power in the most advanced countries should adopt (see also Marx, "Sobre la nacionalización de la tierra," in *Escritos económicos varios* [Mexico City: Editorial Grijalbo, 1962]).

40. The recognition of this equilibrium is expressed in the symptomatic classification into three types of land tenancy made by the *Censo agrícola, ganadero, y ejidal*: properties of more than 5 hectares, properties of fewer than 5 hectares, and ejidos. With that, the government has wanted to have a barometer of the agrarian situation. (From a scientific perspective, this classification is extremely inconvenient.)

41. This is what happened in the 1970s in Peru, where the governing military junta carried out agrarian reform that "state-ized" and created cooperatives on the basis of both the coastal capitalist agricultural enterprises and the semifeudal haciendas of the sierra.

5. Social Classes and Political Power

Epigraph: Miguel Cervantes Saavedra, *Don Quixote*, trans. Samuel Putnam (New York: Viking, 1958), 858–59.

1. Rodolfo Stavenhagen, *Las clases sociales en las sociedades agrarias* (Mexico City: Siglo XXI Editores, 1969), 265.

2. Ricardo Pozas and Isabel H. de Pozas, *Los indios en las clases sociales de México* (Mexico City: Siglo XXI Editores, 1971), 113.

3. Stavenhagen, *Las clases sociales en las sociedades agrarias*, 270.

4. Pozas and de Pozas, *Los indios en las clases sociales de México*, 138–55.

5. Roger Bartra, *Breve diccionario de sociología marxista*, 44.

6. Alexander V. Chayanov, *Teoría de la organización económica campesina* (Buenos Aires: Ediciones Nueva Visión, 1974).

7. It is not possible to consider the peasant as merely someone who works the land and lives in the countryside; his strict definition as a class is indispensable. As an example of the difficulties that the lack of a definition can generate, see David Lehmann and David Zemelman, *El campesinado: clase y conciencia de clase* (Buenos Aires: Ediciones Nueva Visión, 1972).

8. For Pozas, the peasants are simply small and mid-level bourgeoisie. For Stavenhagen, they remain grouped in the class of "property owners" as the

"family" and "mid-level" sub-categories, alongside the "large" agrarian bourgeoisie.

9. Karl Marx, *El dieciocho Brumario de Luis Bonaparte*, in Karl Marx and Friedrich Engels, *Obras escogidas*, 3 vols. (Moscow: Ediciones en Lenguas Extranjeras, n.d.), 1:341. [The English translation here appears in Eugene Kamenka, ed., *The Portable Karl Marx* (New York: Viking, 1983), 313—Trans.]

10. Karl Marx and Friedrich Engels, *La ideología alemana* (Montevideo: Ediciones Pueblos Unidos, 1959), 213.

11. Ibid., 213–14 (emphasis added).

12. Marx, *Capital: Volume One*, 916 [FCE 1:639].

13. Ibid., 915 [FCE 1:638–39]. Of course, the Spanish translation replaces the word *violencia (Gewalt)* with the word *fuerza*. In the French version, revised by Marx, the word *Force* appears (with capital *F*, giving it the apparent feel of violence). Translation problems have been the basis of interpretations suggesting that for Marx, the basis of the modern state is the consensus of the people.

14. Friedrich Engels, Introduction to Karl Marx, *Las luchas de clases en Francia de 1848-1850*, in Marx and Engels, *Obras escogidas*, 1:108 (emphasis added).

15. Karl Marx, *Crítica de la filosofía del Estado de Hegel* (Mexico City: Editorial Grijalbo, 1968), 120.

16. Marx, *El dieciocho Brumario de Luis Bonaparte*, 313 [Kamenka: 310-11] (emphasis added).

17. Karl Marx, "La guerra civil en Francia," in Marx and Engels, *Obras escogidas*, 1:498 (emphasis added). [The English translation here appears in Kamenka, *The Portable Karl Marx*, 511-12.]

18. Marx, *El dieciocho Brumario de Luis Bonaparte*, 315 [Kamenka: 313].

19. Marx, *Las luchas de clases en Francia de 1848-1850*, 134. [The English translation here appears in Kamenka, *The Portable Karl Marx*, 268- 69.]

20. Marx, *El dieciocho Brumario de Luis Bonaparte*, 319 [Kamenka: 318].

21. Ibid., 319–20 [Kamenka: 318] (emphasis in the original).

22. Ibid., 314 [Kamenka: 312].

23. Ibid., 261.

24. *Democratic Caesarism* is the term the reactionary Venezuelan historian Vallenilla Lanz used to justify dictatorship (see Laureano Vallenilla Lanz, *Cesarismo democrático: estudio sobre las bases sociológicas de la constitución efectiva en Venezuela* [Caracas: Tipografía Garrido, 1961]).

25. Louis Althusser, *Ideología y aparatos ideológicos del Estado* (Medellín: La Oveja Negra, 1971).

26. Víctor Flores Olea, "Poder, legitimidad y política en México," in Instituto de Investigaciones Sociales, *El perfil de México en 1980*, 3 vols. (Mexico City: Siglo XXI Editores, 1972), vol. 3.

27. See in this regard the interesting analysis by Luisa Paré, "Caciquismo y estructura de poder en la sierra norte de Puebla," in Roger Bartra et al., *Caciquismo y poder político en el México rural* (Mexico City: Siglo XXI Editores, 1975).

28. For a more general view of the Mexican political system and of the correlation of forces, see Roger Bartra, "Clases sociales y crisis política en México," in *Clases sociales y crisis política en América Latina* (Mexico City: Siglo XXI Editores, 1976).

29. See Pilar Calvo D., "La ideología de la burguesía agraria en México," in *Revista Mexicana de Sociología* 34, nos. 3 and 4 (1972): 713–39.

30. Pilar Calvo D., "La estructura de la burguesía rural: ideología y relaciones de poder en el Valle del Mezquital" (Mexico City: Instituto de Investigaciones Sociales [UNAM], 1973, Mimeo). The stratification that I am proposing closely follows ideas from this research.

31. Ibid., 16.

32. Alonso Aguilar, "La oligarquía," in *La burguesía, la oligarquía, y el Estado,* by Jorge Carrión and Alonso Aguilar (Mexico City: Editorial Nuestro Tiempo, n.d.), 125.

33. On the different class sectors on a national scale, see Bartra, "Clases sociales y crisis política en México."

34. Rodolfo Stavenhagen, "Los jornaleros agrícolas" (Mexico: Confederación Nacional Campesina, 1967, Mimeo), 5.

35. Jorge Martínez Ríos, "Las invasiones agrarias en México o la crisis del modelo de incorporación-participación marginal" (Paper delivered at the Tenth Latin American Sociology Congress, Santiago, 1972).

6. And If the Peasants Become Extinct . . .

1. "Y si los campesinos se extinguen . . . ," *Historia y Sociedad* 8 (1976); "Los campesinos: una extinción imposible en marcha permanente," *Antropología y Marxismo* 2 (1982); "El problema indígena y la ideología indigenista," *Revista Mexicana de Sociología* 36, no. 3 (1974).

2. Karl Marx, "Lectures on the Early History of Institutions," in *The Ethnological Notebook of Karl Marx* (Amsterdam: International Institute voor Sociale Geshiadenis, 1974), 329.

3. Cf. José Luis Piñeyro, "El profesional Ejército Mexicano y la asistencia militar de Estados Unidos: 1965–1975" (Thesis, El Colegio de México, 1976).

7. . . . An Impossible, Ongoing Annihilation

1. This analysis of the crisis was prepared with Gerardo Otero and with the collaboration of Guadalupe Martínez Coria for the compilation of the

statistical data (cf. Roger Bartra and Gerardo Otero, "Agrarian Crisis and Social Differentiation in Mexico," *Journal of Peasant Studies* 14, no. 3 [April 1987]).

2. Robert Wasserstrom, "La investigación regional en ciencias sociales: una perspectiva chiapaneca," *Historia y Sociedad*, no. 9 (1976).

3. Ibid.

4. Daniel Cazés, "Un Camelot sin escándalo," *Historia y Sociedad*, no. 7 (1966).

5. Armando Bartra, "La renta capitalista de la tierra," *Cuadernos Agrarios*, no. 2 (1976).

6. Karl Marx, *Capital: Volume Three*, 249 [FCE 3:157].

7. Armando Barta, "Colectivización o proletarización: el caso del Plan Chontalpa," *Cuadernos Agrarios*, no. 4 (1976).

8. David Goodman and Michael Redclift, "The Transformation Process in Latin America" (Paper presented in the series of discussions organized in March 1978 by the Institute of Latin American Studies, University of London).

8. The Indigenous Peasant and Indigenist Ideology

1. A translation of this chapter was published by UNESCO in *Race and Class in Post-Colonial Society: A Study of Ethnic Group Relations in the English-Speaking Caribbean, Bolivia, Chile, and Mexico* (Paris: UNESCO, 1977).

2. Alfonso Fábila, *Valle del Mezquital* (Mexico City: Editorial Cultura, 1938), 156–57.

3. Ibid., 147.

4. Fernando Benítez, *Los indios de México*, vol. 4 (Mexico City: Ediciones Era, 1972), 10.

5. The interviews were transcribed verbatim from tape recordings made during the interviews. The emphases are mine.

6. Manuel Gamio, *Forjando Patria*, 2d ed. (Mexico City: Editorial Porrua, 1960), 94.

7. Manuel Gamio, quoted in Eduardo Matos, *Arqueología e indigenismo* (Mexico City: SepSetentas, 1972), 183.

8. Gonzalo Aguirre Beltrán, *El proceso de aculturación*, 2d ed. (Mexico City: Editorial Comunidad, 1970), 404.

9. Gonzalo Aguirre Beltrán, "El indigenismo y su contribución a la idea de nacionalidad," *América Indígena* 29 (1969): 397–435.

10. Manuel Coello, S. M. Lara, and H. Cartón, "Capitalismo y campesinado indígena" (Paper presented at a UNESCO conference on interethnic relations in Latin America and the Caribbean, Mexico City, July 1–5, 1974).

11. Roger Bartra, *Estructura agraria y clases sociales en México* (Mexico City: Ediciones Era, 1974).

12. See Sergio de la Peña, *Capitalismo en cuatro comunidades rurales* (Mexico

City: Siglo XXI Editores, 1981), on monetary flows and production in various communities in the Valle del Mezquital.

13. This situation seems analogous to that moment in the history of indigenism described brilliantly by Luis Villoro in which, the destruction having occurred and the Indian's alienation having been consolidated, Clavijero and Friar Servando begin a reevaluation. As Villoro says, "Purified of every demonic vestige only thanks to that death. At that moment, whatever was Indian acquired positive value; and that is the case not because we feel it close to us but for precisely the opposite reason: because we keep it at a distance. If in the previous moment what was Indian had appeared close at hand and negative, it now seems remote and positive" (Luis Villoro, *Los grandes momentos del indigenismo en México* [Mexico City: El Colegio de México, 1950]). I am astonished by the similarity of some historical moments analyzed by Villoro to what I found in the ordering of my anthropological research. That subject would merit a separate study all its own.

14. Since there was not merely a single culture in pre-Hispanic times, one must take into account the numerous indigenous cultures, as well as the distinct Spanish nationalities, Arab culture, and so on.

Bibliography

Aguilera G., Manuel. "La paradoja del campo mexicano: excedentes agrícolas y miseria rural." *Revista del México Agrario* 2, nos. 1 and 2 (1968–69).

Aguirre Beltrán, Gonzalo. "El indigenismo y su contribución a la idea de nacionalidad." *América Indígena* 29 (1969).

———. *El proceso de aculturación.* 2d ed. Mexico City: Editorial Comunidad, 1970.

Aguirre Beltrán, Gonzalo, and Ricardo Pozas. "Instituciones indígenas en el México actual." In *Métodos y resultados de la política indigenista en México,* vol. 6. Mexico City: Instituto Nacional del Indígena, 1954.

Althusser, Louis. *Ideología y aparatos ideológicos del Estado.* Medellín: La Oveja Negra, 1971.

Amín, Samir. *L'accumulatión a l'échelle mondiale.* Paris: Anthropos, 1970.

Barbosa, A. René, and Sergio Maturana. *El arrendamiento de tierras ejidales: un estudio en Michoacán.* Mexico City: CDIA, 1972.

Barraclough, S., and J. C. Collarte. *El hombre y la tierra en América Latina: resumen de los informes CDIA sobre tenencia de la tierra.* Santiago: Editorial Universitaria, 1972.

Bartra, Armando. "Colectivización o proletarización: el caso del Plan Chontalpa." *Cuadernos Agrarios,* no. 4 (1976).

———. "La renta capitalista de la tierra." *Cuadernos Agrarios,* no. 2 (1976).

Bartra, Roger. *Breve diccionario de sociología marxista.* Mexico City: Editorial Grijalbo, 1973.

———. "Campesinado y poder político en México: un modelo teórico." *Revista Mexicana de Sociología* 34, nos. 3 and 4 (1972).

———. "Clases sociales y crisis política en México." In *Clases sociales y crisis política en América Latina.* Mexico City: Siglo XXI Editores, 1976.

———. *Estructura agraria y clases sociales en México.* Mexico City: Ediciones Era, 1974.

———. "La estructura de clases en el agro andino venezolano." *Revista Mexicana de Sociología* 33, no. 4 (1971).

———. "Sobre la articulación de modos de producción en América Latina." *Historia y Sociedad,* no. 5 (1975).

———. "La teoría del valor y la economía campesina: invitación a la lectura de Chayanov." *Comercio Exterior,* May 1975.

———. "Tributo y tenencia de la tierra en la sociedad azteca." *El modo de producción asiático.* 2d ed. Mexico City: Ediciones Era, 1974.

Bibliography

Bartra, Roger, and Gerardo Otero. "Agrarian Crisis and Social Differentiation in Mexico." *Journal of Peasant Studies* 14, no. 3 (1987).

Bataillon, Claude. *Ville et campagnes dans la région de México.* Paris: Anthropos, 1971.

Benítez, Fernando. *Los indios de México.* Mexico City: Ediciones Era, 1972.

Boserup, Ester. *The Conditions of Agricultural Growth: The Economics of Agrarian Change under Population Pressure.* Chicago: Aldine, 1965.

Calderón Martínez, A. "El mercado internacional de productos agrícolas." *Revista del México Agrario* 3, no. 1 (1969–70).

———. "Sobre la articulación de modos de producción en América Latina." *Historia y Sociedad,* no. 5 (1975).

Calvo D., Pilar. "La estructura de la burguesía rural: ideología y relaciones de poder en el Valle del Mezquital." Mexico City: Instituto de Investigaciones Sociales [UNAM], 1973. Mimeo.

———. "La ideología de la burguesía agraria en México." *Revista Mexicana de Sociología* 34, nos. 3 and 4 (1972).

Cardoso, F. H. "Comentario sobre los conceptos de sobrepoblación relativa y marginalidad." *Revista Latinoamericana de Ciencias Sociales,* June–December 1971.

Carrión, Jorge, and Alonso Aguilar. *La burguesía, la oligarquía, y el Estado.* Mexico City: Editorial Nuestro Tiempo, n.d.

Casanova Alvarez, Francisco. "Las élites rectoras como agentes del cambio social." *Revista del México Agrario* 1, no. 4 (1968).

Cazés, Daniel. "Un Camelot sin escándalo." *Historia y Sociedad,* no. 7 (1966).

———. *Los revolucionarios.* Mexico City: Editorial Grijalbo, 1973.

Centro de Investigaciones Agrarias (CDIA). *Estructura agraria y desarrollo agrícola en México.* 3 vols. Mexico City, 1970.

Chayanov, Alexander V. *Teoría de la organización económica campesina.* Buenos Aires: Ediciones Nueva Visión, 1974.

Chen Po-ta. *La lucha de clases en el campo chino.* Medellín: La Oveja Negra, 1972.

Chevalier, François. "La formación de los grandes latifundios en México." *Problemas Agrícolas e Industriales de México* 8, no. 1 (1956).

Ciafardini, Horacio. "La agricultura mexicana: intento de sistematización." *Revista del México Agrario* 3 (1971).

Coello, Manuel. "¿Recampesinización en la descampesinización?" *Revista Mexicana de Sociología* 53, no. 1 (1981).

Coello, Manuel, S. M. Lara, and H. Cartón. "Capitalismo y campesinado indígena." Paper presented at a UNESCO conference on interethnic relations in Latin America and the Caribbean, Mexico City, July 1–5, 1974.

Comisión Económica para América Latina [CEPAL]. *Economía campesina y agricultura empresarial: tipología de productores del agro mexicano.* Mexico City: Siglo XXI Editores, 1982.

Bibliography

De la Peña, Moisés T. *El pueblo y su tierra: mito y realidad de la reforma agraria en México.* Mexico City: Cuadernos Americanos, 1964.

De la Peña, Sergio. *Capitalismo en cuatro comunidades rurales.* Mexico City: Siglo XXI Editores, 1981.

———. "El modo de producción capitalista y la transición al socialismo." *Historia y Sociedad* 1 (1974).

———. "La reforma agraria y excedentes." *Planificación,* nos. 2 and 3 (1968).

Dirección General de Economía Agrícola [DGEA]. *Agenda agrícola.* Mexico City: Secretaría de Agricultura y Recursos Hidráulicos, 1983.

———. "Consumos aparentes de productos agrícolas, 1925–1982." *Ecotecnia Agrícola* 7, no. 9 (1983).

Durán, Marco Antonio. "Los problemas agrarios mexicanos." *Revista del México Agrario* 1, no. 3 (1968).

Durand, Pierre. "La reproduction économique et politique d'une communauté paysanne mexicaine." Etudes mésoaméricaines. Department of Anthropology, Université de Montréal, 1973. Mimeo.

Eckstein, Salomón. *El ejido colectivo en México.* Mexico City: Fondo de Cultura Económica, 1966.

———. *El marco macroeconómico del problema agrario mexicano.* Mexico City: CDIA, 1968.

Emmanuel, Arghiri. *El intercambio desigual.* Mexico City: Siglo XXI Editores, 1972.

Engels, Friedrich. *Las guerras campesinas en Alemania.* Santiago: Editora Quimantú, 1972.

———. "El problema campesino en Francia y en Alemania." In Karl Marx and Friedrich Engels, *Obras escogidas,* vol. 2. Moscow: Ediciones en Lenguas Extranjeras, n.d.

Estadísticas sociales del porfiriato, 1877–1910. Mexico City: Secretaría de Economía, 1956.

Fábila, Alfonso. *Valle del Mezquital.* Mexico City: Editorial Cultura, 1938.

Fauré, Claude J. "Agriculture et mode de production capitaliste." Ph.D. diss., Paris, 1973.

Feder, Ernest. "Campesinistas y descampesinistas: tres enfoques divergentes (no incompatibles) sobre la destrucción del campesinado." *Comercio Exterior* 27 (1977).

Fernández y Fernández, Ramón. *Cooperación agrícola y organización económica del ejido.* Mexico City: SepSetentas, 1973.

———. *Notas sobre la reforma agraria mexicana.* Chapingo: Editorial Escuela Nacional de Agricultura, n.d.

Fioravanti, E. *El concepto de modo de producción.* Barcelona: Península, 1972.

Flores, Edmundo. "Cómo funciona el sector agropecuario de México." *Revista del México Agrario* 2, nos. 1 and 2 (1968–69).

Bibliography

Flores Olea, Víctor. "Poder, legitimidad y política en México." In *El perfil de México en 1980*, vol. 3. Mexico City: Siglo XXI Editores, 1972.

Gamio, Manuel. *Forjando patria*. 2d ed. Mexico City: Editorial Porrua, 1960.

Gill, Mario. *La conquista del Valle del Fuerte*. Mexico City, 1957.

Gilly, Adolfo. *La revolución interrumpida*. Mexico City: Ediciones El Caballito, 1971.

Godelier, Maurice. *Las sociedades primitivas y el nacimiento de las sociedades de clases según Marx y Engels*. Medellín: La Oveja Negra, 1969.

Goldschmidt, Alfonso. *Tierra y libertad: el desarrollo campesino en México*. Mexico City: EDIAPSA, 1940.

Gómez Jara, Francisco A. *El movimiento campesino en México*. Mexico City: Editorial Campesina, 1970.

González Casanova, Pablo. *La democracia en México*. Mexico City: Ediciones Era, 1975.

González de Cossío, Francisco. *Historia de la tenencia y explotación del campo desde la época precortesiana hasta las leyes del 6 de enero de 1915*. 2 vols. Mexico City: Biblioteca del Instituto Nacional de Estudios Históricos de la Revolución Mexicana, 1967.

González Navarro, Moisés. *La Confederación Nacional Campesina: un grupo de presión en la reforma agraria mexicana*. Mexico City: Costa-Amic, 1968.

———. "Instituciones indígenas en México independiente." In *Métodos y resultados de la política indigenista en México*, vol. 6. Mexico City: Instituto Nacional del Indígena, 1954.

Goodman, David, and Michael Redclift. "The Transformation Process in Latin America." Paper presented in a series organized by the Institute of Latin American Studies, University of London, March 1978.

Gratton, Phillippe. *Les paysans français contre l'agrarisme*. Paris: Maspero, 1972.

Gutelman, Michel. *Capitalismo y reforma agraria en México*. Mexico City: Editorial Era, 1974.

Harris, Richard L. "Marxism and the Agrarian Question in Latin America." *Latin American Perspectives* 19 (Fall 1978).

Hernández Segura, Valentín. *Prontuario de la ley federal de reforma agraria*. Mexico City: Departamento de Asuntos Agrarios y Colonización [DAAC], 1971.

Huizer, Gerrit. *La lucha campesina en México*. Mexico City: CDIA, 1970.

Kautsky, Karl. *La cuestión agraria*. Paris: Ruedo Ibérico, 1970.

Kula, Witold. *Théorie économique du système féodal*. Paris: Mouton, 1970.

Lefebvre, Henri. *De lo rural a lo urbano*. Barcelona: Península, 1971.

———. "La teoría marxista-leninista de la renta de la tierra." In *Estudios sociológicos sobre la reforma agraria*. Mexico City: Editorial Universidad Nacional Autónoma de México, 1964.

Bibliography

Lehman, David, and Zemelman, David. *El campesinado: clase y conciencia de clase.* Buenos Aires: Ediciones Nueva Visión, 1972.

Lenin, V. I. "Comentario: Gvozdiev, Los kulaks usureros, su significado social y económico." In *Obras completas*, vol. 4. 2d ed. Buenos Aires: Editorial Cartago, 1969.

———. "El capitalismo en la agricultura." In *Obras completas*, vol. 4. 2d ed. Buenos Aires: Editorial Cartago, 1969.

———. *El desarrollo del capitalismo en Rusia.* Moscow: Ediciones en Lenguas Extranjeras, 1950.

———. "Los nuevos cambios económicos de la vida campesina." In *Obras completas*, vol. 1. 2d ed. Buenos Aires: Editorial Cartago, 1969.

———. "Nuevos datos sobre las leyes del desarrollo del capitalismo en la agricultura." In *Obras completas*, vol. 23. 2d ed. Buenos Aires: Editorial Cartago, 1969.

———. "El problema agrario y los críticos de Marx." In *Obras completas*, vol. 5. 2d ed. Buenos Aires: Editorial Cartago, 1969.

———. "El programa agrario de la socialdemocracia en la primera revolución rusa de 1905–1907." In *Obras completas*, vol. 13. 2d ed. Buenos Aires: Editorial Cartago, 1969.

———. "El programa agrario de la socialdemocracia rusa." In *Obras completas*, vol. 6. 2d ed. Buenos Aires: Editorial Cartago, 1969.

———. "El proletariado y el campesinado." In *Obras completas*, vol. 8. 2d ed. Buenos Aires: Editorial Cartago, 1969.

Ley de Fomento Agropecuario. Mexico City: Ediciones de la Cámara de Diputados, 1981.

Luxemburg, Rosa. *La acumulación del capital.* Mexico City: Editorial Grijalbo, 1967.

Malo Alvarez, Ignacio. *La burguesía y la reforma agraria.* Mexico City: Liga de Agrónomos Socialistas, 1940.

Mandel, Ernest. "La acumulación originaria y la industrialización del Tercer Mundo." In *Ensayos sobre el neocapitalismo.* Mexico City: Editorial Era, 1971.

Mao Tse-tung. "Análisis de las clases de la sociedad china." In *Obras escogidas*, vol. 1. Beijing: Ediciones en Lenguas Extranjeras, 1971.

———. "Informe sobre una investigación del movimiento campesino en Junán." In *Obras escogidas*, vol. 1. Beijing: Ediciones en Lenguas Extranjeras, 1971.

———. "Prefacio y epílogo a investigaciones rurales." In *Obras escogidas*, vol. 3. Beijing: Ediciones en Lenguas Extranjeras, 1971.

Martínez Enciso, Alfonso. "Comercialización, intermediarios y acaparadores de la producción rural." *Revista del México Agrario* 1, no. 1 (1967).

Martínez Ríos, Jorge. "Los campesinos mexicanos: perspectivas en el proceso de marginalización." In *El perfil de México en 1980.* Mexico City: Siglo XXI Editores, 1972.

Bibliography

———. "Las invasiones agrarias en México o la crisis del modelo de incorpora-ción-participación marginal." Paper delivered at the Tenth Latin American Sociology Congress, Santiago, Chile, 1972.

Marx, Karl. *Capital.* 3 vols. *Volume One* translated by Ernest Mandel; *Volume Two* and *Volume Three* translated by David Fernbach. New York: Vintage, 1977–81.

———. *El capital.* Translated by Wenceslao Roces. 3 vols. Mexico City: Fondo de Cultura Económica, 1959.

———. *El capital, libro I, capítulo VI (inédito).* Buenos Aires: Siglo XXI Editores, 1974.

———. *Crítica de la filosofía del Estado de Hegel.* Mexico City: Editorial Gri-jalbo, 1968.

———. *El dieciocho Brumario de Luis Bonaparte.* In Karl Marx and Friedrich Engels, *Obras escogidas,* vol. 1. Moscow: Ediciones en Lenguas Extranjeras, n.d.

———. *Elementos fundamentales para la crítica de la economía política (bor-rador) 1857–1858.* Mexico City: Siglo XXI Editores, 1971.

———. *The Ethnological Notebook.* Amsterdam: International Institute voor Sociale Geshiadenis, 1974.

———. "La guerra civil en Francia." In *Obras escogidas.* Moscow: Ediciones en Lenguas Extranjeras, n.d.

———. *Las luchas de clases en Francia de 1848–1850.* In Karl Marx and Friedrich Engels, *Obras escogidas,* vol. 1. Moscow: Ediciones en Lenguas Extranjeras, n.d.

———. *Miseria de la filosofía.* Moscow: Ediciones en Lenguas Extranjeras, n.d.

———. *The Portable Karl Marx.* Edited by Eugene Kamenka. New York: Viking, 1983.

———. "Sobre la nacionalización de la tierra." *Escritos económicos varios.* Mex-ico City: Editorial Grijalbo, 1962.

———. *Theories of Surplus-Value.* 2 vols. Moscow: Progress Publishers, 1968.

Marx, Karl, and Friedrich Engels. *La ideología alemana.* Montevideo: Ediciones Pueblos Unidos, 1959.

Matos, Eduardo. *Arqueología e indigenismo.* Mexico City: SepSetentas, 1972.

Maturana Medina, Sergio, and Ivan Restrepo Fernández. *El azúcar: problema de México.* Mexico City: CDIA, 1970.

Miranda, José. "La propiedad comunal de la tierra y la cohesión social de los pueblos indígenas mexicanos." *Cuadernos Americanos* 149, no. 6.

Molina Enríquez, Andrés. "Los grandes problemas nacionales." *Problemas Agrícolas e Industriales de México* 5, no. 1 (1953).

———. *La revolución agraria de México.* 5 vols. Mexico City: Imprenta del Museo Nacional de Arqueología, Historia y Etnografía, 1932–34.

Bibliography

Moore, Barrington, Jr. *Social Origins of Dictatorship and Democracy: Lord and Peasant in the Making of the Modern World.* Harmondsworth, Middlesex: Penguin Books, 1969.

Navarrate, Ifigenia M. de, ed. *Bienestar campesino y desarrollo económico.* Mexico City: Fondo de Cultura Económica, 1971.

Nun, José. *Superpoblación relativa, ejército industrial de reserva y masa marginal.* Mexico City: Asociación de Becarios del Instituto de Investigaciones Sociales [ABIIS], 1972.

Othón de Mendizábal, Miguel. "El orígen histórico de nuestras clases medias." In *Ensayos sobre las clases sociales en México.* Mexico City: Editorial Nuestro Tiempo, 1970.

Palloix, Christian. "La question de l'échange inégal." *L'Homme et la Societé,* no. 18 (1970).

Palloix, Christian, et al., eds. *Imperialismo y comercio internacional.* Buenos Aires: Ediciones Pasado y Presente, 1971.

Paré, Luisa. "Caciquismo y estructura de poder en la sierra norte de Puebla." In *Caciquismo y poder político en el México rural,* by Roger Bartra et al. Mexico City: Siglo XXI Editores, 1975.

———. "Obstáculos en la organización de una cooperativa agrícola." *Revista del México Agrario* 4 (1971).

———. *El proletariado agrícola en México.* Mexico City: Siglo XXI Editores, 1977.

Perceval, L. *Avec les paysans, pour une agriculture non capitaliste.* Paris: Editions Sociales, 1969.

Piñeyro, José Luis. *El profesional Ejército Mexicano y la asistencia militar de Estados Unidos: 1965-1975.* Thesis, El Colegio de México, 1976.

Pozas, Ricardo, and Isabel H. de Pozas. *Los indios en las clases sociales de México.* Mexico City: Siglo XXI Editores, 1971.

Preobrazhensky, E. *La nueva economía.* Mexico City: Editorial Era, 1971.

Puente Leyva, Jesús. "Acumulación de capital y crecimiento en el sector agropecuario en México, 1930-67." In *Bienestar campesino y desarrollo económico,* edited by Ifigenia M. de Navarrete. Mexico City: Fondo de Cultura Económica, 1971.

Rangel Contla, José Calixto. *La pequeña burguesía en la sociedad mexicana, 1895 a 1960.* Mexico City: Instituto de Investigaciones Sociales, Universidad Nacional Autónoma de México, 1972.

Redclift, M. R. "El Estado frente al campo." *Nexos* 47 (1981).

Restrepo, Iván. "El caso de los jornaleros agrícolas en México." *Revista del México Agrario* 5, no. 3 (1972).

Restrepo, Iván, and José Sánchez Cortés. "El arrendamiento de tierras ejidales: el caso de Apatzingán." *Revista del México Agrario* 3, no. 1 (1969-70).

———. "Minifundismo y neolatifundismo en un distrito de riego." *Revista del México Agrario* 4, no. 2 (1971).

Bibliography

————. *La reforma agraria en cuatro regiones.* Mexico City: SepSetentas, 1972.

Rey, Pierre-Philippe. *Les alliances de classes.* Paris: Maspero, 1973.

Reyes Osorio, Sergio. "Aspectos de la problemática agraria nacional." *Revista del México Agrario* 1, no. 5 (1968).

Ronfeldt, David. *Atencingo: The Politics of Agrarian Struggle in a Mexican Ejido.* Stanford: Stanford University Press, 1973.

Semo, Enrique. "El desarrollo del capitalismo en la minería y en la agricultura de la Nueva España (1760–1810)." *Historia y Sociedad,* no. 15 (1969).

————. *Historia del capitalismo en México: los orígenes, 1521–1763.* Mexico City: Ediciones Era, 1973.

Senior, Clarence. "Reforma agraria y democracia en la comarca lagunera." In *Land Reform and Democracy.* Gainesville: University of Florida Press, 1958.

Servolin, C. "L'absorption de l'agriculture dans le mode de production capitaliste." In *L'univers politique des paysans.* Paris: A. Colin, 1972.

Shanin, Teodor, ed. *Peasants and Peasant Societies.* Harmondsworth, Middlesex: Penguin Books, 1971.

Shulgovski, A. "El caudillismo después de la revolución, 1917–1930." *Historia y Sociedad,* no. 9 (1967).

————. "Los ejidos y el desarrollo del capitalismo en el campo mexicano." *Historia y Sociedad,* no. 4 (1964).

Silva Herzog, Jesús. *El agrarismo mexicano y la reforma agraria.* Mexico City: Fondo de Cultura Económica, 1959.

Simpson, Eyler N. "El ejido: única salida para México." *Problemas Agrícolas e Industriales de México* 4, no. 4 (1952).

Sistema Alimentario Mexicano: primer planteamiento de metas de consumo y estrategia de producción de alimentos básicos para 1980–1982. Mexico City: Oficina de Asesores del C. Presidente de la República, 1980.

Solís, Leopoldo. *La realidad económica mexicana: retrovisión y perspectivas.* Mexico City: Siglo XXI Editores, 1970.

Stavenhagen, Rodolfo. "Aspectos sociales de la estructura agraria en México." In *Neolatifundismo y explotación.* Mexico City: Editorial Nuestro Tiempo, 1968.

————. "Clases, colonialismo y aculturación: ensayo sobre un sistema de relaciones interétnicas en Mesoamérica." In *Ensayos sobre las clases sociales en México.* Mexico City: Editorial Nuestro Tiempo, 1968.

————. *Las clases sociales en las sociedades agrarias.* Mexico City: Siglo XXI Editores, 1969.

————. "Los jornaleros agrícolas." Mexico City: Confederación Nacional Campesina, 1967. Mimeo.

Tello, Carlos. *La tenencia de la tierra en México.* Mexico City: Instituto de Investigaciones Sociales, Universidad Nacional Autónoma de México, 1968.

Turner, John Kenneth. *México bárbaro.* Mexico City: Cordemex, 1965.

Unzueta, Gerardo. "Relaciones de producción en el campo mexicano, 1939–1958." *Nueva Epoca*, nos. 9 and 10 (1963).

Vallenilla Lanz, Laureano. *Cesarismo democrático: estudio sobre las bases sociológicas de la constitución efectiva de Venezuela.* Caracas: Tipografía Garrido, 1961.

Villoro, Luis. *Los grandes momentos del indigenismo en México.* Mexico City: El Colegio de México, 1950.

Warman, Arturo. *Los campesinos, hijos predilectos del regimen.* Mexico City: Editorial Nuestro Tiempo, 1972.

Wasserstrom, Robert. "La investigación regional en ciencias sociales: una perspectiva chiapaneca." *Historia y Sociedad*, no. 9 (1976).

Whetten, Nathan L. "México rural." *Problemas Agrícolas e Industriales de México* 5, no. 2 (1953).

Wolf, Eric R. *Peasants.* Englewood Cliffs, N.J.: Prentice-Hall, 1966.

Womack, John. *Zapata y la revolución mexicana.* Mexico City: Siglo XXI Editores, 1969.

Zavala, Silvio. *De encomiendas y propiedad territorial en algunas regiones de la América Española.* Mexico City, 1940.

———. *La encomienda indiana.* Madrid: Centro de Estudios Históricos, 1935.

Zavala, Silvio, and Miranda, José. "Instituciones indígenas en la Colonia." In *Métodos y resultados de la política indigenista en México*, vol. 6. Mexico City: Instituto Nacional del Indígena, 1954.

Index

Index

Apertura democrática, 134, 139
Ávila Camacho, Manuel, 35, 118, 151
Ayutla, Revolution of, 31–32
Aztecs, 80–81, 98, 169

Ball, John, 46
Bankers, 68, 132, 133, 134
Banks, 78, 95, 101, 132, 195n.29
Barley production, 76
Barra, Félix, 145, 146
Bartra, Armando, 162–64
Bean production, 156–57, 158
Belgium, 142
Benedetti, Mario, 1
Benítez, Fernando, 169
Boas, Franz, 172
Bonaparte, Louis, 113, 118
Bonapartism, 111, 115, 117–18
Bourgeoisie: agrarian, 3, 26, 56, 57, 65, 108, 109, 119, 122–23, 131, 136, 137–38, 139, 140–41, 144, 145, 159; and agrarian reform, 83, 88–89, 90, 94, 95, 104, 120, 122, 125; agricultural lockout, 145; and agricultural prices, 26, 64–65; and agricultural production, 33, 34, 157; commercial, 122–23, 131; and ejido sector, 96, 97, 101, 104, 105, 120, 136, 139; and elimination of peasantry, 66–67, 105, 136–38; exploitation of peasantry, 13, 15, 65–67, 74, 109, 110, 163; exploitation of proletariat, 23; in French Revolution, 114–15; and ground rent, 3, 22, 137; ideology of capitalism, 7, 19–20; indigenist ideology, 169–79, 181, 185–86, 187; industrial, 26, 64–65, 66–67, 183, 192n.37; monopoly of, 14, 15; and nationalization of land, 103–5, 139; peasants as, 16, 62, 110; political alliance with peasantry, 104–5, 117, 125, 135; political dominance of, 112, 115, 117, 118, 119, 130–35, 142–43; political positions of, 124–25, 129, 141, 159–60; populism and, 119, 124, 125, 139; proletarian struggle with, 19, 94, 126; and Revolution, 32, 118, 132; rural, 24, 31, 58, 66, 105, 107, 108, 120, 121–25, 137, 144; rural bureaucracy, 123–24; as social class, 107
Bracerismo, 141
Bureaucracy, 123–24, 130, 133, 139, 140–41, 143

Cabrera, Luis, 84
Caciques, 99; agrarian reform and, 120–21; and indigenist ideology, 175, 176, 182–83,
185, 186; political influence, 124, 140, 144
Caciquismo, 111, 120, 140
Caesarism (Bonapartism), 111, 115, 117–18
Calles, Plutarco Elías, 90, 119, 131, 135, 145
Calles de Almada, Alicia, 145
Cámara Nacional de la Industria de la Transformación (CANACINTRA), 133
Campesinistas, xii, xiii, xvi
Campesinos. See Peasantry
Cancian, Frank, 162
Capital (Marx), 2, 3, 11, 14, 87, 190n.3, 191n.11
Capitalism: advanced stage, 33–34; agrarian reform and, 20, 94, 118–19; agricultural development of, xii–xiii, 2–4, 22, 30, 32–33, 38, 44, 73; agricultural enterprises, 77, 137; agricultural expansion of, xvii, 31, 140, 149, 151; and agricultural production, 51, 149; agricultural sector, 33, 34, 37, 38, 51–58, 165, 166; bourgeois ideology of, 7, 19–20; bourgeoisie interests and development of, 131, 135, 138; and caciquismo, 140, 182, 185; capitalist mode of production, 2, 5, 9, 17, 29; "dependent," xii, 26, 27–28, 78; destruction of communal property, 82, 84–85; destruction of indigenous culture, 168, 172, 181, 183–85, 186, 188; disamortization laws and expansion of, 88, 89; and disintegration of peasant economy, 13, 22, 34, 73, 93–94, 165, 166–67; in ejido sector, 30, 94, 95, 96, 139; "English path" to, 3, 4, 100; exploitation of peasantry, 63–64, 65, 67, 68, 74; exploitation of wage labor, 18, 51–56, 67; and government agrarian policy, xiv, 32–33, 120, 159–60; and government economic policy, xi, 133–34; ground rent in, 14, 39, 40, 45, 56, 74, 97–98; industrial, 24, 34; internal contradictions of, 58, 72–73, 121, 165–66; "Junker road" to, 2–3, 4, 30, 32, 85, 90–91; and land distribution, 120; and land nationalization, 103–4, 105; land ownership and development of, 58, 79, 82, 90, 92–94, 97–98, 120; latifundismo as, 56–57; market price-setting, 14, 61, 64; Marx on, 5, 8–9, 13–14; Marxist analysis and, 138; Mexican Revolution and, 30, 32, 90–91, 94; noncapitalist modes of production and, 19, 69, 74, 78, 165; and peasant self-exploitation, 15; peasant's existence within, xii, xiii, 4, 11, 13, 20, 45, 47–48, 113, 117, 147, 165; and political power, 111–12, 113, 118,

Index

Index

Index

Labor: collective, 180; cost of, 46–47; exploitation of, 18, 22, 65, 68; free labor, 87, 89; latifundista forms of, 87, 88, 89, 99; nonwage compensation, 10–11, 21; reserves, 25, 34, 39; rural proletariat, 126; social organization of, 107; subordination of to capital, 8–9, 87; superexploitation of, 17, 20, 32, 58, 137; surrendered for free, 16–17, 47–48, 59, 64, 65; technology and, 58; unremunerated, 59–60, 70, 71; value of, 11–13, 20–22, 47, 48, 49, 60. *See also* Surplus labor; Wage labor

Laborism, xvi

Labor unions, 143

Ladinos, 185

Landholding class, 3, 122

Land invasions, 126, 142, 145

Landownership: forms of, 4, 79; limitations on, 133; monopoly conditions, 14, 15, 58, 88, 97–98; nationalization of, 103–4, 198n.39; as obstacle to capitalist development, 58, 79; and political power, 122; private property, 3–4, 14, 79, 86, 88, 97; redistribution, 63, 90, 91, 144, 145–50, 152, 158–59; social functions of, 31, 106

Latifundios, 149; and capitalist development, 2–3, 32, 56–57, 87, 89, 92–93, 100; destruction of, 30, 74, 88–89, 90, 94, 95, 120, 145–46; land ownership, 85–86, 87–88

Latin America, xii, 1, 22, 24–26, 31

League of Agrarian Communities, 119

Leasing, 97–103, 136

Lefebvre, Henri, 194n.15

Lenin, V. I.: and alliance of classes, 160, 161; on capitalist development in agriculture, 2–3, 33, 34, 85; definition of social classes, 4–5, 107; "nonproletarian masses," 27; on peasant labor, 20, 47–48

Lerdo de Tejada, Miguel, 83

Lerdo Law (1856), xiii, 31–32, 83, 92

Livestock production, xv, 44, 76, 150

López Mateos, Adolfo, 135

López Portillo, José, xiii, xiv, 136, 138, 145, 147, 156

Luiselli, Cassio, 189–90n.8

Luxemburg, Rosa, 33

Mao Tse-Tung, 161

Maquiladoras, 76, 77

Marginalism, 22–23, 24–25, 28

Marx, Karl, 1, 191n.33; analysis of class structure, 2, 4; on development of capitalism, 8, 9, 14, 58, 163; and ground rent, 2, 3, 40, 42; on independent existence of the state, 130; on Mexico, 87; on peasant class, xvii, 110–12, 116, 117; on peasant economy, 10–11, 12, 13, 48, 64; primitive accumulation of capital, 3, 8, 33–34, 85; on state violence, 112, 113–15, 199n.13; on subordination of labor to capital, 8–9, 87; theory of modes of production, 4–6, 7, 9; on usurer capital, 68

Marxist analysis, 130; of development of capitalism, 58, 79,138–39; of Mexican agrarian structure, xiii, xvi, 1, 2, 46, 160, 161; populism and, 162

Maximilian (emperor of Mexico), 87

Mayas, 32, 84

Mayeques, 80, 99

Mayo, Valle del, 146

Means of production, 2, 10–11, 15, 18, 106, 107

Mennonites, 92

Merced real (royal grant), 86

Merchant capital, 67, 68–69, 123

Merchants, 39, 76, 183, 186

Mestizos: agrarian reform and, 88–89, 92; indigenist ideology and, 179, 187; and indigenous people, 176, 178, 183, 185; *rancheros*, 91, 92, 100

Methodology, 27–29, 39, 46, 48–51

Mexican air force, 142

Mexican army, 142

Mexican Constitution, xiii, xiv, 83, 88, 118

Mexican Food System (Sistema Alimentario Mexicano, SAM), xiv, xv, 133, 136, 138, 140, 156–57, 189–90n.8

"Mexican path," 31, 33

Mexican Revolution, 160; agrarian reforms, 2, 84, 90, 94, 140–41; bourgeois character of, 101, 118, 122, 123; causes of, 32; class alliances of, 95, 104, 117; creation of ejidos, 95, 101; and development of capitalism, 30, 90–91, 94; institutionalization of, 118, 143; and peasantry, 111, 135

Mexican War of Independence, 82

Mexico: agrarian policy, xiii–xv, 32–33, 189–90n.8; agrarian structure, 1, 2, 29, 33, 43, 46, 72, 136–37, 159; agricultural censuses, 44; armed forces, 142; balance of trade, 67–68; communal property in, 80, 81, 82–85; dependency, xii, 26–27; development of capitalism in, xii–xiii, 33–34, 131; economic development, 25; economic policy, xi, xiv, 24; economy, 23–24, 132;

217

Index

Index

61, 64, 65, 66; forms of exploitation of, 63–69; income strata of, 62, 69, 71–72, 110–11; Indians exploited as, 180; internal colonialism and, 26; kulakization, 62, 65, 139; labor, compensation for, 21, 22; labor, surrendered for free, 16–17, 47–48, 59, 64, 65; labor, value of, 11–12, 13, 20–22, 47, 60, 71; as landholder, 164; land invasions, 145, 146; marginalism, 24–25; market production, 60, 61; merchant-capital exploitation of, 67, 68–69, 70, 123; Mexican Revolution and, 135; minifundista, 94, 107, 110; mythological figure of, xi–xii, 135; political power and, 111–12, 113–14, 115, 116, 118, 119; populist interpretations of, xii, 164, 165; and presidential succession, 129, 130; profits of, 60, 61, 62; as proletariat and bourgeoisie, 2, 16–17, 109, 110, 117, 164, 165; reduction of needs of, 20, 48; revolutionary potential of, 32–33, 96, 110, 161, 164–65; self-compensation as wage laborer, 11–12, 48, 64; self-exploitation, 11, 15, 16–17, 109–10; semi-proletarianized, 70, 71–72, 110; sharecropping, 99; in simple commodity economy, 18–19, 59–62, 99, 110, 161; as social class, 109–21, 160–61, 198n.7; subsistence consumption, 21, 33, 60, 69–70, 155–56, 181; used as wage labor, 37–38, 60–61, 70–71, 72, 76, 77, 189–90n.8; use of wage labor by, 59–60, 61, 62.
See also Proletarianization

Peonage, 87
Peonías, 91
Pequeños propietarios, 123
Peru, 198n.41
Pimentel, Francisco, 169
Poland, 47
Political power, 111–12, 113
Political society, 117
Politics, Mexican, 121, 127; apertura democrática, 138, 139; bourgeoisie and, 118, 119, 124–25, 129, 130–31, 132–33; class alliance in, 117–19, 125, 134, 142–43; indigenist ideology in, 175, 181–84; institutionalization of the Revolution, 118–20, 143; mystery of presidential succession, 128–30; peasantry in, 111, 113, 119, 129, 130, 138, 140–43; stability of, 96, 119
Poll tax, 99
Populism, 127–28; agrarian reform and, 119, 125, 138, 139, 163; and agricultural production, 104–5, 164; Cardenista, 117–18; and

indigenist ideology, 187; "neo-populism," 125; "old-style," 124, 125; and the peasantry, xii, xiii, 119, 137, 139, 160, 161, 165; rural bourgeoisie and, 124, 125; technocratic, 125, 141, 144–45, 147, 187
Pozas, Ricardo, 107, 110, 160, 198–99n.8
Precapitalist forms of production, 103; early Mexican, 86, 87, 88, 89, 91; peasant agriculture as, 2; transformation to capitalism, 7, 8, 85–86
Presidencialismo, 111
Presidential succession, mystery of, 128–30
Prices: capitalist market determination of, 27, 61, 64, 194n.15; crisis of, 159, 166; government price supports, 61; of labor power, 12; monopoly, 14; peasant agricultural activity and, 71; peasant-bourgeoisie antagonism, 26, 64–65, 66; peasant-working class antagonism, 26, 61
Private property, 90, 91–94, 97, 100, 150, 189n.5
Private sector: agriculture, 36, 75, 150; employment in, 147
Profit: average rate of, 14, 42, 49; in class-structure analysis, 2; ejido-land rental, xiv; moneylending, 68; organic composition of capital and, 56, 58, 162–63; peasant-labor, expropriation of, 15, 16–17, 22, 60, 61, 62, 66; peasant right to, 12; in underdevelopment and dependency, 26–27; Valle del Mezquital analysis, 49, 50, 51, 54–55, 56; wage-labor exploitation, 51, 57
Proletarianization, xi, xii, xv, xvii, 24, 37–39, 166; agrarian reform and, 104; and ejido sector, 136, 139, 149; inevitability of, 62, 63–64, 67; political influences of, 141, 147, 164; rural bourgeoisie and, 123; and socialism, 138
Proletariat, xvi–xvii; agricultural, de-peasantization and, 3, 109, 140; bourgeois exploitation of, 23; and capitalist development, 19; in class structure, 107, 113, 135, 160–61; dictatorship of, 4; industrial, 66, 125; peasants as, 2, 109–10, 113; revolutionary consciousness, 116; rural, xvi, 125–26
Protestant Reformation, 85
Prussia, 114
Puebla state, 83
Puente Leyva, Jesús, 39

Racism, 127–28; of indigenist ideology, 170, 172–73, 176–77, 179, 183–84, 185–86

Index

Index

Villoro, Luis, 202n.13
Violence, 31, 32, 112, 115

Wage labor, 115; Agrarian Code and ejido
sector, 101, 197n.36; Agricultural Development Act and, xiii–xiv; de-peasantization
and, 3; development of capitalism and, 2,
149; hacienda, 87; hired by peasants, 59–60,
61, 62; indigenist ideology and, 186;
peasant, as his own, 11; peasant, in simple
commodity mode, 18, 76; peasant, self--
exploitation, 110; peasant, supplementary
income, 37–38, 70; peasant economy and,
137, 165; profit from exploitation of, 51, 57;
rural semi-proletariat, 71–72; superexploitation of, 51–56, 165; unemployment and,
21. *See also* Labor
Wages, 2, 44, 50; industrial, 65; paid by
peasant to self, 11–12, 48, 64; rural proletariat, 126, 166

Wasserstrom, Robert, 160, 161, 162
Water Act, 133, 136, 140
Weber, Max, 23
Weydemeyer, Joseph, 4
Wheat production, 58, 76, 145, 152–54
Wolf, Erik, 162
Working class, xvi–xvii; antagonistic
interests of peasantry, 25–26; exploitation
of, 23; peasant labor and, 64, 66; political
power and, 114, 142–43; rural proletariat in,
125
World Bank, xii

Yaqui, Valle del, 32, 101–2, 145, 146
Yaqui War, 32
Yaquis, 84
Yucatán, 32, 84

Zacatecas state, 83
Zapata, Emiliano, 32